MATTHEW HALL

How to Analyze People

The Ultimate Real-Life Manual On Covert Manipulation By Revealing NLP Secrets And The Completely New Approach To Manipulation Using NLP Techniques

Copyright © 2020 Matthew Hall
All rights reserved.

© Copyright 2020 - All rights reserved.

The content contained within this book may not be reproduced, duplicated or transmitted without direct written permission from the author or the publisher.

Under no circumstances will any blame or legal responsibility be held against the publisher, or author, for any damages, reparation, or monetary loss due to the information contained within this book. Either directly or indirectly.

Legal Notice:

This book is copyright protected. This book is only for personal use. You cannot amend, distribute, sell, use, quote or paraphrase any part, or the content within this book, without the consent of the author or publisher.

Disclaimer Notice:

Please note the information contained within this document is for educational and entertainment purposes only. All effort has been executed to present accurate, up to date, and reliable, complete information. No warranties of any kind are declared or implied. Readers acknowledge that the author is not engaging in the rendering of legal, financial, medical or professional advice. The content within this book has been derived from various sources. Please consult a licensed professional before attempting any techniques outlined in this book.

By reading this document, the reader agrees that under no circumstances is the author responsible for any losses, direct or indirect, which are incurred as a result of the use of information contained within this document, including, but not limited to, — errors, omissions, or inaccuracies.

HOW TO ANALYZE PEOPLE

Introduction *7*

Chapter 1. Neuro-Linguistic Programming (NLP) *11*

Chapter 2. How NLP Works, Importance of NLP, and is NLP Effective? *17*

Chapter 3. Components of NLP and NLP Techniques *22*

Chapter 4. The Swish Pattern *26*

Chapter 5. Hypnosis *32*

Chapter 6. Brainwashing *37*

Chapter 7. How to Use NLP for in Sales *42*

Chapter 8. How to Use NLP in Relationships *45*

Chapter 9. NLP in Business *50*

Chapter 10. Body Language and Behavior Imitation *56*

Chapter 11. Using NLP to Manage People *61*

Chapter 12. Protecting Yourself From NLP Mind Control *66*

Chapter 13. Smart and Wise Goal-Setting Using Neuro-Linguistics *71*

Chapter 14. Introduction of Persuasion *75*

Chapter 15. History of Persuasion *78*

Chapter 16. Six Principles of Persuasion *81*

Chapter 17. Theories on Persuasion *86*

Chapter 18. Persuasion Techniques *89*

Chapter 19. Difference Between Persuasion and Manipulation *95*

Chapter 20. Factors That Influence Persuasion *99*

Chapter 21. Methods of Persuasion and Tricks Used By Mass Media And Advertising *103*

Chapter 22. The Benefits of Learning About Persuasion *106*

Chapter 23. Dark Persuasion *111*

Chapter 24. Covert Persuasion *116*

Chapter 25. Ethical Persuasion *119*

Chapter 26. Difference Between Persuasion and Negotiation *124*

Chapter 27. Deception *131*

Chapter 28. The Dark Triad *137*

Chapter 29. How To Analyze People *141*

Chapter 30. Speed Reading to Understand People *148*

Chapter 31. Advanced Tips and Tricks to Control People *155*

Chapter 32. The Most Powerful Mind-Power Tool *160*

Chapter 33. NLP Conclusion *165*

Chapter 34. Covert Manipulation *169*

Chapter 35. What is Manipulation? *174*

Chapter 36. Examples of Manipulation? *180*

Chapter 37. Introduction on Deception *185*

Chapter 38. Techniques Used in Manipulation: Explication of Different Techniques *190*

Chapter 39. How To Defend Yourself From Manipulation Techniques *195*

Chapter 40. Qualities of a Manipulative Person *201*

Chapter 41. Victim of Manipulation *207*

Chapter 42. Strategies for Seduction, a Person with Manipulation *213*

Chapter 43. Covert Emotional Manipulation: Introduction *218*

Chapter 44. Covert Manipulation in a Love Relationship *224*

Chapter 45. How the Mind Works When It Is Manipulated? *229*

Chapter 46. Hypnosis *234*

Chapter 47. Office Politics or Sociopathic Tricks? – The Workplace Manipulators *239*

Chapter 48. Human Behavior and Manipulation *244*

Chapter 49. Psychological Manipulation *249*

Chapter 50. Turning the Tables *254*

Chapter 51. Stages of a Relationship with a Covert Narcissist *259*

Chapter 52. Covert Emotional Manipulation Methods *264*

Chapter 53. Knowing Yourself *269*

Chapter 54. Psychological Tricks to Examine Human Beings *274*

Chapter 55. Basic Body Language Signals *279*

Chapter 56. Strengthen or Change the Views of Others *284*

Chapter 57. The Art of Persuasion *289*

Chapter 58. Influence Without Manipulation *295*

Chapter 59. Escape or Die *301*

Conclusion *306*

Introduction

NLP refers to the ability to sway interactions with other people. It has several different stages when used, beginning with establishing rapport and ending in getting the desired result. Ultimately, it is guided by non-verbal responses and reactions of the client, which can be used first to create rapport and sway the other person to do what is necessary.

NLP starts with developing rapport, which is typically done through mirroring and matching behaviors. You can cue the other person to begin identifying more with you when you use mirroring first. Following the other person's behaviors as a guide in interacting with him or her, you can begin keying into their desire to like you. They are more likely to identify with and trust you if you are mirroring them. It opens them up to the following step.

You will then be gathering information about the other person's mental state. It is using a study of body language or the way the other person may answer. When you understand the other person's mental state, you can begin understanding what their thought processes are, as well as the wording they use. It is where you start to understand the linguistic and programming parts of NLP. You can understand the other person's mind through understanding their words. You can begin to understand the mindset based on the wording, such as focusing on sensory-based metaphors or focusing on certain tendencies. You understand their programming by watching their body language with their words.

From there, it is time to start coming in on changing their minds. When the other person readily mirrors your interactions, you can begin speaking to the other person and mirroring the behaviors you want. For example, if you wish the other person to be more comfortable with spiders, you make a subtle body language sign that you are comfortable with when you mention spiders. You may learn in a little bit toward the other person, conveying that you are comfortable as you mention the spider. The other person should mirror your response, and as they do so, they tell their minds that there is nothing to fear, nothing to worry about, and that everything is fine.

This sort of process can then be expanded upon to be used for everything from depression to creating self-confidence in another person. It is, essentially, swaying the other person to feel more comfortable with things that may have been uncomfortable before. It allows you to sway opinions, behavior, goals, and more just by tuning into their body language, ensuring that you share rapport, and using that rapport to slowly mold the other person's mind to mimic the one you are attempting to create.

Historically, persuasion is rooted in ancient Greek's model of a prized politician and orator.

To make a list, a politician or speaker needs to master rhetoric and elocution to persuade the public. Rhetoric, according to Aristotle, is the "ability to make use of the available methods of persuasion" to win a court case or influence the public during important orations. On the other hand, elocution (a branch of rhetoric) is the art of speech delivery, including proper diction, proper gestures, stance, and dress. Although Grecian politics and orations seem clearly to be the genesis of persuasion, its use in the rapidly developing world of the twenty-first century goes beyond politics, oration, and other human endeavors.

In the business domain, persuasion refers to a corporate system of influence to change other people, groups, or organizations' attitudes, behavior, or perception about an idea, object, goods, services, or people. It often employs verbal communications (both written and spoken words), non-verbal communication (paralinguistic, chronemics, proxemics, and so on), visual communication, or multimodal communication to convey, change or reinforce a piece of existing information or reasoning peculiar to the audience. Persuasion in business can come in different forms depending on the need of the management. For instance, business enterprise sometimes uses persuasion in cases like; public relations, broadcast, media relations, speech writing, social media, client relations, employee communication, brand management, etc.

In psychological parlance, persuasion refers to using an obtainable understanding of the social, behavioral, or cognitive principles in psychology to influence the attitude, cognition, behavior, or belief system of a person, group, or organization. It is also seen as a process by which a person's attitude and behavior are influenced without coercion but through the simple means of communication. For instance, when a child begs his mother for candy and the mother refuses but instead proffers a better food for the child to eat while also encouraging him to grow more significant. The child gets excited and goes for the new alternative. In this way, the mother has been able to tap into his belief system without any form of duress. Hence, persuasion can also be used as a method of social control.

In politics and governing today, persuasion still retains its role as one of the essential means of influencing the populace's behavior, feelings, and commitment through the power of mass media. For instance, politicians sometimes use social media, television, radio, newspapers, and magazines to persuade people to sponsor their political campaigns. Persuasion in modern politics is also observed through the use of authority in such situations where opponents of one political party influence on cross carpet to the other party with different promises in the form of power and immunity. Also, the court still entertains the use of persuasion during the prosecution or defense of an accused.

Another way to see persuasion is through the intentional use of communication as a tool of conviction to change attitudes regarding an issue by transferring messages in a free choice atmosphere. The verbal, non-verbal, and visual forms of communication are manipulated just for the sole purpose of persuading an individual, group, or organization. Although communication is the most essential and versatile form in which persuasion is manifested, it is worthy to note that not all communication forms are intended to persuade. For instance, the celebration of a newly inaugurated president or governor circulated on the news cannot be classified as persuasion unless intended to impact the country's citizens or react in specific ways.

We go further to look at other possible definition of persuasion in the circular world.

Persuasion is a concept of influence that attempts to change a person's attitudes, intentions, motivations, beliefs, or behaviors. When a child begs his parent for candy and the parent says a big no to him, but the child insists on having candy even while knowing it might not be suitable for his health, persuasion is beginning to occur. The parent will try to proffer a better food for the child to eat instead of the candy. The child gets excited and goes for the new alternative. In this way, the parent has won a banter of persuasion.

On its own, persuasion is a branch of communication and popular as a method of social control. Hence, it is worthy of note that not all forms of communication intend to be persuasive. Persuasion is also a process by which a person's attitude and behaviors are influenced without harsh treatment by simple means of communication. Other factors can also determine a person's change in behavior or attitude, for example, verbal threats, a person's current psychological state, physical coercion, etc.

Having explained the meanings of persuasion, it can be observed that persuasion extends beyond a specific field as there is an intermingling of ideas from different study areas. However, communication and psychology seem clearly to be in use for persuasion to take place. While communication provides the model of how interlocutors in persuasion get messages understood, psychology provides the mental processes model during persuasion.

Now that we know both NLP and persuasion basics, we will now go more in-depth into detail about the subjects connecting to these two from this point and forward.

Chapter 1. Neuro-Linguistic Programming (NLP)

NLP is a fantastic art and science. It is an art since everyone gives what they are doing their own personal and stylish touch, which can never be conveyed with words or techniques. It is a science, and for outstanding results, there is a system and process to discover the models used for outstanding in-dividing in a region. This method is called patterning. In the field of education, guidance, and industry, the models, skills, and techniques discovered can increasingly be used to achieve more efficient communication, have substantial personal growth, and accelerate learning.

Have you ever done something so elegantly and successfully that your time will be cut short? Have there been moments when you were very pleased with what you were doing and how you handled it? The NLP shows you how to appreciate your achievements and arrange them to experience several more moments like this. It is a way of uncovering and unveiling your talent, a form of bringing out the best of yourself and others.

The NLP is a real ability that produces the outcomes we want in the world while at the same time valuing others in the process. It is the p of what distinguishes between the excellent and the nor-evil. It also leaves behind many extremely successful strategies on schooling, therapy systems, business, and therapies.

The History of NLP

The initial version of the NLP of today originated in the early 1970s. At the time, Richard Bandler was a student at the Santa Cruz University of California, met with John Grinder, assistant professor of linguistics.

Grinder, who was especially interested in advanced teaching techniques, was rapidly aware of Bandler's research and held a series of seminars in collaboration with him. Such seminars originally had the classification of group studies. But with growing Bandler and Grinder experience and expertise, the participants encountered more exciting transition processes ever. It culminated in an increasingly close relationship between Bandler and Grinder over the years.

They explored why well-known individual psychotherapists had so much success with their patients in their practice and on what basis this success was based. Several people treating the same patients with the same conditions have struggled to bring about these drastic improvements simultaneously. In Bandler and Grinder's original theory, they believed influential psychotherapists had a common or similar pattern of action in their work with people, based on which they might produce these excellent results. These standard or related behavior patterns are now known as NLP, or magic structure.

So, they started to investigate and evaluate the types of therapy used by the top therapists:

- Virginia Satir, an exceptional family therapist.

- Fritz Perl's, an innovative Gestalt therapist and founder of this direction of therapy, as well.

- Milton H. Erickson, a world-renowned hypnotherapist.

In doing so, the expectations of finding patterns and structures that could clarify these top therapists' success in coping with their clients were always driven.

Despite the three successful psychotherapists' diversity, after long and careful observation, Grinder and Bandler discovered that they used surprisingly similar basic patterns in their work with others. Grinder and Bandler put these basic patterns into writing, refined them, tried them out in their seminars with other students who agreed to do so. Finally, they developed an elegant model to achieve more effective communication, accelerated learning, personal change, and enjoyment, and joy in life. They called it NLP—Neuro-linguistic Programming:

"Neuro" because these are strategies that heavily involve the functions of our nervous system (brain + spinal cord + senses). The point is to perceive more precisely and more, to purposefully change unwanted feelings and behavior patterns in harmony with yourself.

"Linguistics" because it is also very much about the linguistic aspect. We maintain external communication with other people and internal communication with our fantastic "bio-computer"—our brain. Unfortunately, not all of the inputs that we make in this biocomputer are received. Therefore, advanced communication methods are also required here.

"Programming" means that we want to use systematic methods in all of this and not learn through trial and error. It's about discovering procedures and processes that can also be transferred to other areas and people. Many NLP techniques are content-free, which means that the same method can be used for headaches, a phobia, or to build an irresistible motivation. NLP describes procedures and processes that can and are effective regardless of the content.

Based on this approach, NLP developed in two complementary directions:

- In the first direction, as a process for discovering the pattern of brilliant achievements in every conceivable social area.

- The second direction is a compilation of effective ways of thinking and communication used by outstanding personalities in this field.

Beginnings of NLP

In the spring of 1972, Bandler himself offered a Gestalt therapy seminar, inspired by his studies' lack of real significance. It was possible for students in an advanced semester. He focused mainly on studying the therapeutic effects of gestalt work in a group and improving his theoretical skills in practice.

During these seminars, John Grinder became aware of Bandler's research, joining him and his exploration. From then on, both worked together on Bandler's workshops, with John Grinder, a beginner to counseling and psychotherapy.

Between 1972 and 1974, intense and productive cooperation took place, with Grinder benefiting from Bandler's knowledge of psychotherapy and Bandler's knowledge of linguistics.

This combination was particularly useful in modeling Virginia Satir's therapeutic masterpieces, Friedrich Perl's, and hypnotherapist Milton Erickson. When modeling, a person's unique skills are made learnable and accessible through systematic and accurate observation and questioning. Patterns and principles were developed so that interested people could also emulate the skills.

Bandler and Grinder were not primarily concerned with explaining something real but with discovering something useful for others. As proof of the success of their analyses and observations on Satir and Perl's, they saw evidence that in other people, they could achieve the same results as the person who modeled them.

In early 1974, both began designing the first meta-model structures with students held in Mission Street squat, Santa Cruz. To simply put, and the meta-model is a set of particular questions to uncover thinking processes and obtain in-depth knowledge. The starting point for research in the meta-model groups was that verbal communication between therapist and client is central to any therapeutic change work. Consequently, it was believed that common language patterns would crystallize and be cemented in Friedrich Perl's and Virginia Satir's verbal communication, making the dysfunctional processes conscious and causing change.

With John Grinder's linguistic context knowledge, both researchers succeeded in creating starting points for a model that allowed the targeted collection of information about a person's imaginary world. They modeled Perl's and Satir's critical linguistic skills and explained these constructs clearly and thus move them on.

From late 1974, Bandler and Grinder regularly participated in teaching seminars given by hypnotherapist Milton H. Erickson. Again, with the primary objective of researching Erickson's work with people, talking about his language patterns and actions. The findings were refined as with Satir and Perl's, reported in writing, tested for applicability in student groups, and integrated into the current knowledge base.

In 1974 and 1975, more formal communication models became the focus of group study. Since Perl's non-verbal actions often appeared to contribute significantly to the therapeutic impact achieved in addition to language behavior, the beneficial non-verbal elements were then specifically evaluated and attempted to address them. The resulting models were then used for both psychotherapy and daily contact.

Various types of procedures were used and revamped, leading, in addition to Perl's and Satir methods, to the current NLP shape. Bandler and Grinder published their first discoveries in four books from 1975 to 1977. These were:

In 1977, Grinder and Bandler held their first U.S. public seminars. The seminars were received very quickly. NLP's awareness has grown noticeably in the following years and is now used worldwide, especially in therapy, education, and management.

Bandler and Grinder developed reframing in 1982. It shows how one can contact unconscious parts, causing unwanted behaviors or disease symptoms. It enabled changes that were recently only conceivable under classical hypnosis.

1984 introduced the concept of submodalities, inventing one of NLP's most significant and impressive techniques. The submodalities represent a kind of brain programming language that everyone can use if they know the commands. People take information with their five senses, process it, and store it internally as events and thoughts represented in their senses, the so-called modalities. These modalities can, in turn, be specified more precisely, so it is possible to ask more precisely about an experience's inner picture. The fantastic thing about it is that it takes advantage of the fact that the human brain reacts to WHAT we think and how a person thinks, e.g., more in color pictures or black and white pictures.

James developed Time Line Therapy (Zeitlinie) in 1988. This method is particularly suitable for gently healing past traumatic experiences. Using the timeline, unconscious or repressed traumas causing physical or emotional problems can be found and mentally processed.

In 1990, Robert Dilts developed reimprinting to change our childhood's relational structures to limit beliefs and beliefs. An imprint is a decisive experience from which the person concerned has formed a belief or bundle of beliefs that are effective in his world. Such an imprint usually also includes an unconscious assumption of the role by other important people involved. The purpose of reimprinting is to find the missing resources, change the belief, and adapt the role model developed to the person's actual and acute circumstances.

Unlike popular belief, Grinder and Bandler did not create NLP alone. After thirty years of silence, a third colleague now goes public: Frank Pucelik.

Chapter 2. How NLP Works, Importance of NLP, and is NLP Effective?

How NLP Works?

If you are coming across this topic for the first time, NLP may appear or seem like magic or hypnosis. When a person is undergoing therapy, this topic digs deep into the patient's unconscious mind. It filters through different layers of beliefs and the person's approach or perception of life to deduce the early childhood experiences responsible for a behavioral pattern.

In NLP, it is believed that everyone has the resources that are needed for positive changes in their own lives. The technique adopted here is meant to help in facilitating these changes.

Usually, when NLP is taught, it is done in a pyramidal structure. However, the most advanced techniques are left for those multi-thousand-dollar seminars. An attempt to explain this complicated subject is to state that the NLP user (as those who use NLP will often call themselves) is always paying keen attention to the person they are working on/with.

Usually, many NLP users are therapists, and they are very likely to be well-meaning people. They achieve their aims by paying attention to those subtle cues like the eye's movement, flushing of the skin, dilation of the pupil, and subtle nervous tics. It is easy for an NLP user to determine the following quickly:

- The side of the brain that the person uses predominantly.

- The sense (smell, sight, etc.) that is more dominant in a person's brain.

- The way the person's brain stores and uses information.

- When the person is telling a lie or concocting information.

When the NLP user has successfully gathered all this information, they slowly and subtly mimic the client by taking on their body language and imitating their speech and mannerisms. They start to talk about language patterns that aim to target the client's primary senses. They will typically fake the social cues that will quickly make someone let their guard down to become very open and suggestible.

For example, when a person's sense of sight is their most dominant sense, the NLP user will use a very laden language with visual metaphors to speak with them. They will say things like: "do you see what I am talking about?" or "why not look at it this way?" For a person that has a more dominant sense of hearing, he will be approached with an auditory language like: "listen to me" or "I can hear where you're coming from."

The NLP user mirrors the body language and the other person's linguistic patterns to create a rapport. This rapport is a mental and physiological state that a human being gets into when they lose their social senses. When they begin to feel like the other person they are conversing with; it is just like them.

Once the NLP user has achieved this rapport, they will take charge of the interaction by leading it mildly and subtly. Thanks to the fact that they have already mirrored the other person, they will now begin to make some subtle changes to gain a particular influence on the person's behavior. It is also combined with some similar subtle language patterns, which lead to questions and a whole phase of some other techniques.

At this point, the NLP user will be able to tweak and twist the person to whichever direction they so desire. It only happens if the other person can't deduce that something is going on because they assume everything is happening organically or consent to everything.

In NLP, there is a belief in the need for nature's perfection of human creation, so every client is encouraged to recognize the senses' sensitivity and use them to respond to specific problems. NLP also believes that the mind can find cures for diseases and sicknesses.

Importance of NLP

NLP's effectiveness is focused on the idea that your mind and body are all the tools you need to improve your life and your world. It will help you to identify specific goals and act. And by analyzing your behaviors' changes, you can adjust them to produce better performance.

Some clinical studies suggest positive benefits to weight loss, reduced anxiety, and a healthy mood from Neuro-speaker programming. A specific investigation also reveals a positive impact on children's learning abilities with dyslexia, helping them improve their self-esteem by reducing their anxiety level. Here are the other importance or benefits of NLP:

As an adult, NLP lets you take responsibility for events that we feel we can't manage. A person can change his or her responses to past events and control their future through NLP. It is essential to be aware of people's body language in your inner circle and those you want to communicate with. NLP offers opportunities to use controlled and purposeful language. It helps you to monitor your life. With the same mind, you can't make the same mistakes and expect a different outcome. A Neuro-Linguistic (NLP) class is all about YOU; you are the subject. It is more important because it gives you more insight when dealing with individuals when dealing with yourself or yourself as an entity.

NLP helps you improve sales performance, income, health problems, better service to client, family, parenting, and all areas of your life. It allows you to become whole when your relationship with yourself and people is whole as an individual.

NLP helps you focus on your ideas, beliefs, and values. It allows you to understand your brain functions, how it develops patterns, how these behaviors become habits, how these habits become actions, and how these actions become outcomes.

The NLP application covers different professions and vocations in life. It is a highly competent tool for sales degrees, self-help and development experts, parents, teachers, communications, etc.

"You are all you ought to be, and all this is sufficient. Be proud of who you are and love who you are."

Is NLP Effective?

Based on valid, recognized, and established scientific research in sociology, linguistics, and psychology, NLP theories have been largely discredited as pseudo-science. The founders of NLP based their theories on sound scientific research. Still, the scientific community has repeatedly stated that the founders' comments and responses to inquiries have demonstrated that they do not understand the underlying theories they often cite in their work. Also, they have not produced any of their actual scientific evidence to support the claims made by NLP theorists or that their programming sessions bring about the changes they promise.

Mainstream psychology has established through clinical research, practice, and published works the reality of the subconscious mind and the importance of understanding its function to help alleviate, treat, or change harmful psychological developments in individuals. Cognitive-behavioral therapy (CBT) and traditional psychotherapy must meet with fairly rigorous professional standards and are based on proven methods and clinical psychology theories. At the same time, NLP's success record is less consistent and based more on anecdotal testimony.

NLP providers generally have a financial interest in promoting NLP's success, so their testimonials may or may not be accurate. Also, results among people who have completed NLP training sessions are mixed. Some studies have shown that patients who participate in NLP have improved psychological symptoms and a better quality of life. Still, most studies indicate little evidence that NLP can effectively treat any significant psychological disorders, such as anxiety, insomnia, or substance abuse.

However, while clinical studies have discredited NLP as a legitimate form of treatment for severe psychological illnesses, NLP continues to be part of the large, profitable industry that capitalizes on the demand for self-improvement literature. Tony Robbins, the contemporary self-help, self-improvement, and motivational speaking guru, trained with NLP's founders and continues to employ many of their ideas in his famous seminars.

Regardless of all the adverse press reports and scientific criticisms, NLP has spawned a global industry. Companies such as NLP Power, The NLP Center, The Empowerment Partnership, and the founders' own NLP University continue to advertise and promote their services on the internet and provide behavior modification training to a global audience. Many corporations and government agencies also send employees to NLP-based seminars to train leadership teams and sales staff. Thus, while the scientific foundations of NLP have been exposed and discredited, these organizations continue to attract followers and clients who see a benefit in the behavioral changes that result from associating with organizations that provide training in psychological and behavioral change.

Chapter 3. Components of NLP and NLP Techniques

Components of NLP

NLP's core philosophy is built on three essential components. From these components, other researchers and practitioners have expanded upon them. So long as these three components are respected, NLP is believed to work and be effective. To reach their maximum potential, practitioners need to pay close attention to how these pillars interact with one another.

Subjectivity

The first component, or core concept, is subjectivity. It is based on the fact that we all have different perceptions of the world around us. And while there are universal concepts that are believed and accepted, the fact of the matter is that we all have an experience that differs significantly.

Moreover, subjectivity is the basis of human experience. Therefore, we need to engage all of our senses to perceive the world as best we can. It is why educators who implement NLP seek to engage all five senses within the learning experience. That way, learners can get a good sense of the content they are trying to internalize.

Consciousness

NLP is predicated because the human psyche is built on a dual-layer of consciousness and unconsciousness. In this manner, the human psyche uses consciousness to express rationality for the things that we do daily. On the flip side, unconsciousness is the automatic manifestation of the built-in programming that we have accrued throughout your evolution.

Learning

Learning occurs when the conscious internalization of the world around us is achieved through the senses' perception. When a person can internalize content or their particular perception of the experiences they live, they can transform this into learning. It is why experience is crucial to the effectiveness of NLP. Unless a human is unable to experience the world, meaningful learning cannot fully take place.

NLP Techniques and How They Work

Neuro-Linguistic Programming (NLP) tells you that emotions and experiences guide people on their planet's view. It tells us that what you currently see isn't the critical world but a distorted representation supported your beliefs, perceptions, values, and other variables. NLP techniques will help you integrate aspects of your life, improve your quality, and understand how people work. Discover how to use these NLP techniques to enhance communication skills and emotional intelligence that you can use to regulate your life and mind.

Anchoring

The anchoring technique in NLP is important to tug up a particular emotion or put yourself into a specific psychological state, which may be used on yourself or somebody else. It works by integrating emotion with a physical movement, and the anchor laying dubs it. For example, if you decided to tug the thrilling feeling, you'd start by brooding about the days you have been euphoric. You'd wish to tell the account of what went on in your head that led to the present moment. Mention how it feels and enter an excellent deal of detail. Remember the instant, the emotions.

First, confine your right to your left index and middle fingers. Squeeze them twice. Mention your special moment on the second squeeze and strive to feature the feeling. Describe once more how you are feeling, how you think, and clap your hands twice. Let the nice and cozy feeling double once you clap the second time. Roll in the hay continuously for five times.

You'll use those gestures to regain your feeling of happiness. You'd use a fast touch of the arm to secure them if you were to try this to a different man.

Meta Model

The methodology of the meta-model of NLP is usually wont to understand other individuals' concerns. It could even be wont to support others to possess a better understanding of their issues. The aim is to dismantle the conversation, assist you in achieving the basis explanation for the difficulty, and fix it. The response is consciously or unconsciously understood when someone features a question, but the only solution is some things that they are doing not like. The shortage of uncertainty allows the crisis to persist, anticipating that there'll finally be a replacement solution. You'll help them develop how by deconstructing the way someone explains their question.

Mirroring

One of the foremost relevant NLP strategies you ought to learn is mirroring. It'll be very beneficial to be good at mirroring. It's been quite hard to hate someone who knows the way to do that act. Moreover, it's the replication of the individual you interact with (i.e., his/her behaviors). While being subtle and typically subconscious, this simulation is complete. Copying somebody's speech patterns, visual communication, vocabulary style, speed, rhythm, pitch, voice, and volume are ways you'll do that.

Framing

The technique of NLP framing is employed to affect the rise or decrease of the emotional feeling significantly. It is an excellent way to use alongside most of the others. You are going to experience good and bad moments in life. These should enable you to be ready to learn and grow in your life. Nonetheless, memories haven't any feelings connected to them. Such separation occurs because memories and thoughts exist in several parts of the brain. Therefore, at present, you'll experience feelings, then you'll be ready to remember them. The hippocampus is that the brain part that's liable for LTM storage. The amygdala is the brain's portion that regulates feelings. The amygdala will offer you a fast-little reminder of what you feel once you recall a memory from the hippocampus. Simply because of that, the feeling that's important to a selected memory is often modified.

Pattern Interruption

Interruption of the pattern is usually wont to preserve words during a listener's subconscious. One great technique to pair with others is that this technique. To try this, you've got to draw the listener's thoughts into a series or pattern form. When the model gets out of control before finishing the shape, you would like to require them out of the template for a critical juncture. The listener's unconscious is meant to embody the pattern while the conscious mind is overwhelmed at that moment. You'll change the way you think that check out the past, and consider your life with a replacement way of thinking by learning NLP. It can help to enhance your communication skills and enhance your emotional intelligence.

Chapter 4. The Swish Pattern

The Swish Pattern is your answer to powerful and constant change. It is one of the most widely known and widely used NLP tools, and it helps people genuinely create their ideal self and eliminate negative behaviors. Using visualization, the Swish Pattern allows you to take the old images and behaviors you have developed over the years and replace them with powerful, dynamic. All-around better images and behaviors that work for the new ideal life you want to build.

First, though, you need to understand what visualization is:

Visualization

Visualization has gotten a bad rep, mostly because it has been tied up with Oprah's new age movement and the Law of Attraction. Everything can be yours if you just sit down and visualize that it is yours. And that is left behind many bitter and angry people who are ready to say visualization is not good. But, visualization is a tool used by athletes, politicians, and billionaire business people who want to get more and more from their life. Which is all to say many people are wrong.

One of the essential foundational tools for change when it comes to using NLP is visualization. To powerfully use all the NLP tools, you will need to understand what visualization is and how to use it, especially when using the Swish Pattern.

Power of Visualization

Dr. Biasiatto did a study at the University of Chicago, where he took three groups of people and tested their free-throw ability. He took note of each of their scores, and then he had one group practice their free throws for an hour every day for a month. The second group makes them visualize, making free throws for a little bit every day. In the third group, he had to do nothing at all.

In the end, the group that did nothing improved in no way whatsoever. The first group that practiced an hour a day improved their free throws by 24%. The visualization group was just 1% short of people who practiced for an hour a day. They improved at nearly the same rate as those practicing every day through merely the power of mental rehearsal.

Study after study has confirmed that the brain processes a visualized event the same way a real event happens. Athletes who visualize their playing see their muscle fibers activate and their brain process as if they are doing it. Some of the world's wealthiest and most influential people talk about using visualization to enhance their success, get better ideas, and achieve faster.

Visualizing is real. It works when you know how to do it. But, there are a few things that usually trip people up that do not have to trip you up. First and foremost, you do not have to be able to see anything. It is so important because many people think if they are not visual thinkers, then the visualization will not work for them, so they never try it.

Also, though, this will come if you practice visualization enough, your brain will learn to start creating images, and you'll feel a lot better about the whole process. But for many people, they are not visual thinkers, so they're initially just not seeing anything.

It's okay. You do not have to see anything to visualize (as weird as that sounds). Your brain will create experiences for you; if you focus on it, you will access other areas of your body, whether kinesthetic, verbal or anything else.

You will develop the feelings and the skills you are looking for. Now that you understand visualization, let us talk about the Swish Pattern.

The Swish Pattern

The Swish Pattern is a life changer that helps people with weight loss, smoking cessation, better habits, a healthy self-image, a more meaningful and better life. The thing is that you already have your ideal-self likely built inside of you. You know what your life would look like if you did not have your problems and what amazing things could happen with your life once those problems were solved.

You probably have a self-image of yourself that is far and away from your ideal, one that has been built by those problems weighing you down and working on you. It is these two images that you can leverage to make significant changes in your life.

Swish Pattern Step by Step

Step 1: Recognize Your Automatic Reactions

Images, thoughts, emotions, and a host of other things can cause you to have an adverse reaction. Whether you are reaching for a cigarette or a muffin, or it is making you yell and scream, or retreat and cower. We all respond to certain stimuli in remarkably consistent ways with our character that probably does not always help us be the best version of ourselves that we would want to be. You want to find that automatic response for whatever behavior or emotion or anything else that you want to fix. Once you do, you want to narrow down all the images, emotions, and anything else that forms in your mind when you respond in those automatic fashions.

You want to create an ideal image, a simple, powerful one that connects with your emotional state. It should be inspiring, exciting, and something that should make you want to change. You want to create this image focusing on your life would be like without whatever negative automatic response you have.

Once you have these two things, you want to create an image of yourself disassociated from both of these things, almost as if you're watching these two images from a distance, looking at them, admiring them.

Step 2: Determine the Cause of the Negative Image

As we said, you have automatic responses, and hopefully, you will have found them. Now, it is time to isolate what causes these automatic responses. Something brings these negative states to the forefront of your mind. Negative behaviors do not come from anywhere. Find that trigger. Ask yourself, "What Occurs Before This Negative State Begins?" This way, you can imagine the automatic response happening from the trigger and be prepared to create an alternative response to this event in the future.

Step 3: Prepare for Displacement

Take the positive image that you made initially, make it the size of a postage stamp in your mind, and place it on the corner of your developed negative image. You will want to notice a few things from its placement in the corner of the image. Its brightness, it is strength, and everything else that makes it stand out.

Step 4: Swish the Two Images

Now you are going to swish the images back and forth. Making a Swish sound can help because it gives your brain something else to engage with. Imagine the images switching places—the positive one growing more prominent, brighter, and more colorful. The negative one shoots off into the distance of your mind, disappearing and becoming nothing but a memory.

Notice how the further an image travels in your mind, the further the malicious behavior feels a part of you. More importantly, notice how, when the positive image gets brighter, your positive image can feel better.

Step 5: Repeat the Process

Keep repeating the swishing. Bring the old image back to the front of your mind; notice it as it loses color, as it gets blurry, as it begins to lose more and more of its power. You will notice the more powerful image continuing to glow brighter and brighter in the corner, almost as if it cannot be contained.

Keep the process going until the negative image has become tattered, black and white, blurry, and no longer packs the same emotions with it that it once did.

Step 6: Test It

Think about your negative emotion, think about the trigger, and find out if it is now replaced with that more powerful image that you want.

The Swish Pattern is a powerful tool, and it can completely liberate you from your negative behaviors and negative beliefs if you let it and you work it. It is there to help you genuinely transform how you live. You should notice improvement within a few days of using it, especially if you do it every day for a few days until it becomes part of your unconscious. There is no such thing as a transformation without actual work. You are going to have to work at it. The people who complain about the Swish Pattern do so because they thought they could do it once and forget it. But, that is not how it works. That is not how life works. But if you do it few a few days in a row, keep testing it; find where you're feeling weak with it. Within a week, you should see a clear improvement in your malicious behavior and see a positive transformation.

It works, and it works well. As you move through life, consistently trying to make yourself the best version of yourself possible, you will need to use this technique every time you want to end a malicious behavior. The more negative behaviors, beliefs, and emotions you can eliminate from your life, the better your overall life will be. The more you use this, the faster it will work, and the more powerful this technique will become in helping you create the behaviors and strengths you want in your life. You can install everything you want inside of you. You can make your life as exciting and memorable as possible.

The best thing about the swish pattern is that you can do it just about anywhere, and you can control the process. No need for audiotapes or some outside person guiding you through the process; no, you can be in complete control and have full power over yourself.

Start the process now and figure out what you want to change and what negative behaviors you want to eliminate from your life for good. Then create a list of desired behaviors and start to craft out everything that you want to do with your life and what your life will be like if you had these fantastic new behaviors instead of the negative ones you want to get rid of.

The more you design out your amazing future and your amazing life, the more you craft out the opportunity to create something marvelous for yourself to take over.

Chapter 5. Hypnosis

Hypnosis is a position of consciousness that involves focused attention, together with reduced peripheral awareness characterized by the participant's increased ability to respond to suggestions given. Every person has a waking state, a state when they know that they are awake, alert, alive, and in the universe.

What happens is that your attention becomes more and more focused, and your awareness of your environment diminishes. Your attention has more focused on what is inside and lesser on what is occurring outside. It makes you much more aware of your internal images, feelings, and thoughts and less aware of things going on in your surroundings. Usually, it's so pleasant for many people, enjoyable and very relaxing.

Highly imaginative people are usually easier to hypnotize: they have an intense experience of both nature and art. Psychopaths tend to be immune to hypnosis because psychopaths tend to have restricted emotions, but many people are easily hypnotized. Being in a hypnotic state is a regular aspect of human life. Often, creative people use guided imagination in their daily routine without necessarily realizing it as a hypnotic technique.

Three Stages of Hypnosis

Hypnosis is more of an ability than a disadvantage unless you are often hypnotically governed by an external force. Three stages are recognized in the hypnosis field:

Induction

It is the first stage involved in hypnosis. Before a subject undergoes full hypnosis, the subject is introduced to the hypnotic induction technique. For many years, hypnotic induction was used to put the participant into their hypnotic trance, but the definition has altered some modern times. Some of the non-state theorists have comprehended this stage a bit differently. Instead, the theorists understand this stage as the technique to enhance the subjects' expectations of what will happen—defining the role that they will play, getting their attention to concentrate on the right direction and any of the steps that are required to lead the subject into the appropriate direction of hypnosis.

Various induction methods can be applied during hypnosis. The most used method is the Braidism technique. The Braids technique has a few variations, like the Stanford Hypnotic Susceptibility Scale, which is the most applied research tool in the hypnosis field.

For you to apply the Braidism technique, you will have to follow the following steps:

- First, take any object that you can find bright, for example, a watch case, hold it between your middle, fore, and thumb fingers on the left hand. Hold the object somewhere above the forehead to produce a lot of strain on the eyelids and eyes. During the process so that the subject can maintain a fixed stare on the object at all times.

- Secondly, the hypnotist should then explain to the subject that they should keep their eyes often fixed on the object. The subject will also be required to focus theirs mindfully on the idea of that specific object. The subject should not be allowed to think of any other thing or let their mind wander, or else, the process will not be successful.

After some time, the subject's eyes will start to dilate. With some more time, the subject will begin to assume a wavy motion. If the subject involuntarily closes their eyelids when the fore and middle fingers of the right hand are carried from their eyes to the object, they are in a trance. If this is not the case, the subject will be required to start the process again: you should ensure that you let the subject know that they are to let their eyes close once the fingers are carried in a similar motion back towards the eyes again. It will get the subject to go into an altered state of the mind or hypnosis.

Suggestion

At first, the term suggestion was not used. Instead, Braid defined this stage as the act of having the conscious mind of the subject concentrate on one dominant and central idea. Braid did this to reduce or trigger the various regions' physiological functioning on the subject's body. Braid then started to emphasize applying various non-verbal and verbal forms of suggestion to get the subject into the mind's hypnotic condition. These would involve using waking suggestions as well as self-hypnosis. Hippolyte Bernheim, another hypnotist, emphasized the hypnosis process's physical condition over the psychological process that included verbal suggestions. According to Hippolyte, hypnosis is the induction of a physical state that is peculiar and which will enhance the susceptibility of the suggestion to the subject. He always stated that the hypnotic condition that is induced would assist in facilitating the suggestion.

Modern hypnotism applies various suggestions to be successful, such as direct verbal suggestions, insinuations, metaphors, non-verbal suggestions, and other figures of speech that are non-verbal. Some of the non-verbal suggestions that may be used would include mental imagery, voice tonality, and physical manipulation.

One of the distinctions made in the types of suggestions offered to the subject includes those suggestions delivered with permission and more authoritarian. One of the aspects that have to be considered regarding hypnosis is the difference between conscious and unconscious minds. Several hypnotists view this stage to communicate directed to most of the participant's conscious minds.

Susceptibility

It has been observed that people will react differently to hypnosis. Some will find that they can easily fall into a hypnotic trance and don't have to put much effort into the process. Others will find that they can get into the hypnotic trance, but only after a prolonged period and with some effort applied. Still, other people will find that they cannot get into the trance and, even after constant efforts, will not reach their goals.

One thing that has been found about the various subject's susceptibility is that this part remains unchanging. If you have gotten into a trance easily, you will likely be the same way for the rest of your life. On the contrary, if you have challenges teaching your hypnotic star of mind and have never been experiencing hypnotized, then it is probably that you never will.

Two types of victims are considered to be highly susceptible to the effects of hypnotism. These include:

- Fantasizers
- Associates

Fantasizers will have a high score on the absorption scales; they will block out easily the real world's stimuli without the use of hypnosis. They spend a lot of time daydreaming, they grew up in an environment where imaginary play was encouraged, and they had imaginary pals when they were in their childhood.

Associates will always come from childhood abuse or trauma; they found ways to forget their trauma and escape into numbness. When they daydream, it is more in terms of going blank instead of creating fantasies. Both dissociation and fantasizers score highly on the tests of hypnotic susceptibility.

Two groups of people with the highest hypnotism rates include those suffering from dissociative identity disorder and post-traumatic stress disorder.

Effects of Hypnosis

In a trance state, your ability to think logically and critically reduces. You tend to accept any information that is given to you without thinking if it's reasonable and rational or not.

People in a hypnotic state are suggestible. They tend to consent uncritically to any suggestions given to them. Even the strong-willed people can be hypnotized and made to do things that they wouldn't normally do.

Conscious decision making, independent judgment, and rational analysis are all suspended. It is a bonus for leaders who, after all, don't want their members thinking of themselves. Hypnosis is an incredibly powerful set of tools to influence others and manipulate others to do things that violate their ethics and morals.

What Manipulators Say

It is exciting that most leaders usually claim that people can't be made to do things against their will, even when applying mind control hypnosis.

The members are programmed to agree to whatever the leaders say. Therefore, the members will tend to accept the idea. Implicit in the idea is that if the person does something, they do it of their own volition.

When you make your own decisions, you believe more firmly and more committed to the outcome, and the actions and effects of your decision last longer.

Myths About Hypnosis

You should remember that hypnosis is not often a closed-eye process. It's not compulsory to have your eyes closed to be in a trance. Have you ever tried to be on a trip or journey, and when you reach your destination, you do not even remember much of the journey? That is an example of a trance that you were in.

People in a trance state who are driving while their eyes are entirely open and performing; if they see a person in front braking, there's no difficulty in braking themselves and doing what is necessary to avoid accidents. Many have the idea that there are unique hypnotic words to trigger trance. Hypnosis can be triggered in normal-sounding conversations, using the daily words.

Chapter 6. Brainwashing

If you talk to someone and ask them what they think brainwashing is, they may reply that they know because this is a topic that many people have heard about. But most people don't have a full understanding of how this kind of mind control can work. And if you are trying to fight off someone using dark psychology, you must make sure that you understand this topic.

Brainwashing will be the slow process of taking the ideas that a victim has about their identity and their beliefs and then replacing them with new ideas to suit the manipulator's purpose. Brainwashing can occur in a narrow and broad context. For example, a brainwasher could use the techniques to control one person or use those techniques to control a more extensive group's minds all at once.

The Process of Brainwashing

The starting point of brainwashing is the social circumstances and the mental state of the victim. It will be the basis for the rest of the process, and if the manipulator cannot figure this part out, then the brainwashing session won't be successful. Brainwashing is not a process that is going to work out for everyone. It will require an adequate identification of a person looking for something or someone who has a void they are trying to fill.

It brings us to an important point. Who is the ideal victim for a brainwasher? People who have had their existing reality shaken up because of some recent events are excellent brainwashers' targets. If you have lost someone you are close to or had another dramatic or traumatic event in your life, then you may be more susceptible to brainwashing.

Once the brainwasher has found their victim, the process of brainwashing can begin. Contrary to the popular image you may have in your mind about a brainwasher, this person will often come across as someone rational, friendly, and calm. Someone who seems to have their lives together in a way the victim wishes they could have their own. Visualize how it would feel if you were homeless and a celebrity you admired befriended you. It is often how the process of meeting the brainwasher is going to feel for the victim.

The brainwasher is going to get to work right away. The first step for them is to create a rapport and trust between them and the victim. It is going to be done with superficial and deep similarities. The superficial similarities could involve some surface-level preferences, something like enjoying the same food or sport as the other person.

They will then move on to a deeper level of rapport, some that could involve a more in-depth shared experience that they had in the past. The brainwasher will most likely fake these, convincingly, to create these bonds. If the victim shares with the brainwasher that they lost a close relative in the past, then the brainwasher is suddenly going to have a similar story to share with the victim.

This false connection and warmth emotionally are not the only thing that is going to occur. The brainwasher wants to cement that new bond as quickly as possible. It is not unconventional for them to provide favors and gifts to their victim. They could send them a gadget or some other item they may find useful. They may treat the victim to a meal. It is to create a sense of gratitude and indebtedness from the victim to that brainwasher. It is going to soften up a lot of the resistance that the victim may experience.

After the resistance has been stripped away a little bit, the other step will be a sort of romantic presentation. It will involve the brainwasher slowly and increasingly offer a solution to any problems that the victim recently opened up about. It is not going to be a big hard push or sell. Instead, the brainwasher knows how to do this in an offhand and casual way to make sure they don't deal with any negative experiences by pressing the victim. This solution will always be the personality, ideology, or cult that the brainwasher is working to make the victim convert.

When these steps are done correctly, the initial stages will leave the victim wanting more. The victim will want more information and more understanding of the solution that the brainwasher hints at. The brainwasher may even withhold some of this information initially, treating it as something that the victim needs to do some work to attain. Doing this is to push the victim to seek out and accept the information they are eventually going to hear.

After the victim has had some time being spoon-fed snippets of this belief system, and they have shown they will respond well to them, the brainwasher will be careful to reveal the right information at the right time. It is a concept that is called a gradual revelation or milk before meat. It will include the presentation of an easy to accept idea before the controversial idea is revealed.

For example, if the brainwasher is trying to convert the victim over to religious terrorism, they would not start with the terrorism part. They may initially start focusing on the fact that God loves the victim, something that the victim is likely to accept. The more objectionable ideas, such as God wants you to blow yourself up, are ones that are saved until much after in the process. Once the victim has accepted that last part, then this brainwashing session is at a point of no return.

In this situation, you may be curious why the victim is still engaging with the brainwasher, especially when these more objectionable ideas become apparent. There are three main reasons:

The brainwasher has worked on the vulnerable victim. They feel a strong sense of liking the brainwasher, and they want to get the brainwasher's approval.

The victim has invested some time, and in some cases, money, in the process up to this point. It is often known as the sunk cost fallacy. The victim will feel like it is terrible to throw away all the hard work and money they have put into the process.

During this process, the brainwasher has been amassing many sensitive and secretive information on the victim. The brainwasher is often willing to hold this information over the victim to keep the victim on the right path.

The Impact of Brainwashing

The above analysis that we did about brainwashing is going to show how severe this technique can be. It is changing the victim's beliefs and inner identity, and this can be a big deal. Sure, the manipulator will get what they want out of the process, but the victim will lose out on their real identity and often gets so far into the process that they aren't sure what went wrong.

Many different impacts will come with brainwashing after the process is completed. The first one is a loss of identity. Many ideologies and cults feature that the people who go through the initiation process are given a new name. It helps the psyche of the person to detach from their old identity altogether. They can believe things and even do things they would never have done in the past because that older adult they were no longer exists. When this process is carried out the proper way, it can leave a victim feeling like all the parts of their old identity are no longer real or permanent and that they have woken up from a nightmare.

Post-traumatic stress disorder, or PTSD, can sometimes be a hallmark of those who managed to escape or rescued from a situation where they were brainwashed. The victims of these brainwashing endeavors will show some of the same psychological and physical signs as war veterans who were right in the battle. The severity of this traumatic aftermath shows that this type of process, of the manipulator getting more control over the victim, could harm the victim as much as if they went to war.

Brainwashing is something that can have a lasting impact. There are plenty of examples of rescued individuals or who managed to escape from their brainwashing situation, who then went back to that situation of their own free will. Even when they were able to leave the brainwashing and controlling environment they were in, the legacy that came with that process was done so well and ran so deep in their mind that the victim wants to return to it. It shows the power of using this brainwashing process and how much a manipulator could gain.

Chapter 7. How to Use NLP for in Sales

We are all on sale, believe it or not. When was the last time you had to sell an idea you had to your boss or your colleagues or make a proposal to increase your project budget? When was the last time you had to convince your kids to do something they were supposed to do? Whether you sell a product, service, concept, or influence others to achieve the desired result, you sell.

The following 5-step sales process seems to be a simple framework to use and remember:

- Establish and maintain a rapport.
- Understand your client or potential client.
- Define the need/define the value.
- Need/value link to your product or service.
- Close the sale.

Neuro-linguistic Programming is the study of excellence and excellent communication and how to reproduce it. Your ability to communicate effectively is the key to your success in any business interaction. So, let's look at each step of the 5-step sales process and see how NLP fits in.

Establish and Maintain a Rapport

Keeping eye contact while talking or listening to another person is one way to stay connected. Leaning or bending forward and tilting a bit your head to the side while listening shows that you are entirely listening and engaged to the person you're talking to. Uniting and reflecting body, voice, and words is another way to create and maintain relationships. Any resistance you encounter means that you have not established enough relationships and an excellent indicator to go back and build an additional connection. Making a rapport is the first step to getting better results in sales or any communication interaction.

Understand Your Client or Potential Client

The best way to understand your client or prospect is to ask many open questions. Asking questions will allow you to know your client/potential client better and will allow you to identify if it is necessary for your product or service. Find out what is important to them, how they think and process information. Observe their eye patterns as they answer questions to see where they are going to access private information. Look at the main words you use most often. Do they prefer visual words and descriptors such as "I see, can I imagine," or do they incline to the auditory words "I hear what you think," "it sounds true." Or are they more appropriate with kinesthetic phrases like "I understand what you are saying"? I feel your passion. "If you understand the needs of the client or potential client and understand their communication style and preferences, you will be better prepared to communicate with them in a way that works best for them.

Define the Need/Define the Value

Once you have determined the need, you need to define a value. Do you realize it would be useful to solve your problem or improve the situation? Reinforce your value proposition by asking something like, "So it would be useful to answer that, right? Is it something that would interest you or not?" It is an important problem because they may have a need but see no value in solving it. Most sellers spend 80% of their time on people who don't buy. You want potential clients/buyers to buy while ensuring that the value solves their problem is crucial to your sales pitch.

Connect Need/Value to Your Product or Service

You don't sell a product or service in the sales process. You sell emotion. We believe it is our sound mind that makes the decision, but the fact is that all of our memories, feelings, and emotions are stored in our unconscious. Furthermore, the more significant part of our choices is made subliminally. Connecting with your client or client's sentiment is the key to your ability to close a sale successfully. For example, potential buyers looking to buy a new home can see the value of a locker room. You associate it with the sensation she will feel when she wakes up in the morning, approaches her, and feels good when she sees and chooses clothes quickly in the morning. This feeling will connect her to the house they are selling.

Close

If you have successfully followed steps 1 through 4, closing should be smooth. Just ask for a purchase or order. Take advantage of the sale to the end and look for a win-win opportunity.

Chapter 8. How to Use NLP in Relationships

In this part, we will know how NLP can be beneficial to healthy relationships. We will learn what excellent and fulfilling relationships are based on and built upon. We will explore techniques that can strengthen relationships and those that can help us establish healthy relationships. We will talk about the benefits or importance of our mental health and readiness before entering any partnership or relationship and possible outcomes associated with having and not having these factors.

Once you have decided what you want, now is the time to enter into a relationship and have covered your predetermining factors. Now you can begin to open up to the possibilities of finding the right person. Here is when rapport becomes essential. What is rapport? It's your similarities and likeness with someone you are interested in entering a relationship with. It's also the establishment of trust with that person. With rapport, many individual factors can be used for determining compatibility. Some of these are personality types, values, beliefs, culture, political ideologies, interests, religious beliefs, etc. Of course, physical characteristics, such as gender and body types, need to be considered. However, some features can't be overaccentuated because it will mimic the other and cause a loss of rapport.

The rapport established initially, the reasons for your attraction to your partner, and his or her attraction to you must be kept at the forefront of each partner's mind throughout the relationship. It all too familiar for people to enter relationships with guns blazing, meaning being the perfect partner, only to begin to relax and change once the relationship has been established. One partner, or both, will use all available techniques to get the other to enter into a relationship. Once they are in that relationship, the other partner believes they can initially tone down what they were doing. It is one of the typical reasons for relationships ending. Keep in mind, the reasons for someone falling for you are the same reasons that will make them want to stay with you. If you remove the reasons for their attraction, they have no reasons to stay with you. Often, we see children born of relationships used as new reasons, but this does not work. It leads the partnership to morph into, what be, a business relationship. There will be no real emotional connection in the relationship and, even though that couple may remain together, they will lack the comforts and fulfillment of needs they desire.

Now you have identified what you want, making sure the timing is right, and have met that special someone. Now, what do you do? You need to ensure that your significant other feels the same about you. There are several ways in which a person can see that they are loved by the other. These ways should be identified at the relationships beginning. A few methods are by what the other person buys and places he or she takes you. There are also things such as how they touch you, the looks they give, or what they say. Identification of these is essential as they can gauge the continuance of love throughout the relationship.

The best way to determine how you can best assure your partner that you love them is by doing what they tend to do for you. For instance, if your partner puts her arm around you at times to assure you of her love and affection, you can bet that if you do the same, she will believe that you do love and appreciate her. We don't tend to do things to or for others, especially those whom we care about the most, that we wouldn't want to be done to us. Although this is commons sense, it's also an excellent method to gauge or determine how your significant other feels about you. As the relationship progresses, this will come naturally and will take much less conscious effort. Be sure not to allow these things to stop just because the relationship is no longer new.

NLP has devised a few strategies to determine areas in relationships. Areas such as attraction, love, and desire are all strategized with NLP techniques. First, you must know your partner. It means that you should know what those subtle gestures and tones of voice your partner will display depending on how they feel. Know what your partner fears and what he or she wants. You will pick up ideas as to how to carry these things out by merely learning your partner. Be sure never to use this knowledge for manipulation. There isn't a positive outcome in relationships where manipulation takes place.

One technique you can use to ensure that your partner is in love with you and wants you is to remove yourself from his or her presence temporarily. It does not mean that you can tell your wife that you are going to the store for a lottery ticket to not return for a week. However, in short time frames, absence can signal want or lack thereof. Just like the cliché, absence makes the heart grow fonder; this is built on the same premise. When using these kinds of tactics, please never overuse them. Here is some advice. If you are an insecure person needing constant approval and reassurance that you are loved, you should take care of that issue before entering a serious relationship. If not, you will not be the right partner. If your shortcoming does not end the relationship, it could lead it to become a codependent partnership or, at the very least, a very unhealthy relationship. Again, you must first make sure that you are the right candidate for entering into a relationship before taking that other step.

With relationships, you are not merely selling yourself to another, and then the job is over. It's a continuing process forever. Never relax and believe that you have your partner and aren't going anywhere, no matter what you may or may not do. You should always be selling yourself, your worth, compassion, and desire for your partner.

Think of this; You meet someone at the beach or any spot you can imagine. You are both at that exact place at that same time. You may both have everything in common too. However, both you and the other person took different routes to that spot and lived through different circumstances while on the way. Even though you both find yourselves to be at the same point and with the same characteristics, you took different paths there. It means that it's likely that you are not both going to react or respond to every event the same, and those events may lead you to go in different directions. Another way to look at this; you may both like the same sports team. The difference is why each of you has this opinion of that team. One of you may be a graduate from that university, while the other just picked last season's champions. It probably means that the school's alumnus is less likely to decide that they no longer favor that team. Regardless of the possible ways, the ending remains the same. What does this mean? Are we all just merely at life's mercy and subject to emotional trauma at the drop of a hat? Not exactly. Although we may not be able to change the situation when finding ourselves here, we can know why. First, don't give up. Do whatever you can to carry both you and your partner through the tough spot in your relationship, and you may find that you both were able to beat the odds and remain together.

Let's look at what it means to have taken different routes. The recently mentioned scenarios were only metaphors. The location isn't an actual place but a specific state of mind and life situation. Regardless of the spectrum of commonalities you and your partner may or may not have, you both will respond and react to things differently. One of you may be able to brush something, such as a traumatic event, off, but the other cannot do that. Let's look at this. Both you and your wife have religious faith. It is one of the main commonalities you found of yourselves that led to your relationship. Then down the road, your wife either endures a traumatic event or meets an influential person, either causing a dramatic shift in her religious ideologies. What was once the main glue that kept you together has deteriorated to where there is no more left. Not only does she no longer agree with your religious faith, but her newfound beliefs also contradict what you believe. What do you do when faced with this situation? Both of you are firmly holding to your individual beliefs and not willing to waiver. Both accuse the other of being naïve. Neither of you is terrible people, but you are no longer finding the same rapport you once had.

You both joined the relationship only after taking the proper steps and exercised due caution in choosing the other as a mate. Even though this was done, life didn't care about that. Circumstances led to the separation of you and your partner's beliefs, and both of you are much too committed to your independent ideas to compromise them. Therefore, you are now at constant odds, and the negativity within the relationship grows stronger each day. One day, it will lead to resentment and even hate. You have taken the necessary steps in attempting to salvage the relationship to no avail. So, as the very last resort, you decide to part ways. It happens every day.

Like the baggage we carry due to prior bad relationships, we have lessons learned and unique ways of dealing with specific issues based on these lessons. The best thing to do is know what and how things are going, and this can give you a good idea as to what is about to come.

To conclude this guide, NLP is essential and beneficial in the relationship. It isn't just with the beginning of the union but throughout its entirety. You must first know yourself, and then using NLP; you can learn your partner. Knowing your partner can prove invaluable in maintaining a healthy and long relationship. Also, the relationship will be much more fulfilling to both parties. Remember that severe and personal relationships prove beneficial in many areas in life and isn't limited to just the partnership. It's beneficial for both of you as a couple, as individuals, and as part of society.

Chapter 9. NLP in Business

NLP enhances negotiation skills and selling skills. Clients who use NLP in the business report that their managers are excellent coaches, motivators, and influencers.

NLP multiplies excellence in any field. It is a skill known as modeling in NLP; it incorporates all other intermediate skills. It is beneficial in a business organization if, for example, business took good employees from each field and brought them together. The work done will be excellent.

NLP helps to improve communication while doing business. During communication, there is the use of verbal and non-verbal cues. Using NLP, one will be able to understand the spoken and unspoken language of clients and prospects.

It helps one to emulate the successful efforts of other businesses easily. NLP teaches one to understand how successful people work and converse. One can then emulate those using NLP strategies to copy those successes to fit their businesses.

NLP gives one sales staff mind-reading abilities. It enables them to understand non-verbal cues and eye movements, allowing them to answer clients' questions and provide useful information about the products. They also understand how a client feels about the product in question, making it easier for them to close sales.

NLP improves negotiation skills. Negotiation is a critical requirement in the business world—negotiation with vendors, employees' marketers, advertising firms, and many more. With NLP negotiation skills, everyone in the business will be more effective and persuasive.

NLP boosts morale. Why wouldn't one's morale be boosted if everyone in the company or office knows how well and effectively you communicate? One can make themselves apparent as well as able to relate with everyone in the office. It makes the workplace much more fun since there is a better understanding of one another.

NLP is the best client service tool. NLP helps to understand clients' complaints and suggestions after a sale. One can discern if a client is complaining because of awful client service or if he or she is having a bad day. When one's client care can understand the client's non-verbal cues, he will be able to deal with the angry client and make them happy to come again.

NLP can be so useful in boosting your entrepreneurial pursuits. It helps build skills in teamwork, coaching, sales, productivity, personal development, and leadership. For NLP to be useful, there must be potential for growth, and human interaction should be present.

NLP is a useful tool when you are setting and working toward achieving your goals. When you are in a business state, you must set your goals, which are supposed to be achievable, intelligent, meaningful, and measurable. For instance, it will not be realistic for you to set a goal to earn millions of dollars within a month without having logical ways to achieve your goal. Thus, using NLP, it is possible to set and achieve goals for your business. Using NLP will help you change your way of thinking and speaking and motivate you to take appropriate actions toward achieving your goal.

When you are in a business, sometimes you become stressed, but if you apply NLP techniques, it is possible to have a happier and more fulfilling life. NLP includes studying successful people's steps to achieve success, and these successes can come out from any part of your body. These techniques will help you overcome phobias, speak with confidence in front of a large congregation, reduce anxiety, and learn how to be in a healthy personal relationship.

Brain Training Success Techniques

Avoid using weak words, such as try. The type of language you will use in your business matters, and you should avoid using vague language. "I will try to get that book tomorrow"—this sentence is not exactly whether you will do it or not. In a business, make your intentions clear, and avoid giving your clients unclear expectations. When dealing with your clients, only use action-based and positive language.

Away from or Move Toward

We all experience problems and obstacles as we move toward success. The way you tackle those problems matters. If you use NLP techniques, it becomes easier. Entrepreneurs have a way of solving their problems. They tend to break tasks, and then they apply logic to it. Then they look at it objectively by removing emotions from that particular problem. You are supposed to move toward the positive "I am capable of doing this. Although it is a difficult job, it is worth it.' And get away from negativity: "This is impossible. I am not able to do this difficult job."

Direction and Focus

NLP helps you use personality to create focus and direction from both a personal and professional perspective, perfect for direct reports in a coaching setting. It involves having an overview of different areas of both life and work, and this helps you have priorities and identify areas of neglect or drift. It enables us to agree to measurable objectives and actions, sharing benefits to both the individual and the organization.

Improving Personal Effectiveness

Improving personal effectiveness is effective in changing the long-term behavior of a person in the workplace. When employees understand one another, it becomes much easier to respond to one another's and the clients' desires and needs. It has been proven that well-functioning and healthy relationships are essential for success in one's personal life.

In conclusion, applying NLP techniques in your business will make you more successful. It is one of the exciting approaches to your problem, and it is worth trying. It improves your way of thinking and helps you achieve your goals.

How to Use NLP to Gain More Wealth and Get Better Results

It is every human being's wish to gain wealth and receive better results in life. We have different ways of doing so, and by using NLP techniques, it is possible to achieve that. These techniques help you to realize yourself and also the best way you can improve your earnings. Those ways are below.

One Can Make Money Using NLP, Using Various Methods

You Can Make Money with NLP as a Coach

Being a coach has many benefits. One can work from anywhere, work at their time, and work at their pay and price. Coaches help clients integrate their desired outcomes, set timelines and deadlines. Create goals, make them achievable, give advice, make the client see things that they cannot see by themselves, and help them stay accountable for what happens to follow up on what is happening.

One Can Also Make Money with NLP as a Practitioner

NLP gives you a tool to work well with people and almost everything that might be bothering them. It has been discovered that most people are looking for NLP practitioners, and one is very marketable. Being a practitioner helps people to:

- **Conquer fear and phobias**

They have different ways of helping people to overcome fear. Sometimes they expose their clients to what they fear most but in a safe and controlled environment. You will realize that you will learn how to combat your anxiety and fear, and after some time, you will be able to control it. Another way they use is teaching their clients the relaxation technique, which will help control both mental and physical feelings of fear. Some practitioners will suggest you seek medical help if you want to treat phobias, and after taking medication, that phobia will go away. Now you can live in everyday life.

- **Lose excess weight**

They usually suggest methods for us to lose weight. These methods include exercising and always practicing healthy diet habits. You are very aware that if you have too much weight, it can lead to you getting diabetes, affecting your everyday life.

- **Quit bad habits**

Habit is defined as a pattern of behaviors acquired through repetition. We have two categories of habits: good and bad habits. These bad habits make us not live a normal life, and this affects our productivity in life. These bad habits include smoking, gambling, etc. Smoking affects our life as nicotine found in cigarettes makes us addicts, and thus, for your body to operate normally, you have to smoke. There are several ways we can break these habits, but it varies from one person to another. It is broken using the following tips:

- **Identify the trigger.** It is the first step when you want to break the habit. Triggers include those things that go through your mind at that exact time. For example, reflect on what always goes through your mind when you are biting your nails.

- **Then try to replace bad behavior with a healthy one.** For instance, if you want to counteract smoking, try to find a new hobby you can practice during free time.

- **Avoid temptations.** Sometimes habits may be linked to a particular place or people. To break the habit, you have to avoid those friends, for instance, who are always drinking or gambling. That way, you can break the bad habit of drinking alcohol.

- **Keep your focus.** When you want to break a bad habit, you have to stay focused and committed to that. You should keep in mind that you are cutting the bad habit for your good. For instance, when quitting smoking, you are supposed to know that you are doing that to avoid getting diseases like cancer.

- **Never lose hope.** Hope is a pillar that keeps us moving. You should consider that you will face many obstacles when you are trying to leave a habit. Thus, you should have a plan to counter that if it arises. Do it once per day, and never give up.

- **Reward yourself.** When you stay away from a bad habit even one day, treat yourself. You buy yourself a new outfit, or you take a vacation. It will motivate you to keep avoiding the bad habit even though you are the one rewarding yourself.

- **Enhance confidence.** Sometimes we face situations that help us become confident. For instance, when you are having a staff meeting, confidence should be displayed. Practitioners help us boost our confidence by assisting us in identifying our weak points and strong points.

Here, people tend to confuse this with being a coach. A coach is different from a consultant in that a coach doesn't tell people what to do but helps clients find answers to their questions while consultants give specialized advice. For example, a business consultant helps his clients with concrete advice on how to grow their businesses.

You can also make money with NLP as an author. NLP training incorporates accelerated learning, NLP subconscious teaching principles, and layered learning. Becoming a published author increases one's credibility in the field, which will allow you to charge expensively.

You can also make money with NLP as a speaker. It again points to the knowledge one would have acquired from NLP. Suppose one continues with training beyond being a practitioner. In that case, they have the chance to enter a Master Trainer Development Program, where they issue all useful materials one requires to become a good speaker.

Chapter 10. Body Language and Behavior Imitation

Our non-verbal, or body language, is one of the most powerful communication methods we use in our day-to-day experiences. It is the mode of contact that ignites feelings and reactions on our "healthy point." Research has shown that understanding body language improves one's potential to effectively get out of any given situation, whatever one wants.

Have you ever encountered a couple sitting together and got a feeling of exactly how good or bad their friendship was in minutes? Have you ever questioned how you could arrive so quickly at this point without any prior interaction? Whether you are aware of it or not, we spend our days listening to people's non-verbal signals interpreted by their body language and drawing conclusions from our assumptions about them.

The body language shows that we conceal from the world in words and how we feel about ourselves, our relationships, and our circumstances. The individuals we associate with will evaluate our motives. The strength of our interactions, how masterful we are in any particular situation, our level of trust, and our real goals and aspirations by our eye contact, movements, body posture, and facial expressions.

The strength of body language is seen in the resulting emotional reaction. In nearly any case, emotions influence choices and reactions. Non-verbal signals activate emotions that define an individual's core properties, such as truthfulness, trustworthiness, honesty, competence level, and willingness to lead.

Understanding these signals will decide who we are going to meet, the work we are being recruited for, the amount of recognition we are having, and even those elected to powerful political positions.

Why do we not spend years studying and improving successful body language skills for such an immense skill? The fact is that most people undervalue the meaning of body language before they try a better interpretation of human conduct in an intimate relationship or in a competitive market situation to achieve an advantage.

Mastery in body language contains the keys for individuals to perceive the context of particular movements and body expressions and understand how to convey and express signals while communicating with others properly. As a result, there is a significant improvement in the general success of public interactions. The easiest way to continue this learning cycle is to study the simple understanding of the two core body language styles—open presence and closed presence.

The closed presence's body language form is illustrated in individuals who fold their bodies around the body's centerline, which runs straight down the middle of the body from the top of the head to the foot. The physical features that produce this form of appearance are feet positioned beside each other, arms held tight to the chest, hands folded across the chest, slight hand movements kept close to the body, shoulders rolling forward, and eyes fixed below eye level.

The world's signals transmitted by the body language form of closed appearance were a loss of confidence, low self-esteem, impotence, and lack of experience. In extreme cases, the message of needing to be invisible may also be produced. The consequences of this kind of body language on the person expressing can range from actually not having the best possible opportunity to a worst-case situation of harboring a self-fulfilling image of victimization.

By comparison, the accessible appearance is displayed in individuals that build a sense of dominance, control, and leadership by projecting mastery of confidence, achievement, energy, and ability. The physical features include feet held hip apart, freehand movements used in speech away from the body's middle line, elbows held away from the chest, shoulders pulled back, upright postures, and eyes fixed on their listeners' eye level. Such people are viewed as desirable, competent, intellectual, and are quickly seen as achieving success. We consider this form of body language as the "leaders' body language."

The aim is eye contact to enhance body language and to start expressing a transparent appearance. Face contact is one of the social devices that we enjoy most. Someone will alter the way others see them by making direct eye contact while communicating with others. Once people start looking straight into a victim's eyes, they are perceived as confident, trustworthy, and professional.

Hand gestures and facial expressions are the second degrees of improvement that one can create for a transparent face to be seen. Both methods of communicating improve the ability to and accurately convey information. Through skillfully using open hand motions away from the body and expressive facial expression, greater emphasis is produced when communicating through engaging the audience more physically and increasing the amount of knowledge provided during the conversation.

Body language mastery is essential to creating the most powerful presence in all human relationships. Individuals lacking this knowledge are vulnerable to confusion and find their attempts inadequate in expressing their thoughts. With the ability to distinguish between the various body language styles, everybody will achieve the competence required to excel in whatever pursuit they want.

Know and Understand Your Body Language

If you know it or not, body language is a significant force responsible for how everyone you encounter comes up with an opinion on you. Listening skills are a must and very necessary in many careers—particularly in careers where you support others to build positive relationships with clients. Whether you help people maintain their relationships, give people advice for business success or educate people about some other form of issue, they see your body language; displaying strong listening skills makes people feel relaxed.

Poor body language could result in something big being lost in you. It doesn't matter to you! Attentively and sincerely listen to every single word. It is the body language that makes you feel necessary to you and gives them the support they need. Understanding what the signs of a lousy listener are here is significant, and you will seek to rid yourself of all of these. When you have the habit of having your arms crossed around your stomach, whether you tap your feet impatiently, move whether turn and look away too much, or while listening, you tell the other person you're not interested in what he or she does. It will most likely lead to the termination of the partnership, which may cause significant business losses.

Ok, what would you do to continue transmitting constructive messages through your body language to the person you're talking to? You will first try to face the other party squarely on. Look not out to give a constructive signal. So at the moment of contact, we fall into the body's posture. You will take a transparent approach. You never have to leave your arms or legs folded; otherwise, the other guy would think you're not interested in listening to his point.

When you lean over when you speak to someone, your body language suggests you pay more attention to what he or she does. Leaning forward, by comparison, suggests you have little confidence whatsoever. The most pivotal aspect is eye touch. Seek to keep eye contact at all times. When you are looking down or turning down, it shows you have no interest in the topic and feel embarrassed.

However, the importance of a confident stance cannot be overlooked either. You don't want to be too uptight. You need not be too formal when talking to anyone, either. When you believe you have experienced significant defeats in the past due to your bad body language, you can instantly start following the above tips.

Behavior Imitation

Behavior imitation is something that can be used for good and for bad. Often, as children, we mimic the behavior of the people around us. It helps us to learn social norms. Also, it helps us feel like we fit into the crowd. Many traditions have been built off of people mimicking other people's behavior.

As we continue to grow up, we continue to imitate the people around us. Here again, it makes us feel as if we belong. Also, it can help us build relationships and understand the people around us more easily. While many people use behavior imitation for the right reasons, many others don't.

Criminals who are socially awkward tend to act like the people around them. It can make it harder to discern the good guys from the bad guys. It is a manipulation tactic that works quite well when people don't know how to behave appropriately. While some people are very good at mimicking those around them, it will be obvious when others try to do this. Cases of extreme social awkwardness will not allow the person to behave like those around them genuinely. It can be a tip to seeing what they may have planned after.

Another way that behavior imitation is prevalent with criminals is when they idolize someone or something. They will change their very persona to reflect that of which they admire. An excellent example of this is people that still follow the ideals of Adolf Hitler. The new generation of Nazis mimics the ways of old because they still believe his blasphemous thoughts to be true. It is truly scary behavior imitation.

Chapter 11. Using NLP to Manage People

When it comes to managing people effectively, it's essential that you first understand the non-verbal cues they provide to apply your skills toward influencing them. It is a necessary principle in using the NLP technique. Following are a few NLP techniques that can allow you to influence people's perception and thinking:

Deciphering Eye Movements

It is essential to realize and know the meaning of eye movements because each eye movement tells its tale. For instance, when searching for the right word or trying to remember a name, you automatically move your eyes in a certain way (most likely, squinting). Rolling the eyes signals contempt or exasperation.

Winking Indicates Flirtation or a Joke

Widening the eyes signals surprise or shock, even extreme excitement. The eyes can reveal much more about people's mental and emotional status, all on their own.

Once you understand what other people's thought processes are, you can accurately follow a course of action or dialogue which acknowledges the unspoken response, as signaled by the eyes. And as you may know, eye movements complement other communication forms such as hand movements, speech, and facial expressions.

Dilation of the pupils, breathing, angle of the body, and the hands' position—all these are complementary to the spoken message. Still, eye movement is essential in communication because every movement is influenced by particular senses and different parts of the brain.

Here is how you can generally interpret eye movement:

Visual Responsiveness

- **Eyes upward, then towards the right:** Whenever a person tilts eyes upward and then to the right, it means that the person is formulating a mental picture.
- **Eyes upward, then towards the left:** Whenever a person tilts eyes upward, followed by an eye movement to the left, it means the person recalls a particular image.
- **Eyes looking straight ahead:** Whenever someone focuses directly in front of them, this indicates that the person is not focused on anything in particular. That is the look often referred to as 'glazed.'

Auditory Responsiveness

- **Eyes looking towards the right:** When a person's eyes shift straight towards the right, it means the person is in the process of constructing a sound.
- **Eyes looking towards the left:** When a person's eyes shift straight towards the left, it indicates that the person recalls a sound.

Audio-Digital Responsiveness

- **Eyes looking downward, then switching to the left:** When someone drops their eyes and then proceeds to turn their eyes to the left, this signals that the person is engaged in internal dialogue.
- **Eyes looking right down then left to right:** When a person looks down and then proceeds to turn their eyes to the left and then to the right in consecutive movements, it means the person is engaged in negative self-talk.

Kinesthetic Responsiveness

Here, the person looks directly down, only to turn the eyes to the right. That is an indication that the person is evaluating emotional status. It further indicates that the person is not at ease:

- Verbal responses

- Rhythmic speech

The idea here is not to be poetic as you speak, but to speak at a regular pace. The recommended pace of speaking is equated to the heartbeat, say, between 45 and 72 beats per minute. At that pace, you are likely to sustain the listener's attention and establish greater receptivity to what you're saying. While normal conversational speed averages about 140 words per minute, slowing down a little and taking time to pause is highly effective to sustain people's attention. Your regular cadence should be punctuated by fluctuations in tone and emphasis in order not to sound monotonous.

Repeating Key Words

When you try to influence someone, some keywords or phrases carry additional weight as far as your message is concerned. This speaking method is a way of embedding the message in the listener and subtly suggesting that your message is valid and worthy of reception. Repeating key words also suggests commitment, conviction, and mastery of the subject matter.

Using Strongly Suggestive Language

Use a supportive and positive language of what you are saying, using a selection set of strong, descriptive words or phrases. As you do this, you should observe the person you are speaking to closely, in a way that makes them feel as though you see right through them and aware of what they are thinking.

Don't be invasive about this or aggressive. Merely suggest that you have a keen appreciation of what makes people tick by way of your gaze. It places you in a dominant position, especially when accompanied by dominant body language, like "steepling." It helps to use suitable, complementary body language as you speak to underscore the message subtly.

Touching the Person Lightly, As You Speak

Touching the person as you speak to them draws their attention to you in a relaxed and familiar way. By employing this technique, you're preparing the listener to absorb what you say to them, a way of programming attentiveness. Those engaging in inter-gender conversations in the workplace should take great care with this technique, as it can lead to misunderstandings.

Using a Mixture of "Hot" and "Vague" Words

"Hot" words are those that tend to provoke specific sensations in the listener. When you use them to influence someone's thinking, it is advisable to use them in a suitable pattern. Examples of phrases containing hot words are: it means; feel free; see this; because; hear this. The effect of employing these words and phrases is that you're directing influencing the listener's state of mind, including how that person feels, imagines, and perceives.

You're also appealing to the sense most prevalent in the listener's perceptive style (as observed through the movement of their eyes). For example, the phrase "hear this" will appeal to those who indicate a tendency to respond most actively to auditory stimuli.

Using the Interspersal Technique

The interspersal technique states one thing while hoping to impress on the listener something entirely different. For example, you could make a positive statement like:

"John is very generous, but some people take advantage of him and treat him as gullible."

When someone hears this statement, the likely assumption is that you want people to appreciate John's generosity. That is likely to be the message heard, and yet, the subtext is that while John is generous, he is also considered gullible and, thus, at a disadvantage in life when it comes to other people. Your hidden agenda may influence the listener to think of John as gullible, which calls into question his judgment. So, emphasize the words "but" and "gullible."

The word "but" serves to transition the perceived compliment to John to an implicit slight. The techniques just described form strategies in the service of influencing people.

They're not intended to force a viewpoint or to control people's behavior for nefarious ends. These techniques are intended to modify undesirable behaviors, resulting in workplace difficulties, including staff failure to work well together or complete team projects.

They're also accommodating in relationships with young people and children, whether at home or in a learning environment. Techniques of subtle manipulative effects like those described, though capable of influencing people and their behavior, don't amount to anything even approaching coercion. The person being spoken to chooses all responses and is merely influenced or steered toward those responses.

Chapter 12. Protecting Yourself From NLP Mind Control

Now we get how the whole thing works, we're not that fond of it, but we understand the basics. The main question now, though, is how do you guard against it? That's really what we've been trying to figure out this whole time. How do you prevent someone from pulling all that NLP mumbo jumbo on you when you're not looking? This part of the guide is for you because we have a few pointers for you.

Beware of Matchers

The first thing you're going to want to do is to take in and apply everything you've just learned. Remember all that stuff about matching and mirroring? Well, now you need to be on the lookout for it. When you speak to someone you think is trying to control you, make a point to note how they react to your body language. Are they sitting in the same pattern you are? Are they copying your movements as well?

If you're unsure, try testing it out by changing your posture and then wait to see if they mimic it. With pro NLP practitioners, the mimicking may be a bit subtler and a bit more delayed, but the unskilled ones are a total giveaway. They'll copy the posture right away, and automatically, you know what you're up against.

Now that you know, you can either call them out on their behavior or, if you want to have a little fun, start applying NLP on them to confuse them! Not only will you catch them off guard, but if you can pull it off, you can get them to tell you what their whole ploy was all about and who put them up to it. Total win!

Consciously Infuse Randomness in Your Eye Movement

When it comes to confusing your opponent and playing them at their own game, there is little going to give you the same amount of satisfaction as random play. Random eye movements are like going to the gym with your iPod on shuffle. Nobody knows what's coming on after. It's basically like trolling your manipulators in real-time, and it can be quite fun.

Any NLP user worth their salt is going to go in hard with the whole eye movement thing. It is because your eye movements tell them how you assess and store information, which is precisely why some people can tell if you are lying or cheating just by looking at your eyes. When they say your eyes speak volumes, this is what they mean!

So how do you avoid being read by an NLP practitioner? Simple, use random eye movements. As you are speaking, make a point to look left or right or up or down. You can even make a game of it. Left for complex sentences, down for every question, and simple sentences can go right or up, depending on whether they start with a vowel.

Pick Up on Ambiguity

One of the tricks that NLP kind of sneaks in from hypnotherapy is the full use of vague, unclear language. A great example of the use of this technique is Donald Trump's "Make America Great" Again Campaign.

Even though the now-president went around campaigning about making a better version of America, he never really broke down what that meant. It was such a hazy term that it could mean anything to anyone, and that was precisely what he wanted.

Whenever anyone starts using stuff like that on you, such as "release your inner troubles and feel the world move slowly around you in conjunction with your prospective earthly successes." What you're doing is allowing hypnotherapy to program your internal state in a specific form. It helps the other person when they then try to convince you to do something that benefits them.

Anytime you feel that someone is trying to do something like that to you, force yourself to snap out of it and ask specific questions, "What exactly do you mean by 'great'?" or "What potential are you talking about?" Take note; all you have to do is point it out. Once you've done that, you're home free!

Be Hypersensitive to People Permitting You to Do Stuff

The other thing you should watch out for? Permissive language. When a person says something like "you can do XYZ" or "Feel free to make yourself at home" or even something tempting like, "If you want, you can borrow the new Avengers movie from me," what they are doing is preparing you to enter into a trance state. You see, experienced NLP users never outright tell their subjects to do anything. They suggest, recommend, or allow. In this way, the subject feels like they are in control, whereas control was wiped out a long time ago in reality! So then, feel free to say no thanks!

Read Between the Lines

We're onto reading between the lines. You have to keep in mind that people who use or people who are using NLP to control you or to manipulate you tend to use specific controlled langue, and nine out of ten times, you are not going to know what hit you.

How do they do it? Double meanings. And you'll find them in the unexpected places, so skilled NLP users who are good at what they do know how to use double meaning infused sentences to get you to think the way they want you to. Imagine that you are the evil witch's neighbor from the Hansel and Gretel story; now you don't eat kids, but you do have a thing for snacks. Your NLP user, A.K.A "the evil witch" comes up to you and says, "Children make nutritious snacks, just in case you were wondering." Sure the witch claims she was talking about their production capacity, but what you heard and processed was something a little different, and already you're a bit more inclined to take a little nibble.

Be Attentive

You need to be very careful about how much attention you are paying to your surroundings and what's going on in them. We get you that you can't always be super alert, but you need to know that you are vulnerable when you aren't alert. For example, an essential tactic that employers use when negotiating salary packages is waiting until the employee in question seems a little off and then jumping in. Saying that they haven't negotiated a pay difference for Tom, Dick, and Harry and don't foresee a lot of change in the other employees. Not much change at all, they repeat. Automatically, now that you are asked how much change in salary you expect, you say not much change—congratulations! You've just been programmed!

Watch Your Mouth

Another important tip? Watch what you say. Master manipulators tend to create a false sense of urgency to make you feel that you have to do this particular thing by this specific time, or else something drastic will happen. You don't have a choice. You have to do this now! What do you do? Well, nothing. Yes, seriously, nothing. Never make any important decisions at the drop of a hat. Chances are you're not the president of the United States, meaning no nuclear codes lie with you, which of course, means that you don't need to make any immediate decisions without consulting people. You don't have to make any quick decisions at all.

Sit tight. Getting you to commit is a classic dark psychology move to create a sense of obligation after being exploited. Please don't fall for it!

Trust Your Gut

And your final rule, which also happens to be your most important, is to trust your gut. Your instincts know a lot more than you do, mostly because your subconscious mind is processing signs and symbols at a rate your conscious brain can't even begin to fathom. So if it is out there telling you that something is up and that something needs to be done about it, then you need to make sure that you are on your guard ready to get things done because, like a used car salesman, you are more likely than not in the hands of a master practitioner.

Chapter 13. Smart and Wise Goal-Setting Using Neuro-Linguistics

NLP or Neuro-Linguistic Programming explores how you think and feel. It examines the inner language that you usually use to represent your life experiences. It studies human interaction and achievement and uses this knowledge to help you achieve excellence in all aspects of your life.

The concepts behind NLP techniques are based on the fact that you already have the necessary internal resources and capabilities to effectively change your life and the lives of the people around you. NLP helps you in your goal setting and in taking the necessary actions to realize your goal.

Easy NLP Techniques to Help You Achieve Your Goals

Be Specific About the Things That You Want

It repeatedly reiterates what has been echoed: you must have a clear understanding of what it is that you exactly want. You need to have a noticeable or clear vision of what you are aiming for. Look at it this way; imagine you are sailing in the middle of the ocean. Without a clear vision of where you want to go and just going with the flow and where the water will take you, you will fail. If you are blindly going through life, how do you expect to get to where you want to go?

Ask Yourself What You Want

NLP recommends asking questions like: "If I continue doing the things I am doing now, where will I be a year from now?" "Am I happy where I am now and the direction I am going?" "If I am not happy, what should I do instead? What would make me happy?" When you can answer similar questions, it will be easier to identify what you want.

Create Mental Images of Your Goals

The moment you have established what you want to achieve, put them into writing. If buying your dream house, create images of the actual house, including the smallest details as design, location, and neighborhood. You must create powerful internal images and play them on your mind over and over. Be realistic and think about actual colors, what you see around, the smell of the flowers, or the sound of your neighbor's dog barking in the background. Create a "movie" in your mind. Go as far as seeing what you are wearing on that particular day that you are finally buying the house. Make the movie as detailed as possible, as if it is happening. It is bringing visualization techniques to a higher level.

Write Your Goals As If They Are Already Being Realized and Focus on Them

You might find it helpful to use words in the present tense and then create the images. You'll create a more powerful impact if you picture your goal like it is happening right this very moment. Keep in mind that NLP teaches you and allows you to move towards the things you intently focus on. By doing so, you are attracting success. This technique will enable you to influence what the universe gives you. You must maintain your focus on a clear positive image of what you want you to achieve, in this case, buying your dream house. Throughout your journey towards attaining your goal, you have to maintain your focus on that goal.

Use Your Goal As Your Motivation to Keep on Moving Toward It

Think of action items that will bring you closer to your goal. Devise plans of action on how you can continue to move forward. Imagine that you are already there at the "finish line" and look back at how you were able to get there. It might help if you imagine a physical mind with several essential points. It is the path that you have to take to reach the realization of your goal. There may be obstacles, but if you keep your focus on the result, you'll think of ways to overcome those obstacles and continue with your journey. Having a clear picture of the things you have to do to reach your goal helps you achieve it.

Look for a Role Model

Look for a person you can look up to and learn from. Read their success stories. Take pointers from them or if you cannot reach them, find resources that speak about them. Most stories of famous and successful people contain tips and guidelines on how they attained their current stature. Watch video clips, testimonies, and books about them. Learn from their life lessons and mistakes.

Act!

You have the goals, and you have established what you want to do, but you'll never achieve anything if you don't begin to act. Nothing and no one can achieve your goals for you, you have to act, and it is the first step you have to take. Act to begin moving towards the fulfillment of your goals. If you want to buy a house, start saving or considering taking on additional income sources. One small step is actually what you need to get you going.

Plan!

Once you have acted on your goal, you have to make sure that you have a concrete plan to achieve your goal. You have to have a timescale. As you move towards attaining your goal, continue to stay focused, and create positive images of the final goal in your mind.

Exude Positivity

Having confidence doesn't mean you won't fail. It means that while you might encounter challenges, you remain confident to push forward. You might commit a misstep, but if you use that as an opportunity to learn, then you'll get back on track.

Be Flexible

Things do not turn out the way you want to, even if you work hard at it. You need to keep on going, move forward, and try other options.

Keep on Going

You might fail along the way, and you might encounter rejection, but that shouldn't discourage you from continuing to follow your dreams. Keep on moving forward.

Chapter 14. Introduction of Persuasion

Persuasion is the ability to transmit ideas and disseminate them by those who act as recipients. It translates more effectively as the ability that human beings have through a relationship, to convince others. Persuasion is a tool that can be used in fields such as marketing, advertising, and commerce, basically sectors of the economy in which the public is sensitive to various interactions with environmental media and where the decision is the objective of who persuades.

How Does it Work?

Let us elaborate on a scene in which a seller wants his products to be acquired by the buyers; besides being useful, they must be attractive and, in one way or another, more desirable than that of the competition. It is achieved with persuasion, which attracts clients by offering the best product or service attributes, effectively providing comfort to the buyer by relating the most promotional aspects to the most personal. In turn, persuasion generates competition and demand in the market, generating dynamism of intentions and offers that fosters sustainable economies.

Another use of persuasion that we see in a society continually is in the application of the law. In a trial, the lawyers, using the law as the main tool, use the elements in their favor and persuade the jury and the judge that they are valid to win the case.

We are always waiting for others who live in our environment to reproduce or share our ideas; even unintentionally, people seek to persuade others to fulfill their ends. A wife who asks her husband to optimize expenses is trying to convince him that it is the best for both. Either way, each person's ideas will be interpreted as an intention for others to apply and build their ideas based on the initial idea. Persuasion can be so extreme that they can change the way a person thinks. It all depends on what the person who persuades another looks for.

Psychological Tricks to Increase Your Persuasive Power

Evaluate Context and Time

The foundation for increasing your power of persuasion is context and the exact time. The first requirement sets a standard for what is acceptable and can be done, while the right timing makes your chances increase or decrease considerably. Trying to persuade your boss to raise you well when he is nervous or talking about an important issue is not a timely approach. Therefore, having this notion of timing is critical in the persuasion process.

Remember That Persuasion Is Different from Manipulation

To manipulate is to coerce someone into doing something that is not in their best interest. However, persuasion is the art of persuading people to do something that is in their interest and benefits you.

Speak What People Want to Hear

You will not be able to persuade someone who has no interest in what you are saying. Generally, people are interested in themselves and spend most of their time thinking about money, love, or health. Therefore, to increase your persuasion power, it is necessary to learn to talk to people about themselves consistently. Remember: If you show interest in what they want and say, you will always have your attention.

Be Persistent

Have you noticed that historical figures who persuaded large masses achieved this with much persistence in their messages? If you focus on demonstrating value and staying focused, you are much more likely to get what you want.

Greet People Sincerely

We are all affected by compliments, whether we like it or not. And people tend to believe more in someone who gives them good feelings. So greet people when they deserve it, highlight their qualities and achievements. You will see how, practically and honestly, you will be able to persuade someone more easily. Investing in reciprocity is also very effective in this process; after all, when you do something for someone, that person feels compelled to do something for you too. It is part of the evolution of our DNA.

Create a Sense of Urgency

To increase your persuasive power, you need to create a sense of urgency in people by making them want something or act right now. If you're not motivated enough to want something right now, you probably won't like it in the future. Therefore, invest in your power of persuasion in the present, betting on the urgency of things.

Value the Images

Remember: what we see is more important than what we hear. Therefore, hone your first impressions to increase your persuasive power by increasing your ability to paint an image of experience you can offer others in the future.

Be Flexible and Communicate Simply

Have you noticed how flexible children are in their behaviors? They do everything, in every means they can to get what they want from their parents, and most of the time, they can. Therefore, adopting a rigid posture is never a good way to increase your persuasive power. Communicating is also another important point because the art of persuasion is to simplify something so that it is quick and straightforward to understand.

Chapter 15. History of Persuasion

The persuasion can be traced back to Greek origins. It was used as a tool by great orators to get their message across to the common folk. For a country that has created the political frameworks behind democracy, persuasion was immensity popular. If you have ever taken an advanced writing class that went over rhetorical analysis, you might recognize the three rhetorical modes of pathos, ethos, and logos. Aristotle billed these as the three main appeals that an orator could make to move their audience.

Its usage implies that the audience is a malleable entity, like putty. A skilled orator's words can manipulate the audience like a child might manipulate a piece of putty. Other times, persuasion is used to rile up an already popular cause, to begin with, but that had been up to that point undisclosed.

The three rhetorical modes are important because they represent three different attack vectors that a manipulator might use to persuade their audience. Again, any form of persuasion is a type of mental manipulation, but it doesn't become a psychological attack until it becomes malicious. In other words, there is a difference between plain old persuasive arguments and using persuasion to carry out dark psychology.

Regular persuasion is the type that might make you vote for a candidate or buy some product (though some would argue that modern-day advertising has dark psychology aspects). On the other hand, malicious persuasion might entice you to go against your set of morals and beliefs. This sort of persuasion is dangerous because an attacker's arguments may seem very convincing to you when, in reality, they are just cleverly designed to trick you. At the same time, the persuasion is being used to benefit someone else.

The dark psychology mindset tells us that there are people out there with less than kind objectives. They may be after your wealth, your emotional labor, your body, your mind, or just a few minutes of your attention. And all of this is theoretically possible through the levying of persuasive techniques. But first, we should talk about everyday persuasion in the traditional sense.

Modern-Day Aristotle

No matter what persuasive argument you come across, they will have all of the semblances of Aristotle's appeals, mixed in with a modern "secret sauce" that is unique to the persuader (and indeed the situation). It is still worth talking about persuasion and persuasive arguments because they are the cornerstone of all manipulation types. If a manipulator were a boxer, persuasion techniques would be like their left jab. Not as powerful as a KO punch, but still the punch that lands them the most points and slows down their opponent.

A modern-day Aristotle can be anyone. A politician, a used car salesman, even your mother is trying to convince you to move closer to home. All of these would be Aristotle's have something in common: they want something from you. And it is your job to decide whether their needs are genuine and desirable for all parties. They will no doubt stop at anything to convince you that they are. To do this, you have to separate their argument from the chaff. For persuasive techniques, the chaff is usually the bubbly language or the sharp edge in their arguments that cut you into you.

But beware. Just because it cuts you, it doesn't mean that it is deep or meaningful to you in any way. Many skillful persuaders will only pander to already preconceived notions that their audiences may have. They say something that they know their audience will like and instantly become that much more credible.

But someone trying to come up with a novel argument will first have to design a rhetorical strategy using any of the three rhetorical modes available. It is true whether they are trying to form an essay, a speech, or persuade you into doing something. The world of sales is chock-full of strategies used designed to get you to buy. A competent salesperson may try to get to know you first (especially if the purchase is large, like a new house or car). They wish to form a relationship on a first-name basis and then pose as a close friend.

In the world of sales, the only thing that matters is the purchase. If a client decides to buy, then whatever strategies used to make that sale are fair game. It opens the ground for deploying several different types of psychological tricks against the unsuspecting client. For example, a salesperson may introduce them to a high-end item that is purposely out of their buying range and then redirect them towards an item of similar functionality perceived as being more affordable.

A family looking to buy a new laptop for their college-bound son may be directed towards the expensive and latest Apple laptop product only to realize that it is well out of their budget. The savvy salesperson can then walk them to the Windows computers aisle and show them an alternative product that is the same color as an Apple computer but has a different operating system and is slightly less performative. Now, that other laptop may still be a flagship item and have a sizable price tag, but it is perceived as a good buy by the family because the salesperson showed them an item they believe to be state of the art.

Such tricks are less persuasive strategies than they are crude psychological manipulation. More psychological persuasion involves more trickery and deception—the type of things one would expect except dark psychology techniques. Indeed, the salesman trick of going high and then going low can pass as a type of emotional manipulation. It is subtle, but there is clear pandering towards what a client believes their money can buy them. First, they are shown what is considered to be the "it" product. But since they can't afford it, the salesman puts them on an emotional roller coaster of desire.

In a way, it is a projection of what the client believes they deserve. Sure, they can't afford the best, but since they feel like they deserve the best (and since the salesman believes they deserve the best), buying the other best product is an easy choice. And if they can afford the high-end object the salesman shows them first, their job is already finished. In other words, whether the client buys the expensive item or the lesser expensive one, the salesman still wins. It is a perfect example of a psychological manipulation that is difficult to detect in the moment's heat and has a high success rate.

Chapter 16. Six Principles of Persuasion

To learn and enhance the art of persuasion, you need to be aware of the underlying principles that will enable you to harness your influence. Generally, Human beings are a touchy lot; one wrong move and you're going to lose all ability to persuade people to join your team. You need to make critical decisions that are guided by the necessary fundamental principles. Reciprocity, consistency, social evidence, liking, authority, and scarcity are the six principles of persuasion.

Reciprocity Principle

Reciprocity does to others as you would have them do to you. Reciprocity calls for respect and kindness as you go about your everyday experiences. It's a good thing to show kindness to others that makes others feel better about your interaction. Besides that, your way of earning chips that you can cash in after is to do well. If you have been very nice and kind to someone else, you have a better chance that they will be nice and kind to you.

If you are hoping to persuade a person, you must decently behave towards them. Speak a word of kindness, give them a favor, or even buy them a gift. They will be more agreeable after when you need to convince them to do something. After all, you have proved yourself to be a kind human being who cares for him.

The Cohesion Principle

Consistency in persuasion works this way: once you have convinced them to agree to smaller ones, people are more likely to commit to bigger tasks or favors. That is, if you get them to spring a puddle for you, you can get someone to swim oceans for you. A few studies have been done to support this hypothesis. For example, in one study, a group of researchers asked some homeowners to put up a hideous Drive Safely billboard on their front lawn. Very few homeowners declared yes. However, the researchers had to take a different approach to the experiment: first, they got homeowners to agree to the small commitment to putting up a Drive Safely postcard in their home's front windows. Ten days after, they returned with the request for a billboard. This time, despite its lack of aesthetic appeal, more homeowners agreed to put up the billboard. The reason for this is that the homeowners subconsciously felt compelled to keep up with their earlier reaction.

The technique of foot-in-the-door compliance is premised on consistency. It means getting people to consent to a bigger request by first using smaller requests to check the waters. If you want to execute this strategy cleverly, your target will need to be trained to be consistent with their responses to your question.

The Liking Principle

If some people like you, they're more likely to fulfill your demands, no matter what that may be. A person who is unlike and who is also unlikeable will hear no more times than a well-liked person. But how is it that you get people to like you? The secret to being loved is a combination of three main factors, according to science. First of all, people prefer the ones close to them. You must find common ground with them to look close to the person you are trying to convince. For example, many foreigners have learned that learning and speaking the local language is the simplest way to become more likable. You also need and practice to be mindful of is flattery while making yourself more likable. If you are using it well, flattery will open many doors for you.

Citizens prefer those paying attention to them. If you want to ask someone to do something for you, start by offering them a genuine compliment first. Just because this is called flattery doesn't mean you need to be effusive about it. Too excessive in your praise will be counterproductive to your need to be liked. Last but not least, be the kind of person that is usually pleasant and cooperative in achieving mutual goals, and you will be one step closer to being pleasant. If you're always stepping on the toes of others to get what you want, you'll have very few friends, and this won't help your case when you need to convince someone in the future. Remember, being pleasant and cooperative doesn't imply being a doormat. Sometimes, it merely means putting some little effort into helping a person achieve a vital goal. For example, if a colleague struggles with a due report, offer to help them with the printing and mailing process. It's not a lot of work, but you're going to go from an uninvolved, unwritten colleague to a kind and helpful colleague. You can cash this chip after if you wish.

The Authority Theory

Compared to a complete newbie, a person who is an authority figure in a particular field will have an easier time influencing others. If you want to persuade or influence more people to do something specific, you need to build your credibility by making yourself seem like you have expertise in whatever field you play. This principle is a key reason why professionals in their field display their diplomas. Think about it—when, for example, you step into a therapist's office, you would probably deliberately look out for the sort of qualifications they have hanging on their walls. If your therapist has many credentials displayed in this way, you will probably feel a sense of comfort in their expertise and experience. As such, you'll quickly accept and follow any advice they have for you. Essentially the therapist has managed to influence you without even saying a word.

It's a fact that if you're the only one talking about it, your authority won't be taken very seriously. As such, you have to make sure, so to speak, that you recruit others to beat the drums on your behalf. Subtle ways exist to do this. You can identify a field in the office you are passionate about and become that field's office guru. It could be Microsoft Excel or Reporting for some people. The guy known as the Excel office guru will have a much easier time getting things out of people because they already know he knows what he's talking about. He has also proved to be likable and helpful by solving all of their problems with Excel, and his colleagues may want to pay him back in some way. You don't need to learn Excel to make your mark around the world.

Scarcity Principle

The laws of supply and demand are easy and straightforward in economics: when supply is low and demand is high, prices rise. To translate this, the value of scarcity builds. If you are a business person who wants to persuade people to purchase your product or service, it highlights that the product is on offer for only a limited time. Furthermore, let the clients know that they will lose significantly if they do not access this product on time. If the marketing message is packaged in this way, more people will be rushing to beat the time limit on your product.

It is essential to become a scarce product yourself in the business and personal relations world. If you're not there for others whenever they need you, you'll quickly lose your worth. If you want to remain your aura of mystery and power around you, you must learn the art of being inaccessible and unavailable. When you appear, your word will be respected more than a person's word that continuously appears and speaks out of all importance and meaning.

The Consensus Theory

People look at others similar to them in everyday interactions for clues about what to do or say. An individual who is a good influencer knows that buying into their idea is all it takes is one individual, and the whole crowd does. There are different ways you can apply the consensus principle to your benefit. For example, in an office setting, you can get a part of the staff to agree to a cause and champion that causes their colleagues to do so. These colleagues are more likely to be convinced of the worthy cause because their peers have said so.

For example, if you've ever purchased anything from Amazon, you might have seen that it includes a part showing the other items purchased by clients who ordered the product you just purchased. How does that segment affect you as a buyer? More often than not, you'll probably consider buying those other items because they were bought by these clients who have similar tastes and needs to yours. Initially, you may not have planned to buy the additional items, but just the fact that others did it will make you think you also need to. That is, in effect, the principle of consensus.

Chapter 17. Theories on Persuasion

There are a few different theories on persuasion that we should start to understand. Before we talk about these, let's take a more in-depth look at what processes persuasion might be done through. How can we completely change the way we are thinking or feeling based on another person's ability to alter our feelings? There are a few core elements to what persuasion is and what you can use to define this process.

Persuasion is when a message is transferred from one person to the other. This message might be a way of life, such as religion. Have you ever seen signs of someone wanting to share their religion with you? Maybe they have passed free information like brochures or mini booklets to get you on their side. It is an example of how others might try to convince you of their messages. They will be using symbols and words to try and get you to understand where they are coming from. Some will go as far as to scare you as well, making you think that something bad might happen to you if you choose not to follow what they're stating. Persuasion goes as far back as human history does. Some methods of persuasion have been natural in our society. There are other times when persuasion has been a little more forced. Perhaps it is a physical skill ingrained in the anatomy that we use to help us survive. It could simply be a survival tactic or deeply ingrained in our society and the language we use.

Persuasion is always going to be more positive when you can give the other person their freedom to choose. When you take that freedom away and become more forceful, this can turn into manipulation, brainwashing, and other dark psychology methods. We will break all three of these down for you to better recognize the different levels of persuasive behavior. First, let's start to talk about some other theories about how and why persuasion can be so effective.

The first one is conditioning theory. It explains how prolonged exposure could be "conditioning" us to fall more efficiently for a message. It is something easily seen on the level of advertisements. Think of a brand, specifically maybe a candy brand that you like. Whatever this is, recall the last time you saw an advertisement for it. They will use signs of the actual product and what this might look like. In a commercial, they might show someone eating it with the same branded colors in the background. Maybe they have a simple phrase or logo that you remember immediately without even trying. Then, you make your way to a grocery store and see this same product with the same colors and are more inclined to purchase this because you have already been conditioned to do so. If you had never seen an advertisement for the product, you might not notice the display of candy sitting there when you walk in the store, but they have already planted this idea in your head, so you're way more willing actually to purchase this.

The other theory that we have is the cognitive dissonance theory. It states how we will always be looking for ways to connect our thoughts and behaviors with reality. Even if you have thoughts different from what you do, your brain will look for ways to justify this kind of behavior. For example, let's say that you are overweight, and you don't want to be. You'd love it if you could lose thirty pounds. However, you continue to eat unhealthy junk food and skip the gym every day. Your actions are not aligning with your beliefs, and this creates cognitive dissonance. It is essential because it will show how your brain can be persuaded easily even when you know certain information isn't true. Your brain wants your actions to match your beliefs, so it will convince you to do one of two things. You can either find that motivation to go to the gym and eat healthier and then your actions match your beliefs of wanting to lose weight. Alternatively, your mind might instead convince you that there is nothing wrong with being unhealthy. You might assure yourself that what you are told about your health is all a lie, or maybe that you don't deserve even to have a healthy body. Whatever it is, your brain is going to try and fill in those blanks and make you believe something that isn't entirely true, all so that your actions align with your belief. It is something that might end up hurting others in the long run. Think of a crazy cult leader. They will have things that they believe, and after a while, it might not be just enough for them to be the only ones to believe this. Instead of changing their mind about their beliefs, they might try to convince others to believe the same thing in an attempt to validate their perspective. It can be toxic and damaging behavior, but it is something that our brain might naturally do.

These theories are essential to understand because they will start to give you a little insight into how or why someone might be trying to convince themselves or others of their message. We will talk about the basic persuasion techniques that people use soon, but we must first understand the motive. If you can't discover a motive behind someone's persuasion, then they might not necessarily be trying to be manipulative, intentionally or not. Always ask, "Why are they doing this?" whenever you might be questioning someone's goal for whether or not they are manipulative.

Chapter 18. Persuasion Techniques

Persuasion techniques also have their level. Whether you are a beginner, an intermediate one, or an advanced user of persuasion of techniques, you should be able to discern when to apply these techniques to maximize their effectiveness.

Basic Persuasion Techniques

By Association

It is one persuasion technique commonly used by people who are in the early stage of improving their influencing skills. With this technique, you try to link the particular service, product, or idea with another thing that is already liked by your target audience. Association is a powerful technique, although it does not explicitly claim that you will achieve these things.

Let's take an example—associating the concept of 'family' with the brand such as Coke through emotional transfer has been an effective tool for many years. The term 'victory' has also been associated with another brand, 'Nike.'

By Bandwagon

Another persuasion technique that can be used by newbies is the Bandwagon method. What you want to achieve is to make other people realize that 'everyone else is already doing it, and so should you.' Most people want to have a sense of belonging, and they do not want to be left behind. So, in this technique, your ultimate goal is to make sure that your prospect is ready to hop on the bandwagon with you.

By Testimonials

OK, this is probably one of the most common methods, yet it works well despite being around for decades. It is because people tend to pay extra attention to celebrities. Whether we admit or not, following a celebrity or being a fan is one of the guilty pleasures anyone can have. When big brands use celebrities, famous athletes, and models, it is easier to influence people into trying the same product.

By Using Humor

Many of the ads that we usually remember are because of the humor injected into it. When we see them, we laugh, and we feel good. Thus, it becomes a great persuasion tool. When you associate your product or service with something that makes people 'feel good,' it becomes easier to influence them. It performs or works when it comes to relationships too. When you can be intelligently funny to someone, it becomes a lot easier to influence him or her to continue to like you.

By Repetition

As they say, repetition is the key to retention. To influence and persuade people, you should be able to repeat your message subtly and in various ways. Have you ever experienced humming or singing an ad jingle in your head? You may not like the product itself, but since you see the ad almost every day over the Web, on TV, or even in print ads, something about it sticks. When it sticks, it becomes a lot less complex to influence the person.

By Experts

It is a form of testimonials too. Commonly, people would look at the logical reasoning or expert claims behind a particular item. If you are an expert in one area, it would be easier to find an expert testimonial. For instance, if your prospective clients are parents or moms—then the expert should be a mom as well who is known in a particular field.

By Bribery

Yes, we all love freebies, don't we? It is one technique you can employ, as well. When you want to influence people, give them more than they expect—discount, promo, holidays, etc. Influencing people also means giving them good value for money, good returns on their investments, etc. As you hone your skills, you will then influence more effectively using the succeeding techniques.

Intermediate Persuasion Techniques

By Being Charismatic

For instance, if you present yourself to be bold, confident, strong, and sleek, you could expect people to listen to you more. Like, if you get persuaded into buying something if the endorser itself is someone that tickles your fancy.

By Presenting Novel Ideas

People love new things. It is no longer surprising that people place great faith in technological advancements. One method to influence people is by presenting an idea that is new to them. Giving something novel gives them that sense of pride in being one of the first to get it.

By Using Rhetorical Questions

One of the most useful or effective ways to elicit reactions from people is by asking them questions. Questions such as, "Do you want to become a millionaire before you hit 30?" "Do you want to live debt-free?" "Do you want to be as stunning as Monica Bellucci?"—these are all set up to build alignment and to establish rapport before the sales pitch takes over. Usually, these are the type of questions that would capture the attention so that your prospect would stay longer and listen to the sales pitch.

By Nostalgia

It is the opposite method of #9 By Presenting Novel Ideas. In this method, you try to influence people by making them excited about the 'good old days.' As changes come rapidly, some people get tired of it and want to get back to the days when life is simpler. A good example is the revival of the Nokia 3310 in this time of advanced smartphones or that easy-to-prepare food that brings back childhood memories.

By Offering Simple Solutions

We live in a complicated or complex world, and people are continually seeking simpler solutions. If you intend to influence someone or a target market, offer relief by proposing a simple solution to any problem. For instance, advertisers like the concept of 'one-stop-shop' for any particular service, enabling consumers to address their multiple needs in one place.

By Showing Slippery Slope

It is quite similar to using 'fear' as a weapon for influence. Instead of predicting positive results, you can influence people by showing them the looming dangers of not acting and deciding immediately. For instance, to influence and persuade people to invest, you could show the possible scenarios when the recession kicks in. Anything that could give them a picture of what could happen if they do not do something can be used in this technique.

By Presenting Scientific Evidence

In this method, you get to present facts that would eventually influence someone to decide instantly. Many people tend to consider themselves 'people of Science,' or those keen on knowing one product's scientific principle before buying them. For case, if you are trying to sell a collagen-based skincare product, you need to explain the role of collagen and what it does in the biological makeup of the skin. By showing pretty girls using it in ads may not be sufficient.

You will learn the techniques that influencers of the advanced level users. Note that you do not have to jump to this list right away. You can utilize any from the recent list to know which suits your style best.

Advanced Persuasion Techniques

By Analogy

A good analogy helps in influencing people and creates a sense of truthfulness, which helps establish your credibility. A weak analogy, on the other hand, can instantly break interest. When using this method, make sure the comparison is still logical and not over the top.

By Understanding Group Dynamics

It is a more intense version of the 'Bandwagon' technique. Understanding the specific beliefs of a group of people will help understand the influence method to use. For occasion, if you are selling a high-end product, you would certainly look for a market that can afford them. However, you can also capture the market that aspires to be part of the group.

Ad Hominem

It is a Latin phrase that means 'against the man.' In this technique, you do not influence people by attacking a product, but the maker itself. This method is also referred to as 'attacking the messenger.' It takes skills and a colossal amount of research to do this. Incorrect use of this method may lead to other complex problems, so use this with care and discretion.

By Scapegoating Method

It is one powerful method that politicians of today make use of influence voters. They tend to highlight the failures of former politicians or leaders to capture the trust of the voters. Another example is when they blame a particular person, organization, or race for a problem.

One clear example here is when politicians vying for a position in an incoming election would blame the undocumented immigrants for the rising unemployment rate. Unemployment itself is a complex matter that is bound by multiple factors.

Knowing the Right Timing

Timing is of the essence even when it comes to influencing. You need to know what is happening around you, current affairs, and current problems that need immediate solutions. For instance, an ill-timed proposal can instantly go up in smoke when people find the timing irrelevant.

Card Stacking

In this method, you do not tell the whole story but only select the parts considered favorable to your audience or target market. While this could work well, it is imperative to know how you could justify the 'hiding' of the facts. Again, as this is a tricky method, you need to be 'great' to make it work.

As you can see, there are 'dirty' tricks that people can do to influence people. While they are entirely incorrect, it takes a great deal of care, courage, and common sense to use them. If you are not exactly comfortable using advanced techniques, you can still use the beginner and intermediate methods.

Remember, each one of us has an influencing style that we are most comfortable with. Evaluate yourself and find your own. If you have finally grasped how you could do better, it's now time to learn how you could increase your influence in this digital era.

Chapter 19. Difference Between Persuasion and Manipulation

Many people fail to recognize the nuances between manipulation and persuasion. Although both seek to convince someone else to do something else, they are quite different in enough key ways to be classified entirely differently. One is only beneficial to the manipulator (manipulation), while the other ideally, should benefit both people. Because of these key differences, manipulation becomes far more insidious than persuasion. The manipulator sees the other person as a tool, a means to an end, whereas the persuader sees the other person as a partner.

Defining Persuasion

Though persuasion involves changing someone else's mind, it is not necessarily a bad thing—there are plenty of ways to use persuasion innocently or benevolently. Persuasion is any method that will actively change the thoughts, emotions, actions, or attitudes of another person toward another person or thing. This change is seen as a persuasion. It can be done inwardly toward oneself by changing one's attitudes or being done to other people.

Usually, persuasion is used as a form of influence—it is everywhere. It is present in ads, politics, schools, professions, and just about everywhere you could think of. If you can think of something, chances are there is some persuasive layer to it somewhere and somehow.

When persuading someone, four key elements must be present. These four elements are:

- Someone who is doing the persuading

- The message or the persuasion

- A target recipient for the persuasion

- A context that the persuasion is received

Each of these four key elements must be present for something to be considered persuasive. Of course, this means that manipulation would fall within the category of persuasion as well.

Defining Manipulation

In psychology, manipulation is a type of influence or persuasion, but unlike regular persuasion, manipulation is covert, deceptive, or underhanded. It means that, unlike regular persuasion, which seeks to be most honest, manipulation is often untrustworthy. The manipulator will have no concern about lying about the situation or attempting to coerce the target into believing something, so long as he gets what he wants.

The manipulator seeks only to serve himself further—he does not care about the target and does not care about hurting the target. The target is seen as little more than collateral damage—a necessary to get the desired results. As such, manipulation tactics are often quite exploitative and almost always meant to be insidious and harmful.

Successful manipulation requires three key concepts to happen. These three are:

- Concealing the intentions and behaviors while remaining friendly upfront

- Understanding the ways the victim or target is vulnerable and using those vulnerabilities to the manipulator's advantage.

- Being ruthless enough to not care about the harm caused to the victim

Manipulation can take several different forms, but most of them follow the covert, harmful, and causing no guilt to the manipulator.

Key Differences

Ultimately, persuasion and manipulation are quite similar: They are both forms of social influence, but that is where the similarities end. While persuasion is generally positive, even within dark psychology, manipulation is not. Manipulation is harmful, ruthless, and insidious in every way, shape, and form.

When you are trying to choose whether something is manipulative or persuasive, there are a few questions you can ask yourself to decide. This simple test can allow you to analyze what you are doing and say to ensure you are making the best choices. If you are not looking to manipulate, but the questions tell you that you are erring on the manipulation side, you know to tone it down slightly, lightening up on the manipulative factors. These questions are:

- What is the intention that has led you to feel the need to convince the other person of something?

- Are you truthful about your intention and the process?

- How does this benefit the other person?

The persuader will be attempting to convince the other person from a good place—they intend to help the other person somehow. While they may benefit too, they are primarily looking out for the other person's best interest. For example, you may try to convince someone to buy a specific car because it will work better for their family than the person currently looking at. It would be seen as persuasion—you are offering facts about the other car and showing how it would likely serve the person longer and better.

On the other hand, the manipulator is not concerned with the other person's needs—the manipulator will attempt to push for whatever benefits them the most. There is no good intention, and there will likely not be much truth either. It is also not likely to benefit the other person in any way and may even be detrimental. For example, the manipulator may try to sell a car that is no good for the buyer simply because the other car may be worth more money and therefore net a much higher commission. The car is not likely to be very good for the buyer's needs, but that is not the manipulator's concern. The manipulator would see that as something the buyer should know on his own and not bother pointing out how the buyer may be making a bad decision, even if the manipulator knows it was wrong.

Chapter 20. Factors That Influence Persuasion

Before you attempt to persuade anyone, some groundwork goes into the process that must be done beforehand. You will not just walk up to a stranger in the street and try to convince that person that they should buy a house or even a piece of paper from you. You have not assessed that person to determine if they need what you are selling or if that person has the means to buy the item. That scenario is farfetched, but the same principle applies to any situation where persuasion is being used.

You need to put thought into how and why you will approach the person or group of people you would like to persuade. The first factor that needs to be assessed is how easily this person or group can be persuaded. You need to know how much work needs to be placed into making the individual(s) see things in the way you do.

The first factor that determines how easy and straightforward it will be to influence other people is whether you are part of their group. Groups can mean several things. Groups can mean family, workplace, gym, or even a social media group. Being part of the group you would like to persuade does the job that much easier because you are seen as one of them. That relatability makes you more trusted. You also have insider knowledge of what makes the group tick. You know their views on particular matters and are less likely to step on toes when implementing the art of persuasion.

Certain qualities make certain people easier to persuade compared to other people. A person's mental health is one of those qualities. Persons who suffer from depression and other mental health issues are more easily swayed to see things from someone else. It is largely because this person is likely to be lacking in aggression and has low self-esteem, both qualities that also make a person more easily persuaded. It is a point that can tip the scale in any direction, though, as a person with a mental health issue might agree with you to avoid the conflict if they do not but are not convinced or persuaded to your point of view.

As it relates to a lack of aggression, people who are typically not prone to showing aggressive tendencies are more agreeable and less likely to challenge the point you bring across to them. People with low self-esteem do not hold themselves or their abilities in high regard. Therefore, they value the opinion of other people more than their own. As a result, they are typically easier to persuade. Slouching posture and the confidence in a person's tone as they speak are indicators of self-esteem levels. If a person is upright and open in their body posture and speaks with high confidence, this person likely has high self-esteem, while the opposite is true for low self-esteem.

People who are socially inept as also easier to convince compared to social butterflies. People who are impaired when it comes to social interactions typically place the burden of the conversation on other people and are less likely to express their opinions freely. This increases the chances that they can be persuaded without challenging the person who is persuading them.

Once you have determined why a particular individual or group needs to be approached for persuasion, you need to figure out how you will cross that bridge to start the process of persuasion naturally. Coming across as awkward or unsure will immediately put your target's guard up, hence making it less likely that you will sway them to your point of view.

If you are not part of the group that you would like to persuade, you need to get the right introduction into that group. Walking or calling will likely not work as we are naturally suspecting people we do not know. This person does not know you or what you stand for and, therefore, will not trust what you have to say. It is why salespeople who cold-call have so much trouble getting a foot in to make the sale. The potential client does not know or trust the salesperson.

Getting someone that the target already knows and trusts is better for forming that bridge. People tend to think that the connections of the people they already know and trust are likely trustworthy because people tend to form connections with people who hold similar views and beliefs.

Sometimes though, it is not possible to get an introduction through a mutual connection. Therefore, as a persuader, you need to be still able to finesse your way into building that connection with the intended target from scratch. Even though cold calling is a sales strategy that many salespeople hate participating in, many salespeople find great success with the technique because they have mastered making the potential client or client comfortable in their company and, further, trusting the message delivery. This mastery comes from having great listening and communication skills.

The first thing that effective listening does is to allow the persuader to observe the target's language. Language, in this instance, refers to the jargon that the target understands or recognizes as applicable. A computer salesperson will have to learn a particular language that includes memory capacity, hard drive space, and monitor resolution. He cannot hope to sell anything to a computer fanatic if he does not understand these terms and others related to computers.

A master persuader knows how to ask questions that allow him or her to gather information about the one to be persuaded and then listens effectively to gain pieces of information that can make it easier to persuade the target. For example, a door to door salesman can walk up to your door to make a sale. However, if he wants to have an effective campaign, he will not just start selling to you. Even if you want or need the product or service that he is selling, you will be wary of this stranger who has come up to your door and is not very trusting of what he has to say.

Instead, a savvy salesperson will work to get you comfortable, perhaps asking about your day or even picking up on your body's cues about how you are feeling. If you are feeling harassed, he might sympathize with you. If you are in a festive mood, he might enhance that feeling by being equally expressive, hence building a feeling of camaraderie between the two of you.

Then, he will move onto asking questions and making the meeting about you and fulfilling your needs. Many salespeople's mistakes are talking about themselves rather than allowing their clients to talk about their needs and wants. Always make it about the person you are trying to persuade. Asking questions and listening to the target makes them think that you care about their needs and wants; you respect their beliefs and, thus, have their best interest at heart. It creates conditions where this person is more likely to actively listen to what you have to say and be persuaded.

Even when the conditions are prime for stating your point, remain subtle. There is a notion in marketing that people are less likely to buy when they know they are being sold. The same applies to the art of persuasion. Suppose a person knows that you are actively trying to change their point of view. In that case, if that is plainly stated, the person will likely put up mental guards to prevent them from being persuaded even if the material being imparted is helpful to them. A person is more likely to be persuaded if their guards are down. Therefore, you need to be low key about how you impart your persuasion. That is not mean that there are not instances where being blatant with persuasion does not work, but most often, the subtle route yields faster and better results. Subtle methods of persuasion include storytelling, drawing comparisons, and recognizing the integrity of the target.

It is also essential that you learn and understand to agree with your target even when you disagree with their view. You will never see you agree with anyone every time, and that applies to the target of your persuasion as well. While you must agree with your target as often as possible to indicate that you value their opinion, it is also okay to disagree at times. It would be best if you disagreed since you are trying to convince the target to take on a different perspective. The key is to do so diplomatically and respectfully. Keep your posture and body language open and engaging. An agreeable attitude must be maintained even when you are disagreeing.

Chapter 21. Methods of Persuasion and Tricks Used By Mass Media And Advertising

Usage of Force

The manipulator may decide to use some degree of force to successfully persuade the victim to think in some specific way. It is, however, dependent on the situation at that particular moment. It is seen to be deployed in instances where both the manipulator's ideas and the victim do not seem to match up. The type of conversation they are having don't seem to bear fruit, or where the subject appears to be irritated or frustrated with the turn the conversation has taken. It may be classified as a scare tactic by most since it gives the victim minimal time to think logically of the events that seem to be transpiring instead of when the victim is in a normal state of mind.

A manipulator is usually inclined to use force as a method of persuasion, generally at that particular instance, when they may have hit a wall on their journey of persuasion. They may also do this if the manipulator feels as though he is losing control of the grasp he had on the victim or when the victim presents them with solid evidence of the manipulator contradicting them.

Asking Leading Questions

Another method that a dark manipulator skillfully uses is to ask leading questions. It could be considered one of the strongest verbal techniques because they ask the victims questions to obtain a specific set of responses. For example, a dark persuader may ask their target,

"How bad do you think these people are?" This issue already means that the individuals at issue are certainly bad to a certain extent. Dark persuaders ask these leading questions such skillfully that they instantly feel the victim is whipped up to leave the vessel and only go back to the questioning line where the victim appears to be in a relaxed position. Dark manipulators also use their real intentions to mask dark persuasion. To be easily exposed to dark persuasion, the dark manipulator hides his true intentions from the outset. Otherwise, he will fail. Skilled persuaders may mask their real intentions in several ways, depending on the individual victim and circumstance.

Create a Need

If it is executed professionally, the victim will be eating out of the persuader's palm in no time. It means that the manipulator will need to tap into their victims' fundamental needs, such as their need for self-actualization. In most cases, this technique will work well for the manipulator because the victim will need these things. For example, food is usually something that we as humans need to survive, and a prolonged lack will cause a big problem

Utilizing Illustrative and Words

The choice of words one chooses to use comes a long way in the success of using persuasion. There are many ways in which you can phrase sentences when talking about one thing. Saying the right words in the right way will make all the difference when attempting to use persuasion.

Tricks Used by Mass Media and Advertising

The media uses two main methods to persuade the masses. The first is through the use of images, and secondly, the use of sounds.

Media Persuasion by the Use of Images

Our sighs and visual processing areas of the brain are very powerful. Just think about it for a minute. Have you ever thought of a person without ending up picturing how they look? It is because of this that makes imagery and visual manipulation a preferred method by the media. Companies will often include split-second images of their product or individuals inserted into an advertisement that seems quite innocent by face value. It is usually a form of subliminal persuasion.

Media Persuasion by the Use of Sound

Sound is yet another trick that is used by the media in the persuasion of unsuspected victims. Some people usually underestimate the powers that exist within the sound. But how will you answer this? How many times have you listen or heard a song somewhere only to have it loop through your mind continuously? Songs usually influence us even though we are not aware of it despite knowing we are listening. It is what the media tends to exploit in their quest for persuasion of the masses. An example of this is seen at McDonald's. The melody "I love it" is often repeated in a manner that persuades the victims to purchase their meals continually.

Chapter 22. The Benefits of Learning About Persuasion

Your power of position will be one of the easiest ways to have persuasion. People with more real or perceived power will have more influence. However, people with power tend to talk more than others, interrupt conversations, and force the conversation to go in specific directions, thus damaging the power of their position. A person who controls their power of persuasion by engaging in meaningful dialogue can be even more influential.

Emotional control is critical. Letting your emotions run your conversation can be detrimental to your influence, but allowing emotion to pepper your argument or persuasion can be powerful. Think about how best to show your passion for your perspective or way of thinking and use it wisely. Sometimes, a well-placed expletive or watery eye can showcase how deeply you feel about what you are speaking about. Sobbing or turning red while cursing is the opposite. No matter how knowing you are on a topic, being too emotional can degrade your authority quickly.

Passion links well with expertise. When a person is knowledgeable and well prepared and passionate, they are an almost unstoppable persuasion force. It is especially helpful if you are not in a position of power in the conversation. It is a terrible truth that experts can be ignored if they cannot communicate their knowledge well, and people with little experience can be followed because they can sway a crowd with a stirring oration.

The final pillar of persuasion in communication includes controlling the connection. It is not the most powerful pillar, but it is essential. It is not just through conversation and verbal information but over your body language and understanding how others present themselves.

When you are dedicated to communicating with people, you need to be aware of these pillars of persuasion and control almost any situation with the correct words or actions. The following are here to guide you in understanding how different conversational tactics can provide you with the ultimate influence in any scenario.

Persuasion is a strong and valuable skill that not everyone has, but everyone should have. It comes in handy throughout your life in virtually any aspect of your existence, from sweet-talking your way into free movie tickets to convincing your boss you deserve a raise. By learning about persuasion will provide you with the following benefits:

In Your Personal Life

Your Relationship with Your Spouse

They say a good marriage or romantic relationship is all about compromise, but if you've ever been in a relationship, you know that's not always possible. You have to pick one side or the other, and why wouldn't it be your side? Far from being unfair or manipulative, having the ability to convince your significant other can improve your relationship because you have fewer fights about your disagreements and lack of compromise.

Your Relationship with Your Friends

We all have that one friend who always makes terrible life choices, and no one can get through to them and steer them towards the right path except you, that is. If you have influence and persuasion skills, don't keep them for yourself. Use them for good, not evil. Repeat these lines:

- "No, maybe you shouldn't marry that guy you just met."

- "Yes, limiting your day drinking is a wonderful idea!"

- "Please get that weird rash checked at the doctor."

- "Stop stealing from your workplace; you're going to get in trouble."

In Your Professional Life

Get Paid What You Deserve

Negotiating falls under persuasion, so really, absolutely everyone should have this skill. No matter if you're haggling at the market or talking a higher salary, you need to have the ability to convince your 'opponent' that you deserve this, and you should have it.

It's mostly applicable in the workplace, where—let's be real—no boss will ever willingly part with their money and hand it over to you. It's your job to convince them to do it. You've earned it, you deserve it, and it's rightfully yours. You have to ask for it, but you have to know-how, and persuasive skills help with that.

Earn the Trust and Respect of Your Boss

But of course, your only interaction with your boss isn't the yearly salary tug-of-war. If you're ever going to attain your career dreams and climb the corporate ladder, you need to have an excellent relationship with your boss, which means winning their respect and their trust.

You can accomplish that by becoming their go-to person. Offer your bright ideas, come up with solutions to problems the company is facing, persuade them to implement your suggestions, and that they're the contribution the company needs right now. In time, you will reap the rewards when your boss comes to consult with your first.

Be a Good Leader to Your Colleagues

To be effective in any leadership position—whether you're a manager, a team leader, etc. you need the power to convince people to:

- Do what you tell them
- Take you seriously

Your persuasive abilities will prove invaluable to a position like this if you want people to respect you, your work, and your ideas. It should be obvious for everyone that your way is the right way, and there will be minimal dissent if you have the necessary influence over them.

In Everyday Life

Persuasion is of unbelievable and utmost importance in our world today. Almost every human interaction involves an attempt to persuade or influence others to the speaker's way of thinking.

It is true, regardless of professions, age, sex, philosophical beliefs, or religion. If you can persuade other people, then you have a power that you can use to make your life better. Think about every person in your entire life who had influenced you to do your best and become successful.

Persuasive people can improve lives, avoid wars, and keep adolescents free from drugs or alcohol. However, some persuasive people can also destroy lives, start wars, and convince kids to try drugs or alcohol. That means persuasion is a powerful ability you can use for positive or negative things, depending on your motives. On the contrary, it would be best to use this power to attain self-improvement and overall growth for the entire community.

Get Out of Paying Tickets

Legally, a ticket is a mandatory consequence of breaking the law in some way, by speeding, failing to wear your seatbelt, talking on your cell while driving, etc. Practically, however, a ticket can be a negotiation, as long as you have the necessary skills.

Get into Coveted Clubs or Restaurants

How many times have you stood in line for hours to get into a popular club or restaurant, only to be turned away at the door by an unfriendly bouncer or snotty hostess? Well, let's see if you need to have a reservation. If you're persuasive enough, you can influence any menial gatekeeper and convince them to just let you through without needing to jump through fiery hoops or grease the well-meaning palms of anyone. Talk about some sweet perks!

Get Important Information

Do you feel like you're always being left out of the loop when it comes to important info among your family or group of friends? You don't have to guess what the drama is if you can convince someone to tell you, even if they promised they wouldn't.

If you can talk the talk well enough, you can convince anyone to tell you anything. Gossip from your friend preferred client sales dates from sales attendants, where they keep the extra free peanuts from the flight attendant, you get the idea. Sweet talk yourself into perks and valuable info.

Chapter 23. Dark Persuasion

The diversion between normal persuasion and dark persuasion is that dark persuasion does not always justify moral justification. While a normal persuader may try to persuade someone for that person's good, a dark persuader does so with motivations that aren't always good for the other person. They try to get a full grasp of the understanding of the person they wish to persuade, and they take pains to do so because they know what the biggest motivation is.

While persuasion always has moral implications, a dark persuader does not concern themselves with these implications. They are aware of them but choose to place their eyes on their objective(s) instead.

Persuasion is a psychological phenomenon in the everyday life of a human being. It is either that you are the one trying to persuade someone else or you are being persuaded. What makes the difference between dark and normal is the motivation behind it. In mass media, politics, advertising, and legal decisions, persuasion comes into play all the time. The outcome of practicing it in these fields is determined by ways of persuasion, which will influence the subject of persuasion.

There are some obvious and crucial differences between persuasion and other types of mind control, such as brainwashing and hypnosis. While these two requirements that the subject should be isolated to change their minds and identity, persuasion does not also require isolation.

To get to the goal, manipulation is used on one person. Although persuasion can also be done on a single subject to change their minds, there's a possibility of using it on a large scale to change a whole group's minds or even an entire society.

For this reason, persuasion is a more effective mind control technique and perhaps more dangerous because it can change the minds of many people at the same time instead of the mind of just one person at a time.

Several people make the mistake of thinking they have immunity to the effects of persuasion because they believe that they will always see every sales pitch that comes their way. They believe they will always be able to use logic to grasp what is going on and then find a logical conclusion.

Thanks to the fact that people are not always going to fall for everything they hear, this may be true if they use logic. It is also possible to avoid persuasion because the argument does not augur well with the person's beliefs, no matter the argument's strength.

Nevertheless, some people know how to use persuasive messages to encourage people to patronize the latest gadgets or products in the market. This act of persuasion is very subtle, so the subject will not always identify it, so it will be quite challenging for them to always form an opinion about the information they will get.

Every time persuasion is mentioned, one likely thinks of it in a bad light. They automatically think of a conman or salesman trying to change their perspective and eventually push them until this change is achieved.

While dark persuasion is prominent in sales and conning practices, there are also ways that persuasion can be used for good, like in diplomatic relations between international bodies or in public service campaigns. The contrast only lies in the way the process of persuasion is brought to play.

Dark Persuasion Techniques

When a person is willing to change their subject's mind by persuading them to do something contrary to their initial state of mind, the persuader will have some well laid out techniques to help them achieve their goals.

Each day that passes, the target is going to face different types of persuasion. For food makers, their goal will be to get their target to try out their new recipes or have them stick to the old ones, while studios will flash their latest blockbuster movies on the faces of their targets.

Whatever the case may be or whatever product they are selling, their main aim is to make more sales, and that is why they are trying to persuade you. They really couldn't care less about how this will impact you, and this is the reason why they must be very careful and skilled in the art of subtle persuasion to ensure that they do not tip you off or get you agitated. Since there are also many other brands trying to persuade you, they must find a unique way to impress their views on you.

Due to the influence of persuasion on a wide range of people, the techniques used in it have been studied for many years, dating back to ancient times. It is because influence is a very useful tool in the hands of a wide range of people.

Starting from the early 20th century, the formal study of these techniques began to grow. Remember that the goal of trying to persuade people is to push a persuasive argument on an audience and have them convinced. They will then internalize this message and adopt it as their new attitude or even way of life. For this point, there is a great need to discover the most successful persuasion techniques. Three dark persuasion techniques have proven to be of great value over the years.

Create a Need

It is one of the most fruitful ways of changing their perspective or way of life. The person trying to persuade a target will either create a need or capitalize on a need that the subject already has. If this is done properly, it has the potential of appealing a great deal to the target.

It means that to be successful, the persuader must appeal to the needs that are of more importance to the target. It may be their need to fulfill their dreams or boosting their self-esteem. It may also be their want for love, shelter, or food.

This method will always work out well because there is no way the subject will not need it. Since there is no way the target isn't going to have dreams and aspirations, the persuader will only have to find ways to make the victim understand how they can easily help them achieve those dreams.

The persuader may also tell their target that the target will realize their dreams if they make specific alterations to their beliefs or perspective. Doing this, according to the persuader, will give the target a higher chance of achieving success.

Appealing to Social Needs

The other technique that the persuader can use is identifying the target's social needs. While this may not yield as many results and the target's primary needs will, it is still an essential tool in the persuader's hands.

Some people are naturally drawn to crowds and desire to be wanted. They always want to have specific items, not because they need them, but because it comes with certain prestige that makes them feel like they belong to a higher class.

The notion of appealing to the target's social needs is obtainable through many TV commercials where viewers are encouraged to buy a product not to be "left behind." When they can identify and appeal to the target's social needs, the result is they can reach a new area of the target's interest.

Making Use of Loaded Words and Images

When someone is persuading someone else, they must be careful with their choice of words as words can make all the difference. While there are many ways to say a thing, one way of saying it may be more potent than the other.

When it has to do with persuasion, one of the essential things knows how to say the right thing at the right time. Words are always essential tools in communication and knowing the right call-to-action words.

Dark persuasion is one of the most powerful dark psychology concepts, but sadly it is always overlooked and underestimated. It may be because, unlike the other methods of mind control, persuasion leaves the target with a choice. In the other mind control methods, the target is forced into submission. Sometimes, this is done by putting them in isolation not to have any say in the outcome.

When it comes to persuasion, the chips are laid bare (although with an ulterior motive in dark persuasion) so that the target is left to make the decision that they think will suit them best.

Chapter 24. Covert Persuasion

Covert persuasion typically addresses the exact prediction of human behavior in any given context. Numerous attempts have been made in history to categorize people to understand them better and anticipate their behavior. A brief overview of this initiative shows various of the most famous names in psychology, consumer behavior, philosophy (NLP), and business from the periods of Aristotle, Freud, B.F. Skinner, Jung, Carl Rogers, Abraham Maslow, and William James, to the more modern brains of psychology, industry, and marketing, came up with some brilliant ways of understanding our collective thought and decision making to persuade us and influence and direct our behavior.

The Hermann Brain Superiority Predictor, the Myers Briggs Type Indicator, and the Language and Behavioral Profile are some examples of attempts to categorize us all. Of course, there are the endless personality tests that try to determine if you are well suited to a sales career. Moreover, there is the Enneagram of individuality and, obviously, the traditional 4-quadrant explanation of us as a Relator, Socializer, Thinker, or Director.

There is a famous theory that all of our actions stem from our need to avoid grief and attain pleasure. But it's not as easy as that. There's also the whole area of language analysis where it's assumed the words you're using will dictate your feelings. The labels (words) you put on your experiences determine your emotions.

Examples of Great People Manifesting Effectiveness of Covert Persuasion

Everything you have or will ever get, become, do, or learn, you'll get with and through others. Life is but persuasion! The world is the perfect context for persuasion and convincing. Marketers and advertisers are making virtually endless attempts to understand every one of us accurately. Every year they will spend hundreds of millions of dollars trying to catch our attention, convince us to buy their product or service, sample their offer, vote for their candidate, and donate to their cause. In reality, if you live in the US, each year, you alone are the recipient of more than $3,200 of marketing and advertising messages. That's a lot of money that's invested in convincing people.

Persuasion techniques help you understand and apply these to achieve your goals in the real world. Starting with the self-talk inside your mind that is important for the trust required to manipulate others, all the way to the final action of communicating straight to the one you want to convince, your target, are all here.

Through mastering the powers of persuasion, you will find it easy to get more of what you want and when you want. If you are in sales, you will now have tools at your disposal, which will double or even triple your profits and commissions if you consciously and regularly put the ideas and techniques to use every day in your work life. It sounds insane, but you're not going to be in the first 1,000 to tell us this was what happened. If you're in business, you have to convince colleagues, managers, and superiors to go along with your proposals. Here you will find plenty of methods that you can use instantly to persuade others to think your way covertly.

Persuasion strategies also include phrases that are more convincing when it comes to your personal and business life. Combining these terms with powerful stories will help you convince more people, more often.

The strategies and techniques would encourage you to have more of what you want more often by subtly or covertly persuading the other person to think your way. It doesn't take any more time to achieve it; however, you get everything you want, and you don't have to compromise or give up anything.

The persuasion methods often consist of powerful hidden powers like emotions and the influence of well-structured, well-thought-out, result-based questions.

Persuasion starts in the mind. Many words are written about how the human brain works, and many different opinions and hypotheses on how we think precisely. Yet, one thing is sure. To convince someone else to believe your way, you have to sync your mind with theirs. Effective persuasion begins and ends when a "mind meld" of real meaning, emotion, and comprehension is present. So how do we create this mind meld? How do we become more adept at persuading other people to think our way? The answer lies in knowing what motivates the other person and pushes him. Equipped with that experience, you can organize your thoughts and demands so that other individuals with little or no questions can easily and quickly embrace them. They will see you as much as they do and feel compelled to satisfy your requests.

Persuasion bypasses the vital human mind component without the message recipient being aware of the process. It is a question of getting through both resistance and response. It is achieved when one person sends a message, and it is received from the recipient without any critical thinking or questioning.

Persuasion is sometimes about controlling and handling the "state." What is the state of mind of that other person? For example, in the selling atmosphere, the consumer does not have to buy the product or service; in fact, purchasing is not an indication that there has been Covert Persuasion. An individual without money could easily be convinced and put in a purchase state, whereas he did not have the money.

Chapter 25. Ethical Persuasion

With persuasion and manipulation so closely related and only differentiated in a few key ways, you may be wondering how to keep your persuasion ethical. You may even be wondering why anyone would want to persuade, even ethically. There is a simple reason for this: Persuading others can often be quite beneficial to the other person, especially when you do so to better the other. Think of the best leader you may have ever encountered in your life. Perhaps it was a teacher that just had a way about him that always swayed people to behave. His very presence was enough to keep even the most troublesome students in line, even though those students rarely wanted actually to be in class. He could genuinely keep people involved in class and appeal to everyone, keeping even the students who would largely avoid learning in school engaged. He was able to do this through the persuasion of his own. Does this make the teacher a bad person? Not at all—he knew how best to deliver his messages to his targets, and in doing so, he was able to persuade those around him to pay attention.

Ethical persuasion can be used in a wide range of situations; it can be used with your children to keep them behaving well. It can be used at work to defuse stressful situations. It can be used to come to some agreement with a spouse or friend. There are endless possibilities for ethical persuasion if you are willing to give it a chance.

Remaining Ethical

While it may seem challenging to juggle ethics when attempting to persuade someone else of something, there is a helpful anagram to help you: TARES. It stands for truthfulness, authenticity, respect, equity, and social responsibility. When you keep this in mind while attempting to persuade those around you, you will be better able to keep your behavior in check. Remember, persuasion, in the right context, can be beneficial to everyone involved. It does not have to be avoided simply because it falls within the same category of social influences as manipulation. If done correctly, persuasion is a powerful tool that will enable you to continue to act ethically while still persuading someone else to do what you see is right.

Truthfulness

When you test your persuasion and intent, start first with analyzing the truthfulness of what you are saying. You want to remain truthful and honest when attempting to persuade those around you for a good reason—you want the other person to be informed. When staying ethical, you should recognize the other person as their person with their own free will that deserves respect, just as you would want for yourself. You would not want someone else infringing upon your own free will, and as such, you should make it a point not to infringe on the free will of others either.

When testing for truthfulness, ask yourself if what you have said is true. Beyond that, though, you must ask yourself if you have omitted any information you felt would negatively influence the person or keep the person away from acting in the way you would prefer him or her to do so. You must make sure that you are truthful in your communication as well as in your lack of communication—make sure you leave no pertinent information out, regardless of whether the other person has asked about it or not. You want to make sure that the other person is as informed as possible because you want the other person to willingly agree to do what you ask without coercion and manipulation.

Authenticity

The other test for ethical persuasion is determining the authenticity of what is being presented. At a glance, this may seem similar to verifying truthfulness, but it goes a little further. In truthfulness, the important part was making sure that everything was accurate and reported wholly and truthfully. With authenticity, you are checking the integrity of the message you are trying to convey. You must ask yourself whether you are doing what you are doing with good intentions. It means that you are not stereotyping, generalizing, or using fear to scare the person into an agreement with you.

Ultimately, you must make sure that the message you are conveying is done for good reasons. An easy and straightforward way to test for this is to ask if you would buy into it if you were presented with just the information on its own. For example, if you are trying to persuade someone to buy a car and you were in that person's situation, such as buying a family car that will fit three car seats, would you take the message you are presenting as honest, authentic, and trustworthy? If you feel as though you would agree with the reasoning being provided, the message is likely authentic. If you think that you may have a problem with the information presented, you should probably reevaluate the situation and your behavior and words. To make sure you are lining your persuasion up with ethics.

Respect

Then, you want to evaluate to make sure you are acting and persuading with respect. Are you recognizing the individual needs of the person you are attempting to persuade? Is what you are saying something that you would be comfortable announcing to other people as well, or would you be embarrassed or ashamed to be trying to persuade a perfect stranger of the message you are delivering? For example, if you aim to persuade someone to buy a minivan, are you appealing to some gender stereotype, or are you genuinely offering up the benefits a van has to offer entirely neutrally, such as talking about how spacious the seats are and how nice it is to have doors that slide open instead of swinging open when trying to keep track of kids.

Suppose you feel that your message hinges upon something stereotypical in any way or are not tailored to the individual. In that case, you are attempting to target with your persuasion, and you should probably look into ways to change the message. Just ensure that what you are attempting to persuade the other person is not offensive, nor is it done offensively. For example, you should not say that the other person must not be educated because they are from a specific minority with a lower rate of higher education. Because of that, they likely want this one specific car that many lower-educated minorities ask for. That would not be appropriate in this situation—it does not respect the individual as a person and is not respectful in general. Avoid the stereotypes and seek to get to know and understand the individual you are helping to ensure that the information you present is as relevant, respectful, and persuasive as possible.

Equity

The fourth step in analyzing your persuasion, then, is equity. When you are attempting to ensure that your message is equitable, you seek to ensure that both you and the other person are on an even playing field. It is incredibly essential that you are not looking to lead by coercion or by playing upon the other person's ignorance. You should seek to make sure that you are offering up as much information as possible to ensure that they feel that an informed decision is possible when trying to persuade the other person.

Often, when people attempt to persuade others, they play off of a lack of information. When someone is misinformed, it is much easier to take advantage of that misinformation. For example, if someone came in for medical treatment and asked for something far more expensive and far more than the person needed, it would be unethical for the doctor to accept that without ever talking about less invasive options appropriate for treatment. You want to do the same and precisely with your persuasion. Back to the example of the car salesperson, if you have someone coming in to trade in his car because he has hit 100,000 miles and the person has always heard that after 100,000 miles, the car is no longer reliable and needs to be replaced. As a salesperson, you may have thought it would be the perfect opportunity to get in an extra sale. Still, as the conversation continues, you learn that the person is not in a good place to get a new car but felt that he had to do so merely because of the mileage, even though everything was working correctly. It would be unethical not to point out the information you know would keep the person from buying the car because not pointing that out would only take advantage of his lack of information on the topic. That is not equitable—the other person deserves an even playing field when making decisions, even if giving that information can cause the person to decide against what you are attempting to persuade him to do in the first place.

Social Responsibility

Finally, the last method to check for ethical persuasion is social responsibility. It is when you stop to see if your persuasion is beneficial advice as a whole. If it is not, how can you change how you are persuading to ensure that you are doing so in a way that protects those who may be at a disadvantage? Remember, the point of persuasion is to convince people to do things on their own—it is not intended to be harmful to other people, nor should it cause others distress.

Suppose your persuasion is generally a good thing and will not have negative implications to the world at large, for example. In that case, you are not persuading someone to think of something in a racially biased manner, and it has passed through all of the other steps, then your persuasion method is likely to sound, and you are free to move forward with it. If it failed anywhere along the way, you would likely want to make sure that you are working to make your persuasion methods more ethical. Remember, ethics are respectful. They treat people with basic human decency, something that everyone deserves.

Chapter 26. Difference Between Persuasion and Negotiation

What Is Negotiation?

Negotiation is a way of resolving differences. It is a mechanism through which consensus or agreement is achieved while disagreements and conflicts are avoided. In any conflict, people understandably try to accomplish the best result (or perhaps an entity they represent) for their status. However, the foundations for a successful outcome are the core values of fairness, mutual benefit, and relationship maintenance.

In many situations, specific negotiation types are being used in international affairs, law, administration, industrial disputes, or intra-regional relations. But in a variety of activities, overall negotiation skills could be managed to learn and applied. Negotiation experience can help solve the conflicts between you and anyone.

Negotiation Phases

A formal negotiation strategy can be beneficial in securing a favorable outcome. For instance, in a job situation, it may be appropriate to schedule a conference where all the parties concerned will interact. The negotiation process contains the following phases:

Preparedness

A decision must be made before discussions. About when and where to talk about the issue and who will be involved. It is also beneficial to establish a limited period to avoid more conflicts. This phase consists of making sure all the relevant facts are known to explain your position. In the above example, the knowledge of your organization's "rules" for which assistance is given is included when aid is not deemed appropriate and the reasons for such refusals. The rules you can adhere to in preparing talks may be in the organization. While addressing the dispute, planning can help prevent future disagreements and unintentionally waste time during the session.

Talk of the Matter

Individuals or representatives of each side put the case as they choose, i.e., their awareness of the situation, forward during this stage. In this step, key skills involve interviewing, listening, and explanation. It is sometimes helpful to note all points rose during the debate stage if further clarification is necessary. Listening is essential, as it is simple to make the error that you talk too much and listen too little when there is conflict. Each hand should have the same chance of presenting its case.

Objectives Clarity

The aims, interests, and views of the dispute's two fronts must be clarified from the discussion. Such considerations should be identified as objectives. Through this explanation, absolute mutual respect can often be found or created. Clarification is an integral part of the negotiation phase. Unless it is overlooked, difficulties and challenges to obtaining a positive outcome can occur.

Discuss the Win-Win Results

In this phase, a win-win situation is focused on where the two parties feel their views are considered. This phase concentrates on what is called a win-win output. Generally, the best result is a win-win outcome. It may not always be feasible, but this should be the final goal through mediation. Various strategies and sacrifices suggestions need to be considered here. Commitments are often positive choices, often more beneficial than holding the initial positions for all concerned.

Agreement

Accord can be established after attention has been extended to recognizing the opinions and desires of both parties. To reach an acceptable outcome, everyone concerned must remain open-minded. Any contract must be made clear so that the decisions have been taken on both sides. The intervention plan must be followed to carry out the determination under the agreement.

Non-Agreement

If the negotiation process breaks down, and no agreement is reached, another meeting is expected. It prohibits both sides from engulfing themselves in warm debates or disputes that not only bother wasting time but can also affect future interactions. The negotiation phases should always be repeated at the upcoming meeting. Some new ideas or desires must be addressed, and the condition revisited. It could also be useful to look at alternatives and to mediate in another individual.

Informal Discussions

Sometimes, more unofficially, it is necessary to negotiate. In those cases, it might be difficult or essential to take the above steps officially if there is a disagreement. However, in various casual settings, it can be beneficial to remember the main points in the stage of formal negotiations.

The following three components are essential and will likely affect the outcome of negotiations in any talks:

Attitudes

The attitudes to the system itself, for instance, attitudes towards problems and individuals involved with the individual case or attitudes aligned with social acknowledgment requirements, have strongly influenced all conversation. Know always that: mediation is not a place for personal successes to be accomplished. The need to bargain with the government can be resentful. Through bargaining, characteristics may affect the actions of a human, such as that of individuals.

Awareness

The more awareness you have of the issues concerned, the greater your involvement in the negotiation process. Well-preparedness is essential, in other words.

Gain as much knowledge about your assignments as possible about the issues. Therefore, it is essential to understand how things are resolved because mediation can require different approaches in various situations.

Interpersonal Competencies

Strong interpersonal skills are important to successful talks, informal settings, and non-formal or less formal or one-to-one meetings. Such competencies include:

- Successful verbal contact
- Hearing
- Project study
- Solving question
- I am deciding
- Stability
- Tackling difficult circumstances

Are Negotiation and Persuasion the Same?

Negotiation is defined as two, or even more, people interact to reach an agreement on one or more issues and talk with another person to agree.

Persuasion can be described as the act or method of manipulating or moving to a new opinion, place, or course of action—through argument or intercession. It's the key to all discussions to transfer somebody to a new post or action path. Throughout immobilization negotiations, two parties try to find a compromise. It is mainly the case. While anyone may try to negotiate, an efficient and persuasive negotiator typically works more successfully.

Bringing up persuasion as a negotiation strategy means looking at the various types of conviction values related to property transactions; there are six different opportunities for self-interest, individuality, comparison, swap, sameness, and logical sense in property negotiations.

In the other perfect world, everybody would agree with you, and you would still be correct. About 99% of the time is not like that. What are you doing? Frequently people use manipulation to manipulate their stance on the other side. Persuasion is perfect if it succeeds because it does not cost you much but often does not succeed, so that you may have to bargain. So, what the distinction between persuasion and bargaining is.

It is best to switch to a dictionary to describe persuasion. The meaning 'to persuade' of Merriam-Webster is 'to compel (somebody) to do something by questioning, debating, and giving reasons.'

A brilliant short book called "Eristic Dialectic, the Art of Being Wrong" has been published by Arthur Schopenhauer and is still one of the day's popular rhetoric. Its 38 stratagems educate you about using logical errors, false proposals, generalization, and other handy instruments. There are some essential differences in both processes: the point of persuasion is to say, and trade is a negotiation. Strategies of persuasion are to explain, to promote, to manipulate, to inspire, to argue, to advise, and to contest.

On the other hand, negotiation implies that concerns, desires, shortcomings, motivations, and goals can be considered so that a better understanding can be made available from both sides. There is not strictly exclusive convincing and mediation either.

Both could be close to their results or goal. All strategies are very successful, and citizens are often persuaded that they prefer their reasoning and beliefs above compromise. The other party's reasoning and views tend to us not to be particularly interested. The individual may find it difficult to change his position, but we still choose it as persuading is which we've developed with since childhood and used again. Negotiation is challenging because we must be attentive to the other party's views, values, and reasoning and consider ways of dealing with them.

If we speak about compromise, there is some uncertainty about whether we say mediation or coercion. Negotiations, in their very essence, warrant a rapprochement between the two sides to reach a compromise. Convincing or manipulating, though, is the process of making the other party do what they want.

The Art of Convincing Is Often Termed Negotiation

Good negotiation leverage you will learn when and how to use effective skills to be a good negotiator. It is probably happening at times when you seem unable to agree on negotiations. In these cases, it is also necessary to understand how and when to persuade efficiently.

Use of Queries to Help Persuade Others to Compromise

Comments are high as they speak to the other arm. Yet reacting to what is being said is the real art of interrogation. It doesn't mean that you hang on each word. "The detection, selection, and interpretation of keywords that turn information into intelligence" is the definition of Mullender's listening. His conceptual model is 'information you use for your benefit.'

In sales situations, implied and explicit requirements are the keywords that a client of our SPIN Selling Skills model would listen to. An effective sales representative can turn that information in the form of profit statements into intelligence.

The profit statement requires that sellers dive into issues or perceived concerns, precisely the same as that recommended by Mullender, to "steer anxiety" in circumstances of recovery. You will define the specific desires (what the other side wants to do about this) and render helpful suggestions only by finding the real source of the pain. Unsurprisingly, in these cases, Mullender points to SPIN as a "stunningly clever" template.

Ultimately, while talks can be seen as a separate part of a process and a different ability to sell/persuade, a successful leader must still be willing in a negotiating scenario to execute suitable persuasive techniques. They recommend that negotiators develop strong selling strategies and negotiation skills to help them produce win-win outcomes. It is why they support

What Should You Select?

Seek first to convince and see whether it fits for you. Though, we were all on the other hand of someone who told us constantly that we don't approve. It cannot be very pleasant. Although persuading and bargaining, know when you hit an impasse.

The persuasion of sound is always stronger than the power of language. When you have the point of no-return, substitute the tone to be more convincing or switch your bargaining dialogue—you are much more likely to get a response. The persuasion of sound is always better than the persuasion of words.

Chapter 27. Deception

When someone is trying to deceive another person, the intentions are usually going to be pretty bad. It is a useful tool for being a dark manipulator, but you have to remember that most people will not be happy if they find out it is being used against them.

Perceiving Deception

Suppose the subject is enthused about maintaining a strategic distance from deception in their life to keep up a key decent way from the mind games that go with it. In that case, it is as frequently as conceivable a sharp plan to understand how to recognize when deception is going on. Reliably, it is difficult for the subject to find that deception is going on, except for if the master goofs and lies are clear or noticeable, or they repudiate something that the subject undeniably knows to be genuine. While it might be difficult for the chairman to cheat the subject for an important stretch, it will, by and large, happen in typical ordinary nearness between people who know one another. Recognizing when deception happens is regularly hazardous, considering the path that there few pointers that are completely solid to tell when deception occurs.

Techniques Used in Deception

Deception is a type of expression that utilizes lies and omissions to persuade the victim to fit into the world that the agent wants. A form of interaction or communication has to be involved. Deception can manifest itself in different types, according to the situation where it is applied. It is challenging to tell when someone is trying to deceive others. Luckily, though, there are a few components that, when identified, point to the likelihood of deception being involved. After many years of studying deception, psychologists have developed three classifications of deception: camouflage, simulation, and disguise. Out of the three classifications of deception, we can identify the common techniques used in deception. Let us first define the classifications.

Camouflage

Camouflage is the first classification of deception. The deceiver works to conceal the truth of their intentions in a way that the subject cannot decode. Just like the typical camouflage deployed by animals and plants to hide from predators or to approach prey without being detected, deceivers make use of methods that are hard to detect without extra observation.

Simulation

The second classification of deception is simulation. Simulation is the act of imitating to be something. In deception, simulation is defined as exposing the victim to false information as a tool of misleading them. There are three types of simulation described below.

Fabrication

Fabrication means altering reality. The deceiver can use a real thing and change it to work in their favor. For example, they can add or reduce details to a story to make it better or worse to convince the subject. A real-life example is when a suspect in court over stealing tells the judge that they stole food because they were almost starving, yet they intended to sell their loot for financial gain.

Mimicry

The second type of simulation is known as mimicry. Mimicry is defined as the art of imitating to ridicule or confuse a situation. In deception, mimicry happens when the deceiver pretends to be something or someone that they are not. A deceiver might steal an idea from someone, and instead of citing the owner; they use it as their own. An example of mimicry is when an author uses a famous writer's name to fool readers to purchase their book.

Distraction

The final type of simulation is called distraction. Distraction is the act of cunningly forcing the victim to shift their attention from reality and focus on falsehood. To divert the subject, a deceiver can use a form of bait, which might appear to be more convincing or beneficial than the truth.

Disguise

The third classification of deception is a disguise. Disguise is defined as the act of faking a different appearance to conceal one's identity. When it is being deployed, the deceiver puts up the impression of being somebody or something different from what they are. Practically, disguise means the agent keeps something from the victim, as their intentions, what they do for a living, etc.

Lies

A lie refers to the agent's act in making up and feeding the victim information that is not true. When presenting a lie, the deceiver makes it appear as a fact, thereby making the subject absorb it as the truth. Lies are the most common techniques used in deception since they divert the victim from verifiable facts and make them easy targets of manipulation.

Concealment

Concealment is the act of preventing something from being recognized. In deception, it is mostly deployed by the use of half-truths. While giving information, the deceiver intentionally omits some essential parts to keep some truth from the receiver. While the deceiver will not have lied to the victim directly, they will have ensured that the most important information has been kept from them.

Creating Illusions

Deceivers are experts at creating convincing illusions. Once they have acquired the subject's attention, they demonstrate imaginary pictures that sway them into partnering with them. They come up with illusions that appear to be realistic and workable in every way. The first step of creating the illusions is to explain their "ideas" to the target's mind. After that, they pull back a little to wait and see if the subject will develop an interest in the illusions.

Equivocations

Waffling is the application of ambiguous language to hide the truth. Ambiguous language can be indirect or contradictory. The equivocations' objective is to confuse the victim, so they are not aware of what is happening. If a deceiver is asked a question, he avoids giving definite answers and provides general responses. They can also be used by the deceiver to escape blame if they are found out. If they are suspected, they give many explanations about whose aim is to confuse the accuser.

Understatements

An understatement is a situation that has been minimized but can cause more effects than what has been portrayed. The deceiver delivers a statement to their victim while making it appear like a small deal than what it is. However, the statement can influence the victim more than they have been made to believe.

Exaggeration

Exaggeration is the opposite of an understatement. It is whereby a situation is overstretched or overstated to alter it. The deceiver might not be lying directly to the victim, but they turn a situation into a far bigger deal than it is. Exaggerations can be used to convince the victim in a situation where they would not be, had they been given the genuine version of the situation.

Seduction

Seduction is typical on social media, where a person can write an attractive bio about themselves and top it up with carefully processed photos or videos to catch others' attention. The problem is that both the bio and the media provided by such people might be false and only intended to lure followers or lovers.

Rationalization

Rationalization is the deployment of weak or far-fetched arguments with the intent of convincing someone that something is more pleasant than it appears. In the context of deception, the agent comes up with clear ideas to convince the victim to do something difficult to accept or is unpleasant under normal circumstances.

Playing the Servant

Another method used to deceive people is playing the volunteer or servant role. In this case, the deceiver hides their agenda by making their victims believe that they are doing something for a noble cause. The subjects are less likely to suspect that someone is up to some mischief, who claims to be doing something to assist others. Therefore, they end up trusting them and concurrently lowering their defense mechanisms. Once the deceivers have their way, they unravel their evil plans.

Diversion

Diversion is the action of changing the natural or acceptable course of something. In deception, diversion is a tricky endeavor that aims at destroying a subject. Mind controllers are aware of the human traits which direct their responses, behaviors, and personalities, such as self-esteem and discipline.

Playing the Victim

Deception takes a lot of consideration for emotions. A deceiver uses playing victims to appear weaker or hurt, whereas they are the ones in control. The idea is to make others believe that they are victims of circumstances to evoke sympathy, compassion, and pity from the people they look forward to deceiving. Once a victim shows some form of concern for the deceiver, they cooperate with them and become easy to deceive.

Chapter 28. The Dark Triad

Often, abusers fall within this category—the dark triad. The dreaded three personality types combine to create a human storm capable of destroying lives so utterly that the individuals have little hope of reassembling them without intensive professional assistance. These personality types are dark—they do not care about people and encompass everything wrong, and everything toxic about humanity. They are often monstering within human skin, staring out into the world, and looking to wreak as much havoc as they can as quickly as possible. These three traits are Machiavellianism, narcissism, and psychopathy. They are dangerous enough on their own, but when you find an individual who harnesses them all, be forewarned—you are better off leaving while you still can and escaping all of the nonsense altogether as quickly as possible.

Machiavellianism

If you had to simplify Machiavellianism into the shortest possible phrase— "The ends justify the means." Though never directly stated by Niccolò Machiavelli, an Italian politician and philosopher from the 1500s, this phrase came from the text he wrote in The Prince in 1513. He informed the prince that was being instructed within the document to present himself in one way, honest and benevolent, even though he was ready to behave as harshly as necessary because everyone can see a person. But very few people will ever actually get close enough to realize the truth. The message is essentially summed up by saying that the ends justify the means, meaning that it was acceptable to lie because it made the prince more well-liked. A well-liked leader is far more likely to be a successful leader that can maintain power.

Drawing from that principle, Machiavellian people are adept at appearing how those around them wish to see them. They will say whatever those around them want to hear because they know that it is unlikely that those around them will ever know the truth, and telling them what they want to hear makes them happier and gets the Machiavellian person what he or she wants. Then, getting the desired result, the end justifies the means of lying, even though lying is typically considered morally wrong and reprehensible.

This personality type is quite insidious—you never know whether you see what you are getting. The Machiavellian individual is deceitful and a master at deceiving people around him or her. They will only tell the truth if it is beneficial to them or is the most desired result, which it usually is not. They assume that it is more important to seem desirable and make good connections than developing proper relationships. Still, when you see people as nothing more than a means to an end, you are not likely to ever want to develop a relationship with others. When people are nothing but means they have been dehumanized, it turned into nothing but tools to be utilized to get what you want in any way possible simply because you want that result. Ultimately, despite the immorality of the behavior, you will do whatever it is that you must get the result you wish to only because it will get you what you want, and that is all you care about at the end of the day.

These people should never be trusted—they always have an ulterior motive, no matter how truthful they may seem in the moment. There is always something motivating them to behave in specific ways; whether it is innocent or not is up for debate. You are better off avoiding and not trusting this person whenever possible.

Narcissism

The other one is the narcissist—those with narcissism have a narcissistic personality disorder. It is characterized when an individual present with a grandiose sense of self, meaning he is quite egotistical and believes that he is far superior to a pervasive lack of empathy and an excessive need for admiration and attention. The narcissist thrives off of getting his or her sense of self-justified through actions such as praise or admiration—they only see themselves as worthwhile if others around see them as worthwhile first. They want to be recognized as worthy and will do whatever it takes to get that.

It means that narcissists are often willing to lie about who they are or what they like. They have no true sense of self beyond someone that desperately seeks the approval and admiration of others, no matter what the cost, and is willing to do whatever it takes to get it, even if that means lying about who they are.

The narcissist typically creates an alter ego of sorts, a persona that he presents to the world that is everything he wishes he was—charismatic, powerful, influential, and well-liked. He then utilizes several dark psychology manipulation techniques to keep people under the spell he seeks to create. He creates a sense of self and then always plays mind games and manipulates those around him. Only those who get close to the narcissist to be trapped in his web of lies beyond hope of getting out ever see his true self. The malicious individual lies beneath the persona, lurking for the first possible chance to lash out at those around him.

After snaring a victim within his trap, he will systematically manipulate the other person, conditioning them into doing whatever the narcissist desires. Over time, he can mold his victim into the perfect source of constant admiration, something referred to as his narcissistic supply. He will then always utilize manipulation and mind control techniques to keep his new toy under his thumb for as long as possible, attempting to break down his victim by any means necessary systematically.

Psychopathy

Psychopaths suffer from their personality disorders, in which they are often characterized through a series of persistent antisocial actions. They almost always lack any real sense of empathy—the innate human ability to connect emotionally with others at any meaningful level. This lack of empathy makes them incredibly dangerous. Without empathy, which is a built-in red flag system that lets us understand when something is wrong with those around us, particularly in regards to our behaviors to others, the psychopath has no real fail-safe to his or her behaviors—he will continue to push and push, even with the most aggressive behaviors, simply because he does not feel any need to stop. For those who do feel empathy, the pain they, themselves, feel as they harm someone else is usually enough to make them stop. The pain and guilt become overwhelming, and they stop before making it worse. The psychopath, however, does not feel that.

Beyond the lack of empathy and, therefore, remorse, psychopaths typically exhibit disinhibited behaviors—in simpler words, they are impulsive. A thought will pop into their mind with some random impulse, such as stealing a purse from someone or deciding to hurt another person, and they are far more likely to act upon it simply because they like to act upon their impulses.

Psychopaths are frequently also bold—they do not fear anything they are approached with. Consequences are not intimidating. People are not intimidating. Even dying or being harmed is not intimidating to the psychopath. The psychopath is incredibly tolerant of danger and is frequently noticed to have high confidence and assertiveness. Even though he is not likely to want to do anything meaningful with that confidence—he sees no point in engaging in social conventions.

The Dark Triad

With those three personality types now described in an easy-to-understand manner, you may now be wondering what happens when the three are combined. The results are an aggressive, toxic individual who does not care to act in a normal manner. They are fantastic at exploitation, lacking the empathy necessary to impede such negative, harmful behavior, and having the right amount of lack of impulse control to encourage it. They manipulate, they hurt, they steal, and they lie. They are callous, meaning they do not care about others' feelings and revel in seeing people hurt, angry, or sad. Research has shown that people with the dark triad personality type all enjoyed seeing people with negative expressions on their faces.

Ultimately, those possessing the dark triad are not forces to be reckoned with—they will do anything that will hurt you if you wrong them, and they do not care enough about social conventions to be held back from seriously harming you.

Chapter 29. How To Analyze People

It is the knowledge of the character by the features of the face and hand. It is about moving from an empirical art to an observation science. The character is not independent of the physical constitution. The state of our body conditions it. On the other hand, the body is influenced by the emotions of the soul.

Life is due to a double movement: a dilation movement and a conservation movement, which analyzes any human being's personality.

The Dilation-Expansion

Its adaptability characterizes it to the environment, an externalization of intuitive and affective tendencies, sociability, cheerful humor, need to be in groups, intelligence adapted to the useful and directed to practical realizations.

The Conservation-Seclusion

Oppositely manifests itself, with an elective adaptation to a privileged environment. Since withdrawal is a defense process, it acts only in a medium that does not suit you.

While the expansive individual is a friend of the whole world, disperses his activity in all directions, reacts impulsively, is determined, and has a sensory intelligence of immediate contact, the withdrawn has only friends of choice. If he does not have them, he prefers loneliness, concentrates, and is only active in some directions. It is not resolved unless he has reflected, does not trust his sensory impressions, and is more idealistic, replacing reality with abstractions, distrusting his senses, and reason.

The Expansive Individual

It is characterized by having a thick structure, colored and warm skin, wide round face, largemouth, snub nose, large eyes, and a smiling expression, with ease and abundance of exchanges.

The Retracted Individual

It is thin in nature, short limbs, dry and cold skin, and pale dye. The face is elongated, narrow, and bony. It is economical, selective in the exchanges, smallmouth, narrow and bony nose, sunken eyes, hermetic face, and little communicative.

The Expansive-Retracted

It is an intermediate of the recent two; the face is rectangular, large eyes slightly sunken. It opens or closes, depending on the situation.

Physiological Tricks to Analyzing People

In valuing people we have just met, we are often victims of our psychological mechanisms. It can lead to misunderstandings and preconceptions that eventually affect our ability to socialize. The best way to counteract these mistakes is to know how to identify them, so here are the common mistakes we make when valuing others.

Confuse Personality and Situations

When we observe someone's specific behavior, we immediately think that they act according to their personality. Instead, when we think about our behavior, we usually value it based on the situation in which we find ourselves.

For example, we know that we are distant when we are worried about something. However, if a person you just met acts in this way, you may directly assume that he is a jerk. To avoid falling into this trap, we should always consider the so-called situational conditions when valuing other people.

Confirmation Bias

Once we have a specific idea about someone, we usually see everything they do through the filter of these preconceptions. For example, if you consider a co-worker to be selfish, you look at the behaviors that confirm it, but not those who deny it.

Although our first impressions are usually quite reliable, they are not infallible, so it is essential to consider our judgments as we continue to relate to that person. The best way to prevent confirmation bias is to seek evidence that challenges your initial assumptions actively. Psychology calls this process "positive DE confirmation of expectations."

The Wavy Effect

The wavy effect is a cognitive bias whereby we make a generalization wrong from a person's single characteristic. The variable that most causes this effect is physical attractiveness; that is, we tend to value those who seem attractive to us more positively. Similarly, we also tend to value better those who resemble us.

An effective way to understand how it works is to identify when it occurs in critical situations. For example, when you hire someone for a job or when you are in a situation that involves many new people. If we pay attention, we will see that, in both cases, we tend to gravitate towards those people with whom we share certain features, whether physical or cultural background.

Let Us Influence the Past

A bad experience with a postal officer can lead us to assess all civil servants negatively. In the same way, knowing a person who reminds us of someone from our past can influence our judgment about that new person. For example, if the most undesirable person in your class at the school was named Alberto, you will have more difficulty positively assessing a person with that name.

One way to avoid this negative influence is to pay attention to our reactions' proportionality and identify when we approach a situation with a negative or defensive attitude.

The Supposed Similarity Bias

Usually, we tend to assume that others think like us and have our same preferences. But obviously, this is a mistake. If you want to skip this type of cognitive prejudice is to create a habit of warning people about diversity in people's preferences and expectations. That is, allow people to let you know that their comfort zone is different from yours.

Secrets of How to Analyze a Person

You surely wanted to be able to read the minds of other people more than once. With the aid of their formed instincts, some are spared, but if you are not so wise, you have only one way out: learn to decode the body's language.

It's no longer a secret that we get 55% of the information with the aid of non-verbal communication. Face expressions, emotions, and actions of the body will strip anyone's disguise and reveal their true thoughts and feelings.

Closing Your Eyes

If a person closes his eyes, talking to you, you must know that he is trying to hide or protect himself from the outside world. That doesn't mean I'm scared of you. Alternatively, the other way around, He wants to take you out of his dream area. You may already have bored it. Open and bam your head! You're done.

Protecting the Mouth by Hand

It's a vivid example from childhood that we all come. Remember, when you didn't want to say anything, you covered your mouth with the palm of your hand. It's the same person. Many fingertips, fist, or palm allow us to express the words. Sometimes with a feigned cough, we mask it.

Biting the Rim of Your Glasses

Does your buddy intentionally bite his glasses rings? Try to encourage and support him. He must surely be concerned about something, and he wants to feel safe at his subconscious level, as in childhood with the mother's breast. By the way, the same applies to a pencil, pad, finger, cigarette, or even chewing gum in hand.

Stroking the Chin

The person is trying to decide this way. Your attention can be focused downwards, sideways, to the left, or any other side at the same time. He doesn't know what he sees at that exact moment because he's immersed in his feelings.

Crossed Arms

One of the most repeated movements. It is not shocking that many people feel very comfortable with this posture, as this gesture helps separate themselves from others. When we're not happy with something, we use it several times. The crossed arms are a clear sign of your interlocutor's negative attitude.

Self-Exposure

This posture is more accessible, right? When a woman wants to like a friend, by revealing her best sides, she starts to reveal herself. She straightens and bends her thighs to show her breasts. The folded arms below are a clear signal of the interlocutor's attention.

Leaning Forward

Normally, he leans forward when a person feels concerned for their interlocutor and needs to contact him or her. The feet that remain in the same place at the same time, but the body moves unconsciously.

Leaning Back

If the individual leans against his seat's back, he clarifies that the conversation is boring. In your interlocutor's company, you can feel uncomfortable.

Handshake "Glove"

It indicates you can trust him if your interlocutor embraces you with both paws.

Squeeze with Palm Up

The palm-up displays sensitivity, protecting the interlocutor's face, but only if achieved at once. If the hands were already holding for a particular moment, and then somebody placed the hand palm up, it may signify a desire to show who is in charge.

Squeeze with a Touch

The person can touch the forearm, elbow, or back of the person he greets with a single hand. This personal space invasion shows the need for contact. And the smaller the body becomes, the more important it is.

Straightening the Bond

It depends on the situation here. If it's a man who does it in a woman's presence, he may very much like it. But this gesture can also mean the person is not feeling comfortable. You may have been lying or just wanting to leave.

Collecting Non-Existent Hair

The gesture of repression is thus called. We use it most of the time to express their overt dissatisfaction. We don't express their opinion freely, in other words, but we certainly disagree with what's going on around them.

Feet on the Table

This expression can mean many things: bad manners, arrogance, the desire to show off as a great boss, or health concern. Nonetheless, psychologists tend to believe that it would be safer to use it at home or in your relatives' company, even if you are very confident in this role.

Riding the Chair

A chair is not a saddle, and the back is not a shield, although it seems to be in some respects. It was also designed for other uses. This way of sitting around is troubling so many people, so we feel a lot of hostility from the "hung" individual at the intuitive level. Powerful men usually use this position.

Eye Contact

The eyes are the soul's mirror as well as a natural interactive device. There we can read all the interlocutor's feelings and emotions. Lovers look at each other's heads, expecting unintentionally to see how they get larger. And this shows a lot as, relative to their normal state, the pupils will increase in size up to four times. By the way, if the person gets mad, their eyes become like accounts because of the pupils' full reduction.

Chapter 30. Speed Reading to Understand People

If you are ready to read other people, then this is the guide for you. Ultimately, being able to read other people is highly essential. If you want to understand what is going on in someone else's mind, you need to tell what is going on with their bodies first. The truth is, people are quite easy to learn to read if you know what you are doing. All you have to do is make sure that you are looking at specific clusters.

Ultimately, we all communicate with people in different ways. We have both verbal and non-verbal signals that we give off at all times. However, the bulk of our communication is non-verbal. We have plenty of body language that we use in different ways to understand what is going on with other people. We look at proximity to each other and general demeanor to figure out what is going on inside one person's mind to get more information from them. When you do this, you learn to recognize how you can interpret what they are about to do, if they are going to do anything at all.

Within this guide, we will take a look at what it will take for you to begin understanding other people at a glance. You will learn how to understand the basic expressions, attraction, closed behavior, assertiveness, and dominance. All of these are important in their ways, serving essential roles that you can utilize. All you have to do is make sure that you know what to look for!

Reading Expressions

Ultimately, we have seven primary expressions—these are known as our universal expressions because you can spot them pretty much in any culture. Every one of us knows what a smile is, and you can recognize it immediately. That is because a smile is an expression that is considered universal. Let's look at the six universal emotions now so that you can better see what to expect with them.

Happiness

Happiness is easy to understand. When you see someone that's happy, you can recognize it by the smile primarily. However, the most obvious sign of happiness is the crinkle in the eyes—this is how you know that the smile and happiness are legitimate.

Sadness

When it comes to sadness, you can identify it by the fact that the entire face melts. You can see that the eyebrows go down. The corners of the mouth do as well, and the inner corners of the brows go up. There may or may not be crying involved as well.

Anger

Anger is defined by three primary characteristics, aside from the demeanor that goes with it. Usually, someone who is angry will have their brows lowered while pressing their lips together firmly. Alternatively, the mouth may be open, bearing teeth and squared.

Fear

Fear is usually shown as brows up high on the face, but still flat, with the eyes widened. The mouth usually opens widely as well.

Surprise

The surprise is similar to fear in people, but the marked difference is that the jaw lowers alongside the mouth's opening, and the eyes are usually opened wider, showing whites on both sides. The brows are also arched instead of just raised.

Disgust

Disgust is noticed primarily by taking a look at how the face comes together. The upper lip goes up, rising slightly. The nose bridge usually wrinkles as well, and the cheeks pinch in and up to try to protect the eyes.

Reading Attraction

When a person is attracted to someone else, they show undeniable body language as well. In particular, you can expect to see all sorts of specific actions. The body does not usually lie, and because of that, you can look directly at the behaviors that someone is doing to figure out if they are attracted to you or not. In particular, you want to look for the following behaviors:

Sustained Eye Contact

You will see that the other person will maintain eye contact more when attracted to you. Additionally, they will usually look away and then glance right back to see if you're still watching them.

Smiling

There is a reason we assume smiling is flirting—it happens often. The flirty, attracted smile usually lasts longer and includes flirty eye contact, and fleeting, but regular.

Self-grooming

Men and women both do this—they brush their hair with their hands, adjust their clothes, and otherwise tamper with their appearance when they are flirting or talking to someone they find attractive. If they do this regularly, they may be attracted to you.

Looking Nervous

Being nervous is a very normal thing when attracted to someone else, and this usually shows itself through fiddling with something repeatedly.

Leaning in

Typically, people will lean toward things that they are attracted to, and people are no exception to that rule. You will also notice that the feet will point at the person that the individual is attracted to.

Licking the lips

This is a common one, but it is subtle and easy to miss. However, you can notice it if you pay close attention. Usually, it is noticeable by a quick part of the lips and a small suck or lick.

Reading Assertiveness

Assertiveness is calm, confident, and in control. Effectively, if someone is assertive, they behave as if they are in control—they take charge, are comfortable with themselves, and won't go out of their way to overstep on other people. They sit back and allow things to play out without letting anyone else dominate them. The most common signs of assertiveness include:

Smooth Body Movements

When you are assertive over something, you don't have jerky movements. They are smooth and in control without much of a problem, even when energized or emotional. The voice sounds smooth as well, and they slowly and steadily look about.

Balanced

The assertive individual is usually upright, relaxed, but also well balanced and comfortable.

Open Body Language

Usually, these people will show that they are open to engagement without threatening or provocative. They do not block off their bodies at all and show open hands as well.

Eye Contact Regularly

Eye contact is usually steady and maintained comfortably without much of a problem.

Smiling

There are plenty of polite smiles and listening well with this body language as well. Usually, you can expect the other person to be quite comfortable, and they will smile efficiently and appropriately.

Firm

While they are firm, they usually have a solid stance without much of a problem. They are not confrontational and typically show that they are willing to listen, but they are also firm. They do not escalate anything and tend to avoid aggression in any form.

Reading Domination

Domination is a little more than assertiveness. Usually, with assertiveness, you see someone that is showing that they are confident without being threatening. However, with dominance, you can expect to see a much more threatening demeanor. A dominating body is going to show signs such as:

Facial Aggressiveness

You will be able to see the aggression in the face—usually in the form of frowning and sneering or even snarling.

Starring

The aggressive individual will usually stare at someone they don't like or may also squint or attempt to avoid looking at someone entirely.

Widebody Stance

They will usually stand out with their shoulders widened and may even hold their arms wide open as well. They may also stand with their hands placed firmly on their hips in a crotch display.

You may notice sudden movements that the aggressor is very rough with his movements, moving about suddenly and even erratically sometimes. It is a good sign that they are not in a perfect spot and may do something else aggressive.

Large Gestures

You may notice that as the individual moves, he will signal with aggressive, almost too big or wide movements that get close to you without ever getting close enough to touch you.

Reading Closed Behavior

Finally, let's go over closed behavior before we continue. Closed behavior shows that the individual is not interested in engaging with the other party at all. When you see closed behavior, you know that the individual will not want to engage with you; you will see that they want to be left alone. You can expect to see symptoms or signs of this sort of behavior, such as:

Crossed Arms

This is perhaps the most telltale sign. When someone feels closed off, they will almost always cross their arms and keep their hands near their bodies. When they speak during this time, they will keep a monotone voice. Think as your sign that you create a barrier between yourself and the other party with your arms. You want to be alone, so you close yourself off entirely.

Crossed Legs

You can also cross off legs as well—when you do this, you see that the knees are across from each other when sitting down, or they can cross the ankles as well. It creates an even more closed off image that shows that you are defensive and unwilling to listen or change your viewpoint on something.

Looking Away

It is also prevalent to see that the closed-off person wants nothing to do with those around them. They don't want to look at the person that is engaging with them.

Leaning Away

You may also see that the closed-off person wants nothing to do with getting close to the individual engaging with them either. Instead, they will pull away and lean back, trying to put as much distance between them as possible.

Feet Turned Away

Look to the feet when you want to know how engaged someone else is. If you see that the other person is standing away, feet pointing away from you, they are closed off and don't want to engage in the conversation at all.

Chapter 31. Advanced Tips and Tricks to Control People

So you're playing the seduction game and leading someone to get intimidated by you? Again, manipulation is a powerful weapon in your arsenal that can be used negatively or positively to achieve your objectives with the person, even though it may have largely negative connotations. There are plenty of psychological tricks that can be used to get close to a person or lead them to be intimate with you.

Exercise due caution and diligence when it comes to using these techniques because your dignity and reputation are at stake here. Playing with other people's emotions always to have your way will make you come across as distrustful, deceptive, and selfish.

Flattery

Flattery is a brilliant way to break the ice with someone you've just met or lead someone you know for ages to do what you want. Ensure that you disguise flattery (however fake it is) in the garb of genuine and specific compliments.

For example, instead of telling someone how lovely they look in a particular piece of clothing, say something like, "I love how the color of your eyes is beautifully complemented by what you are wearing." It sounds more genuine and invariably draws the person to you.

There is a secret strategy when it comes to resorting to flattery. Identify an area where the person is slightly insecure and needs reassurance. Use specific compliments related to that area to win over the person. For instance, if someone has issues related to speaking confidently in public, tell them that they have a wonderful voice texture or always use the right words while talking. It directly squashes their concerns and insecurities and makes them feel nice about an area they aren't too sure about.

Make Them Indebted to You

It is another slightly insidious strategy that can be used to seduce a person or get them to do what you want. It is a universal strategy that is effective across cultures, classes, and genders. You make the subject feel indebted to you by doing them a series of favors. In their mind, they become obliged to you even though they didn't ask for it.

You create a misbalanced equation where you are the giver, and they are the receiver. To make the equation more balanced, they know they have to pay you back in some form. Take advantage of this titled balance and get them to do what you want by straightforwardly asking them when the time comes. There are high chances the person has already mentally conditioned himself or herself to pay you back. Evil as it sounds, the tactic is used by several people who will fund others' lifestyles to make them feel indebted to the manipulator. The subtext is, "I own you because I pay for everything you use." It may start with small things that the subject voluntarily opts for, which then becomes impossible to get out of.

Use Shame or Guilt

There's no denying that the manipulation seduction game can get sneaky and complicated with blurred right and wrong lines. However, the manipulator widely uses another technique to charm people into going out or sleeping with them. It comprises inducing feelings of guilt or shame on the subject.

If the manipulator's requests are continuously turned down, he or she will make the subject feel guilty or shameful about refusing them. For example, "You know how lonely I am, living all alone away from my family. I've had a very rough and lonely childhood where no one ever loved or cared for me. You are also adding to my feelings of being lonely and uncared for with your cold and disinterested attitude. I know the world is against me, and no one wants me."

Manipulators know how to induce feelings of guilt by pushing the right emotional buttons. You will make more sweeping statements (no one loves me, the world is against me, or I've had a rough childhood) rather than state-specific instances. Manipulators cleverly study what makes the other person feel guilty and target those areas to get what they want.

Another disturbing yet highly successful seduction manipulation technique is to make the other person feel shameful about their past actions repeatedly. Though it may help you get what you want in the short run, it will certainly not set the basis for a healthy, rewarding, and meaningful relationship in the future.

Steer the Conversation

Seducers who've mastered the art of manipulation will almost always hold the remote control of a conversation to lead their subject into doing what they want. For example, if you want to sweet talk with a date, spouse, crush, or friend who is nagging you about something, you steer the course of the conversation by changing the topic to a more favorable one.

"Hey, I just saw a gorgeous blue, low-cut outfit that would look flattering on you at Mary Ann's boutique the other day" or "I saw the most jaw-droppingly beautiful house at Lakeview Lane on my way to work the other day, what do you think about living there together?" It takes the conversation from a rather unpleasant tone into a more welcoming and inviting tone that sets the pace for wooing someone or triggering feelings of intimacy in them.

False Logic

Teens and adolescents mostly use this one, but there's no denying that plenty of adults resort to it too. The logical fallacy or false logic creation technique comprises creating a seemingly false argument and making it sound that it is indeed true. When you tell someone that if a particular thing is true, they will not do something that you deem undesirable.

For example, "if you love me, you will get married to me immediately" or "if you trust me, you won't hesitate to go to bed with me" You are challenging them to prove their feelings and emotions by getting them to do what you want them to.

Make it Appear Normal

So what you as a manipulator are doing here is making the subject feel like what you've asked for or what you want them to do is normal. To do this, you stealthily use numbers, statistics, and research findings for your advantage. You make someone feel like they think differently, while what you are asking for is normal. This way, they are led into believing that something is wrong with their thinking.

For example, "statistics reveal that 75% of people end up sleeping with each other right after the first date." You establish that it's a norm and that most people would do it, and they are crazy or abnormal if they think otherwise.

Silent Treatment

Seduction experts using manipulation know how to use the silent treatment all too well. It works like magic when you're getting someone to obey your wishes. When you remain silent, it impacts the other person by making them feel like they have done something wrong or hurtful.

They become even more eager to make up for it when they realize that you are hurt, angry, or upset with their actions.

The Mirror Effect

As someone who uses the mirror effect manipulation technique for seducing the subject, you attempt to establish a level of trust and emotional comfort by convincing the other person that you are exactly like them. The manipulator pretends to have the same background, values, interests, personality traits as the subject. You may also share fake stories, secrets, or confessions to build a sense of trust, familiarity, and emotional proximity with the other person. You let them know what they want to hear emotionally, and they return the favor with what you do to them, often sexual.

It is the basis of most seduction-manipulation techniques. Manipulate someone's emotions to lead them to think and feel in a particular way, and then get them to bed with you.

Create a Compelling Want

Seduction is all about creating a compelling desire and then presenting yourself as the source for fulfilling it. It is pretty much what every advertiser, salesperson, and internet marketer use. They create a specific thing in their prospective clients' lives and then present their products or services as the only solution.

Build a strong need for what you have to offer. Make them feel like they need you to fulfill their physical and emotional objectives. Do not be afraid to show them how you can help them or what you can offer them. Strut your strengths and tease until they are convinced that you've got what they need!

Maintain a little distance from the subject to show them what they desire is slightly out of their reach. They will be yearning for you more when they realize that you have everything they want and are yet out of their reach. It makes them strive for your attention even harder!

Chapter 32. The Most Powerful Mind-Power Tool

Humans spend countless hours seeking new ways to work just about anything. Through endless hours of research, they pour over books and journals looking for the message that will tell them the secret to harnessing mind power. Many never realize that the most powerful mind power tool is already on board and just aching to be used. It is the human brain, the mind itself.

Every time a person practices a new habit or thinks a new thought, they make a new pathway in the brain. Every time the habit is used, or the idea is thought, the nerve pathway becomes even stronger. The human brain is wired at birth to be an efficient machine, and it is ready, from birth, to make an ever-increasing amount of nerve pathways and strengthen the pathways used the most.

Sometimes thoughts and habits need to be changed for the improvement of the person. When people decide that they would like to change their lives, there will be a period of adjustment. It is true whether the change is mental, emotional, or physical. During this period of adjustment, there will be some level of discomfort. When a habit or a thought is already formed, it has made its path in the brain. When a stimulus is seen or heard, the message travels along the preset nerve pathway to the brain's spot that controls that thought or habit. To change a thought or a habit, the nerve path must be changed. Until the nerve path is changed, the old nerve path will remain in the brain. The brain's discomfort is trying to access the old pathway, and the new pathway simultaneously automatically. It is painful for the brain to do.

It is easy to become frustrated when the brain goes back to its old thought and habit patterns. Never fall into the habit of placing blame on a lack of willpower. Willpower has nothing to do with it. It is a challenging thing to override preset pathways in the brain. The brain is a very powerful tool. When will power fail, and mistakes happen, always remember to use kindness and compassion to deal with the failure? The brain is very efficient at doing what it does. The only way to change the brain's pathways is to keep working on new pathways that will eventually obliterate the old, undesirable ones.

The brain needs a clear understanding that changes are about to occur, and new pathways are about to be laid down. Remind the brain that new habits and new thoughts will be replacing the old ones. Blaming failure on a lack of willpower is a self-defeating statement. The process of making new nerve paths in the brain takes hard work and time. It will help to keep reminding oneself of the impending change. By doing this over and over, it makes the process no longer about possible character flaws. The focus is now put on the habit of thought that is being built.

Is it possible to build new nerve pathways in the brain? Yes, it is possible, and it can be done. If more proof is needed, compare the adult brain to the baby's brain. Every current habit and thought a person has the direct result of practicing them repeatedly until they created a brain pathway. New pathways can be created. The baby's brain has no idea of anything. It has no thoughts or habits. Every nerve path currently in the brain was practiced until it became a part of the brain. Think of the baby. The baby lies around day after day and does baby things. Then one day, the baby notices the shiny rattle that mommy is waving in front of its little face. The baby wants the rattle. As the baby is waving its tiny arms around, the mommy puts the rattle close enough so the baby can touch it with its wavering hand. After a few of these sessions, the baby gets the idea that it can touch the rattle if the arm is in the air. A nerve pathway is beginning to grow. So the baby decides to lift its arm to reach for the rattle actively. The baby will be unsuccessful because the arms will wave wildly and will not connect with the rattle. One day, the baby will grab the rattle, and the nerve pathway is then complete.

While this may seem like a straightforward example, it is precisely how nerve pathways are created in the brain. Every action, thought, or habit has its nerve pathway. All pathways must be created. No one was born knowing to sit in front of the television and mindlessly eat dip with chips. No one was born lamenting the excess pounds they carry in strange places. No one was born hating their body; all behaviors are learned, good and bad. And the bad ones can be replaced with good ones.

So if the ability to program negative thoughts into the brain exists, then the ability to disrupt those negative thoughts with positive thoughts also exists. The brain can be reprogrammed. It is a powerful tool, and its main function is to turn thoughts into reality. The brain is always working, so why not use the brain's power to benefit rather than harm? Just because a particular habit or thought has been around forever, it does not mean it needs to stay. Use the brain's power to choose new habits and thoughts to focus on and replace the brain's old, negative thought pathways.

The new thought needs to be believable; the new habit needs to be doable. It does not look really good to try to stick to a habit that is impossible to accomplish or to try to believe an unbelievable thought. After years of seeing an obese body's reality, it would be nearly impossible to suddenly believe that the mirror image is that of a skinny person. But the brain will likely accept something that mentions learning to take care of the body or learning to accept the body to correct its flaws. The brain will turn a belief into reality. Believing a positive thought will lead to a different result than the ending where only negative thoughts are present.

Be prepared to repeat and repeat some more. The primary key to being able to make a new habit stay is repeating it constantly. The more a new, desirable habit is practiced, the more the brain begins to accept it. The nerve path becomes stronger every day. With constant practice, this new nerve path will become the path the brain will prefer to use, and the old one will cease to exist.

In any case, be sure to allow enough time to create a change effectively. Accept the starting point and continuously visualize the ending point. Accept that the path to the goal of a new habit or thought will not be easy or perfect. The path will rarely travel in a straight line. Sometimes people fall entirely off the path, and that is okay too. Do not get sidetracked by the idea that this journey will be comfortable and carefree because it will not be. Just keep thinking of the new nerve pathway created by the new thought or habit, and it will eventually become a reality.

Most of the pathways in the brain are stored in the subconscious mind. It is the part of the mind that is always working without always being thought of. Think of learned skills like tying shoes, zipping a coat, and pouring milk into a glass. These were all learned behavior whose nerve pathways are firmly set in the subconscious part of the mind. This part of the brain is the bank of data for all life functions.

The communication between the conscious mind and the unconscious mind works in both directions. Whenever a person has a memory, and emotion, or an idea, it is rooted in the subconscious mind and translated to the conscious mind through mind power. The subconscious has the power to control just about anything a human regularly does.

For example, during meditation, steady, deep breathing is usually practiced. The control of the breath is brought from the subconscious mind and given to the conscious mind to control the breathing. Once a pattern of deep, steady breathing is begun by the conscious mind, the subconscious mind takes over and keeps the set rhythm going until it is told to stop. It is done by a conscious end to deep breathing. The subconscious mind also processes the great wealth of information received daily and only passes along to the conscious mind those necessary for the brain to remember.

When sending thoughts from the conscious mind to the subconscious mind, the brain will only send those thoughts attached to great emotion. The only thoughts that remain in the subconscious are those that are kept there with strong emotions. Unfortunately, the brain does not know the difference between positive emotions and negative emotions. Any strong emotion will work. Both negative emotions and positive emotions can be quite strong. Also, unfortunately, negative emotions tend to be stronger than positive emotions.

Step one in learning to use the subconscious part of the mind's power will be to eliminate any thoughts that come with negative emotions. Also, negative mental comments will need to cease. Fears will usually come true, precisely because they are drowning in negative emotion. Negative ideas need to be eliminated because they can be very harmful roadblocks on the road to harnessing brainpower.

One best practice to use to get rid of negative thoughts is to counter them with positive thoughts. It will take time and practice, but it is a very powerful and useful technique. Whenever a negative thought pops in the conscious mind, immediately counter it with a positive thought dripping with strong emotion. The actual truth will come out somewhere in between the two thoughts.

Another way to counter negative emotions is to delete them, just like using a remote control. When a negative thought comes into the conscious mind, imagine destroying it. Imagine writing that thought on paper and burning it. Imagine pointing a remote control at the thought and pressing a huge delete button. Whatever form used to imagine deleting the thought, the important thing is to get rid of it before taking hold in the subconscious mind.

Find something energizing and use it to reach a goal. Those things that are found to be energizing bring boundless energy to positive thoughts. It is often necessary to invent motivation to learn to create new habits and thoughts, at least in the beginning. But with a bit of practice and a lot of positive thought, new positive habits will soon be burned into the subconscious mind, and the old negative thoughts and habits will fade away.

Chapter 33. NLP Conclusion

You learned all about NLP, persuasion, and other subjects connected to these two. Remember all of the body languages you were taught—out of everything, that maybe one of the best skills to foster and develop. You learned of several different ways people can control, influence, and persuade other people to do what they want or need. You learned all about how people prefer to interact with others and genuinely and naturally develop the persuasion and influence that so many people desire. You were also taught how to develop several social skills that are of the utmost importance if you wish to be successful.

Ultimately, the information should guide your behaviors. Let this allow you to go through your life, be informed, and aware of how your behaviors influence others. Focus on those around you with their body language and see how easily your behaviors can sway them. Learn from negotiation skills to ensure that you can get what you want while still giving back to others. Remember how to keep your interactions with those around you ethical, even if you understand how to take over and manipulate them into obedience to do whatever it is you are seeking.

Neuro-linguistic Programming practitioners and trainers have put forward exemplary approaches and techniques to persuade, which can be used in various environments. Studies state that these techniques develop personal performances and help the individual maintain good intrapersonal and interpersonal relationships.

To persuade someone entails a process of altering and rebuilding their opinions, beliefs, values, and behaviors towards an outcome. Humans are programmed to find it extremely difficult to move out of their comfort zone, no matter their comfort zone. For some individuals, even if their comfort is unhealthy, they wouldn't mind staying in it because, well, it's comfortable.

Persuasion is just not about forcing an individual to behave how we want them to behave; it is about allowing them to come out of their comfort zone to achieve a higher comfort zone after the discomfort of the change subsides. Simply put, an individual who regularly smokes will keep smoking because it is his comfort zone. To persuade or convince him will be a pretty challenging task because quitting is uncomfortable for the person. During the non-smoking period, this person might go through considerable discomfort. Still, afterward, he will experience a higher comfort zone due to the absence of his unhealthy behavior.

For persuasion to be successful, the person tries to persuade the individual to figure out what is essential to the individual. The persuader should identify factors that can eventually give the individual a higher level of comfort. For a person who finds staying at home and shunning social life comforting, the persuader should discover a factor that can allow them to move outside the box. By helping them realize that although going out can be, they will have a higher sense of comfort once they achieve their goals. This process needs a skilled persuader to assure the client that the behavior change will make them feel more comfortable.

Advantages of NLP

These NLP techniques can increase the level of influence that you exert on others. Companies that engage in marketing and sales depend entirely on persuading their clients or clients to buy their products; the strategies presented in NLP guide these sellers and dealers to increase the chance of influencing their clients in making decisions. NLP also increases the person's performance; NLP helps you modify and replace your negative behaviors with more positive ones. These strategies also help you to improve your leadership style. Being humble and non-judgmental allows you to have a better communication style, even outside the persuasion process.

Essentials for Persuasion

Empathy

This is an essential quality that a persuader requires. You should not only be thinking about yourself, but you also should try to put yourself in the other person's shoes and think about how they might be feeling. Empathy also helps deter you from being judgmental.

Listening Skills

Only a good listener will persuade another person; a person who is always ready for an argument will never be a good listener. If you want to be a good and positive persuader, you need to listen to what the other individual says and pay attention to their body language.

Indirect and Clever Commands

People tend to be more responsive to suggestions than questions. For example, instead of using the words "Would you like to go to the concert?" You can say "Come, let's go to the concert"; this motivates a more positive response from the individual.

Restrict the Choices That You Provide

Try not to allow the individual to say "No." Taking the same example, instead of asking, "Will you be able to stay long at the concert?" ask them, "Would you like to stay here for three hours or four?" The latter question makes it hard for the individual to say a "No."

Allow the Person to Visualize

Successful persuaders always help the client, or the individual visualize to convince them. An example would be, "this concert will make us scream the lyrics of our favorite songs."

Always Make It Simple as Possible

Trying to convince the other person by bragging will only be a failure; keep it as simple as possible and remember you should never put their views down.

You can use the information you were provided for good. You can use it to better your relationships, your career, and your social life. If you understand how people interact with others, you can ensure that you are interacting positively. You can make every interaction with other people positive and fulfilling for everyone involved. Above all, you can naturally develop the skills you need to create and earn your leadership skills. People will naturally seek to follow you if you build your NLP and persuasion techniques. People will listen to you better if you have advanced social skills. You can use it to your advantage to ensure that you and those around you are happy with life. Use your enlightenment and knowledge for good, and go out there, armed with the knowledge you need to persuade others, both for your benefit and theirs.

So, what are you still waiting for? It is time to embrace this guide so that you'll allow the light inside you to radiate without fear of hurting others of being all that you are meant to be. This guide will help you overcome manipulation so that you can shine brighter!

Chapter 34. Covert Manipulation

Numerous people in the world do not realize that mind control has become a dangerous aspect used by different people to control others and resources. Mind control is used in different aspects of life, and the list below might surprise you by the extent to which it has expanded in modern-day life. When we think of mind control, some of us assume that it is a direct way of getting into the brain and influencing the very mechanism in which we think. However, mind control is much greater than that, and its effects are putting control of the world in a few elite hands.

It is necessary to consider how agencies, companies, and even individuals practice mind control, as it is an important aspect of NLP manipulation. Mind control is basic to begin with, but it can also be complex in practice because different people use different aspects of technology to control those around them. The following list is but a taste of the different approaches to mind control in the world.

Mind Control with NLP for Love and Relationships

We will learn what truly good and fulfilling relationships are based on and built upon. We will explore techniques that can strengthen relationships and those that can help us establish healthy relationships. Many factors play a role in good relationships. We will discuss the importance of our mental health and readiness before entering into any partnership or relationship, and possible outcomes associated with having and not having these factors.

We all want and need certain things. There are basic needs for all of us, and one of the most crucial ways we can have our basic emotional needs met is with healthy relationships. We all want to be loved, desired and needed. We all long for compassion and understanding. All of these can be acquired in good and healthy partnerships. Likewise, a bad relationship can be devastating. Most of us carry around baggage, such as negative emotions, fear, and anxiety from previous unhealthy relationships. This can place barriers between us and others when we find ourselves in new relationships. True fulfillment usually can only be found in the emotional qualities of our relationships.

Every good relationship begins with a clear and comfortable frame and state of mind. The maturity of both parties is a factor, as well as timing. Your goals and wants need to be compatible with the person you want as a partner. Your values and beliefs need to match. These ideas and characteristics are tangible and very important in the overall health of any relationship. If you find yourself in a great relationship, the benefits are numerous. You will gain confidence and a feeling of self-worth that can't be matched. Just as important, you must also remember to transmit this to your partner. You should always treat your partner exactly the way you want to be treated. In doing this, and having this knowledge, you can know what it is that your partner wants. You just need to see what it is that your partner is doing and take it from there.

Before we can be the kind of partner we should, we must first be good within ourselves. If you enter into a relationship, while you have self-doubt or internal difficulties, you are entering a partnership that is doomed from the start. A perfect couple consists of two people who can function well as individuals but function as a partner just as well, if not better. This is the first step in entering any relationship. You must be good with yourself. This is a must and shouldn't ever be compromised. The second important point that needs to be addressed is establishing what, or who, it is that you desire. This is your personal decision based on your personality, desires, ideologies, and belief system. It does not matter what others believe you need or what you think you should have. What matters is what you want.

The next part of entering into a good relationship is timing. This isn't just important to you, but it's also important with your partner. Are you looking for "Mr. Right" or "Mr. Right Now?" Are there things going on currently in your life that may prohibit your success in the relationship? Are these things not only able to hinder you, but are they able to hinder your partner as well? Timing is important and crucial to the longevity of the relationship. If you are a point in your life where other priorities take precedence with you, you should wait until those priorities shift. You can become capable of making your partner the priority that he or she deserves.

Once you have decided what you want, have concluded that now is the time for you to enter into a relationship, and have covered all of your predetermining factors. Now you can begin to open up to the possibilities of finding the right person. Here is when rapport becomes important. What is rapport? It's your similarities and likeness with someone with whom you are interested in entering a relationship. It's also the establishment of trust with that person. With rapport, many individual factors can be used for determining compatibility. Some of these are personality types, values, beliefs, culture, political ideologies, interests, religious beliefs, etc. Of course, physical characteristics, such as gender and body types, need to be considered. However, some characteristics can't be over accentuated because it will mimic the other and cause a loss of rapport.

The rapport established in the beginning, the reasons for your attraction to your partner, and his or her attraction to you must be kept at the forefront of each partner's mind throughout the relationship. It all too common for people to enter into relationships with guns blazing, meaning being the perfect partner, only to begin to relax and change once the relationship has been established. One partner, or both, will use all available techniques to get the other to enter into a relationship. Once they are in that relationship, the other partner believes they can initially tone down what they were doing. This is one of the most common reasons for relationships ending. Keep in mind; the reasons for someone falling for you are the same reasons that will make them want to stay with you. If you remove the reasons for their attraction, they have no reasons to stay with you. Often, we see children born of relationships used as new reasons, but this does not work. This leads the partnership to morph into what can be seen as a business relationship. There will be no real emotional connection in the relationship and, even though that couple may remain together, they will lack the comforts and fulfillment of needs they desire.

Now you have identified what you want, making sure the timing is right, and have met that special someone. Now, what do you do? You need to make sure that your partner feels the same about you. There are several ways in which a person can see that they are loved by the other. These ways should be identified at the relationships beginning. A few methods are by what the other person buys and place him, or she takes you. There are also things such as how they touch you, the looks they give, or what they say. Identification of these is important as they can gauge the continuance of love throughout the relationship.

The best way to determine how you can best assure your partner that you love him or her is by doing what they tend to do for you. For instance, most likely, if your partner puts her arm around you at times to assure you of her love and affection, you can bet that if you do the same, she will believe that you do love and appreciate her. We don't tend to do things to or for others, especially those whom we care about the most, that we wouldn't want to be done to us. Although this is commons sense, it's also a great method to gauge or determine how your significant other feels about you. As the relationship progresses, this will come naturally and will take much less conscious effort. Just be sure not to allow these things to stop because the relationship is no longer new.

NLP has devised a few strategies to determine areas in relationships. Areas such as attraction, love, and desire are all strategized with NLP techniques. First, you must know your partner. This means that you should know what those subtle gestures and tones of voice your partner will display depending on how they feel. Know what your partner fears and what he or she wants. You will pick up ideas as to how to carry these things out simply by learning your partner. Be sure never to use this knowledge for manipulation. There isn't a positive outcome in relationships where manipulation takes place.

One technique you can use to ensure that your partner is in love with you and wants you is to remove yourself from his or her presence temporarily. This does not mean that you can tell your wife that you are going to the store for a lottery ticket to not return for a week. However, in short time frames, absence can signal want or lack thereof. Just like the cliché, absence makes the heart grow fonder; this is built on the same premise. When using these kinds of tactics, please never overuse them. Here is some advice. If you are an insecure person needing constant approval and reassurance that you are loved, you should take care of that issue before entering into a serious relationship.

If not, you are not going to be a good partner. If your shortcoming does not end the relationship, it could lead it to become a codependent partnership or, at the very least, a very unhealthy relationship. Again, you must first make sure that you are a good candidate for entering into a relationship before taking that other step.

With relationships, you are not simply selling yourself to another, and then the job is over. It's a continuing process forever. Never relax and believe that you have your partner, and he or she isn't going anywhere, no matter what you may or may not do.

Many divorcees have made this mistake countless times. You should always be selling yourself, your worth, compassion, and desire for your partner.

Chapter 35. What is Manipulation?

When coming from a psychological point of reference, manipulation is mostly about perception. How we perceive things or actions determines our laws, social formalities, and even our lives.

The manipulator changes these norms with tactics. The determination of the positive or negative connotation of these actions remains subjective. Psychological manipulation is often considered devious. With the subject of dark psychology, we can take into account that the manipulation practiced is often exploitative at the expense of others.

So, what is the manipulation of the dark?

Sources tell us that it is concealment—hiding in the shadows knowing when to strike. It is also a false front, hiding true intentions. When we are talking about this level of deception, we are talking about hiding aggression. When we take, there is a certain level of aggressive behavior that happens. A small part of manipulation is hiding that aggressive behavior so that the victim sees only good nature.

This is accomplished in various ways and means, one being knowledge. When we allow another to know us, we display vulnerability along with strengths. The knowledge of these personality traits can give the manipulator the ability to maneuver around without any alarms going off.

The effectiveness of manipulating those strengths and vulnerabilities arrives when the dark practitioner knows what is vulnerable and what inspires pride.

A reoccurring ideology that drives us to war takes into consideration that war is more negative than positive. We want to avoid it. The manipulation process sees pride in all of us and plays to that pride. It is our strength. However, when used to drive an army to slaughter others, the intention of our pride has been manipulated to enforce the agendas of others.

There is ruthlessness when we talk about psychological manipulation. When dealing with someone other than the pure psychopath who feels little to nothing, ruthlessness can be measured. Often soft ruthless behavior can sneak up on its prey and snag it before it knows what is happening. This harm of the prey becomes less than even a momentary qualm in the mind of the manipulator.

Often the practitioners of dark psychology use aggression and fear to drive us. The less dark side still falls into the category of knowing what weakness is, and that weakness leaves the individual open to control.

How the manipulator uses that control determines the severity of manipulation. There are positive versions of manipulating others, such as convincing someone that they are not doing well and need help. However, we are looking at the darker side of this. The manipulator uses their control skills to get what they want—and the cost does not apply.

There are many ways to move another into a place of being controlled. From the positive to the negative, psychological manipulators utilize all tactics.

When positive reinforcement is used, the charm is displayed. A forced smile or laughter can trigger laughter in all of us. As when we were infants, we copy what we see. When we see tears, we want them to stop. When we see a smile, we find ourselves smiling as well.

Using positive reinforcement, the manipulator can shower money, charm, and gifts to get us to feel something. The usage of these things allows control of us on an instinctual level. We follow those who tell us what we want to hear.

Psychological manipulation can also implement negative reinforcement. This is a form of deflection—a substitution of one thing for another.

Often, we have things we need or have to do, and we do not really want to do them. The psychological manipulation of negative reinforcement uses that power of negativity to lure the subject from their original need, pushing them toward something they want to be done instead. The long game, a slow play of putting tasks into another's life and then controlling those tasks, so that the manipulator can get what they want, is an extremely effective and subdued tactic.

Sometimes only partial reinforcement is required to gain control. We are talking about elevating the fear or doubt regarding the tasks needed to be done. The partial is the long play. It knows that in the end, the victim will lose. It knows that by planting small seeds now, victory will eventually happen. It knows that we all have our weaknesses and that by planting even a small seed, we can take someone to that weakness. An individual trying to work toward something they already were shaky on or had doubts about, will listen to the lie and flow with that idea, and use it to their own destruction.

The partial manipulator only needs to put the thought in mind, knowing the weakness is already there and utilizing it will take their prey to a destructive end.

Psychological manipulators flat, outright punish. From an actual physical lashing to the victim's passive-aggressive playing, punishment is very effective when one wants to control another.

We skulk, cry, yell, nag, and go completely silent. This is the blackmail of the manipulator. It inspires guilt in us. That "wanting to be the better person" rises to the front, and we do what the manipulator wants.

When the manipulator sets free the crocodile tears, we have no idea if they are real or not. The degree of crying is not up to us to determine. Only the manipulator knows if the tears are legitimate or not.

In this case, the trap is often sprung from the victim's side. They walk up to the hurt individual to help, only to find that the manipulator is just lying in wait to strike.

One extreme version of manipulation is violence.

Violence triggers something inside us. We often do anything to avoid it. The manipulator knows that violence strategically applied can make us go into a state of avoidance. There incites the control. Physical violence can have mental scarring. The manipulator causes the scarring. It places violence in tactical places to get the result they want.

Some would say this is the darkest of the dark.

Taken to the individual, this can mentally damage them for a long period of time, if not permanently. Placed on a world stage, it can lead all the way up to the physical conflict of genocide.

The manipulation process in dark psychology is normally not a single move. It is a complex series of moves, often with the outcome only known by the manipulator. The motivations of manipulators are as convoluted as human nature.

Mostly it is about gain. Manipulators of the dark want to gain something. When we speak about gain, we are talking about power and influence, control and manipulation over others. The trophy is up to the individual. This can be everything as to gaining affections, to money, and even to life itself.

It is about gaining for their own personal reasons and gratifications. The taking of others and making the power and control their own. Selfishness to the extreme. The mind of the dark practitioner sees the ultimate win as gain over others.

They have power. Superiority is the power over another, and taking of someone else's power makes them feel superior. This is a huge driving force behind the manipulator. Often, in the case of immature individuals driving manipulations toward superiority, any is pushed aside for just the feeling of being superior.

In relationships, it is about control. The manipulation of power can put one in control. Although we have looked at the role of the vampire and power, and we know who really has control.

This feeling of control can be overwhelming to the mental state of the dark. Almost drug-like, it is a feeling of emotion that is most logical. Control is one of the easiest manipulation tactics to achieve with only logic to guide. It drives not only the victim but the manipulator as well.

Psychological manipulation can also be about self-esteem. The self of the manipulator is always in question. This is one of the reasons they manipulate, to define themselves. How easily they are able to manipulate another can tell the dark that they are better than others. That weakness and strength can be measured in the tactical playing field of the hustle.

This defines who they are. Can they manipulate? Yes? They are stronger. No? They are weaker. It is a measuring device for self-esteem.

However, we are not saying it is the only device for measurement. Self-esteem can be measured by far less damaging means.

The mind gets bored, and what do we do when we get bored? We seek entertainment. How do we achieve entertainment? We manipulate.

We all do it.

Let us assume we are bored, and we want to remove or alleviate that boredom with something else. Do we just sit back and wait for something new to happen?

No. We actively search for something to replace boredom. Manipulation can take place on many different levels, as well as the severity of which they are applied, from picking up a crayon and coloring to taking a mental absence to massacre everyone around you.

The dark psychological manipulator is bored most of the time more than most. The psychological manipulator will often use manipulation to determine their own validity of feelings and emotions.

What this boils down to is that manipulation applied in relations with others helps the manipulator to regulate reactions to validate or not validate their own emotions. The manipulator measures the self and their self-esteem by how others handle their personal self-questioning.

This happens when the practitioner does not have a grasp on what emotions are. They look at their own emotions as invalid and manipulate the situation in such a way as to validate them.

We are stuck with ourselves, and we cannot get away. Psychological manipulators validate or invalidate themselves by the tactical controlling of others. It is an interesting way of viewing life, although there is one form of manipulation that we all idolize—the con. One common form of manipulation is convincing of another to make their money yours.

This is a hidden agenda of the criminal. This form of mental manipulation preys mostly on the elderly and the rich. However, we all can fall to this form of manipulation. What we choose to spend on and what we do not is our response to a form of psychological manipulation.

Something happens when the buck is passed over. We go from manipulation into action. Something drives us. It is within us, and it is outside forces that drive. What causes this drive and the drive itself is called persuasion.

Chapter 36. Examples of Manipulation?

It is worth noting that manipulative people don't always come out of nowhere. Often we find individuals with this behavior in the workplace, at school, and in the family. The characteristics presented above are shaped according to the mode of friendliness. Here's how to deal with manipulative people in these environments:

At Work

In a professional environment, the manipulator is the employee always ready to help, but remember, it's compulsive help. He stays at the heels of colleagues, reinforcing how much he loves helping colleagues who have difficulties in their tasks. The manipulator on the desktop can stay up and even take a break in the office, all for the "pleasure of helping others." The targets of "goodwill" are charmed with such dedication.

The manipulator is seen as the company's legal person, employee, and fellow stick to for all work. However, this establishes a relationship of dependence. Whoever is the target of "goodwill" is being placed on the web. The one who receives the "help" loses his autonomy since he cannot act without asking for the manipulator's opinion. Consequently, he loses confidence and does everything not to lose this "friendship." When the victim begins to perceive himself as such and tries to escape, the manipulator reverses the roles and convinces his prey that he is bad. The prey, in turn, accepts such a condition and follows the will of his tormentor.

How to Get Rid of the Manipulator at Work?

Be firm and kindly dispense unsolicited favors. When the manipulator takes the day off to flatter you, return the compliments, but make it clear that you are just doing your duty, and anyone else would do the same. The manipulator will be amazed at your steadiness.

In School

At school, the manipulator is the perfect colleague. The manipulator targets unpopular students who are constantly ridiculed.

The manipulator praises the high notes. You are sure that the "new friend" is the best student. When his grades are low, he places the teacher's blame because the teacher certainly did it to harm him. He does not hesitate to defend injustice. There is no bad time that prevents you from helping with the activities, and the manipulator makes a point of doing the work with you. The target of such unknowing friendship reveals what time he leaves home, what time it takes to drive there, reveals possible enmities with other students, tells of his fears and anguish. The manipulator reveals nothing about his life.

When the victim realizes that something is strange and tries to disengage, the manipulator feels extremely offended. He places the "friend" as an unjust person, unable to recognize true friendship. The manipulator depreciates the "friend," listing his defects, and claims that he will return to being a solitary person and be ridiculed if the friendship ends. The prey, who already had low self-esteem, is even more vulnerable. Thus, the victim believes the manipulator, apologizes, and no longer measures their efforts to do all the manipulator's will, so afraid of losing the "friendship."

How to Get Rid of the Manipulator in School?

If you feel that you are being cheated again, move away slowly. Speak only as necessary and ask other people's opinions on how to deal with the situation.

In the Family

In the family, the manipulator sticks close to that shy relative and is considered good by everyone. It may be that cousin who always compliments, even when the victim has done something that isn't so great. The manipulator justifies his "object of affection" blockades and believes that his target is wrong. He insists on telling us how much he loves us and is happy to be with such special people.

The manipulator is always ready to go to the mall, help with school activities, go to the doctor's office, and do some repairs. However, when the target begins to be bothered by the excessive clinginess and flattery, the manipulator turns the tables and lowers his victim. The manipulator underscores his lack of social skills and how he is seen as lonely, poor, and a failure unable to have friends. The sentences that the victim says will continue to be seen as unimportant. The already emotionally unstable target agrees with everything, apologizes, and resumes "friendship," doing everything according to his tormentor's will, afraid of not being able to count on such a valuable person.

How to Get Rid of the Manipulator in the Family?

Family ties make things harder, but we must put an end to this vicious circle. Ask the opinion of people outside the family spectrum. Even if it is not possible to cut the manipulator out of the conversation, talk only when necessary.

Differences Between Male and Female Manipulators

The behavior between men and women is different in several respects. On the question of manipulation, there are also singularities.

Men

Male manipulators have the following characteristics:

- Shy: the manipulator observes the behavior of everyone around him. He transmits fragility and submission to convince himself that he is a needy person.

- Handsome: manipulators are always friendly, extroverted, and know how to live life. They show extremely worried and attentive with their "friends," but they make a point of showing who is in charge. The victims do not feel the courage to disagree with such a nice man, but when he goes to a boring event, he does not bother to disguise his boredom.

- Altruist: he gives many gifts, does numerous favors, always intending to receive something in return. When it is not "reattributed," it gives people a sense of guilt.

- Seductive: vain and attractive. He looks into others' eyes, asks embarrassing questions, and loves to make a mystery of himself.

- Worship: has excessive admiration for diplomas, pompous professional curricula, and social projection. He subtly shows contempt for those who do not have the same knowledge. He loves to embarrass people, monopolizes conversations, and gets annoyed when someone interrupts his speech.

Women

Manipulative women behave in the following ways:

- In front of everyone, they are true porcelain dolls. However, when the target moves away, she's stupid with people. When the victim returns, she will be candid with him/her.

- Use beauty as a weapon to get what she wants. It seems absurd to someone not to praise it.

- She uses a sensual tone of voice and promises a thousand wonders to those who satisfy her requests; she wants the target to guess her wishes and surprise her with trips, restaurants, and luxury gifts. She becomes angry if her requests are not answered.

- Her emotions can be radical. When you are right, she wants to prove that it's better that you are wrong. When she is wrong, she does not admit it and insists until someone believes in her.

- They cry too much. If the victim wants to go out with other people, she cries because she was "betrayed." If she is asked how the car got scratched, she cries because she was accused of being a bad driver. She is "fragile" to the point of not carrying a suitcase or not being able to open the car door.

Manipulative people enter our lives because they see that we are going through a moment of vulnerability. We feed these people by providing intimate information. However, if we allow them to enter our lives, it is up to us to remove them from the scene. The task is difficult, but these tips can be useful:

Do not feel guilty for not satisfying the wishes of the manipulator. Often they are irrational and seem like things a child who wants attention at any cost may request. Ask probing questions; question what will change if you attend to the manipulator's wishes. Ask yourself how your feelings were before and how they are now. Learn not to speak to those who do not do you good; this means you must avoid saying yes to the manipulator.

If none of this works out, move away. If it is not possible to physically get the person out of your life, move away emotionally, and speak only about the basics. Remember that manipulative people are "toxic people," non-evolved beings who want to suck energy and steal others' autonomy. No one deserves to live in the shadow of others. No one deserves to live, having to consult someone at every step. Emotional independence is the key to a happy existence.

Chapter 37. Introduction on Deception

What is Deception?

How can deception be defined? Deception, alongside subterfuge, mystification, feign, deceit, and beguilement, is an art employed by an agent to spread beliefs in the subject, which are untrue, or truths coated with lies. Deception involves numerous things, for example, dissimulation, sleight of mind, suppression, cover-up, propaganda, etc. The agents win the subjects' favor; they trust him and are unsuspecting of his propensity to be dubious. He can control the subject's mind having won their confidence and trust. The subjects have no doubts about the agent's words. The subjects trust the agent completely and possibly plan their affairs based on the agent's statements.

The deception practiced by the agent can have serious consequential effects if discovered by the subjects. How? The subjects will not be disposed to hearing his words; neither will they accept them anymore; no wonder the agent must be skilled at the deception technique. He must create an escape route to cover up if things boomerang and still retain the trust his subjects have in him.

Deception breaks the laws that govern relationships, and it has been known to affect negatively the hopes that come with relationships. Deception does occur now and then, resulting in feelings of doubt and disloyalty among the two people in the relationship. Nearly everyone desires to have an honest discussion with their partner. However, if they find out that their partner has been dishonest, they, in turn, need to find out how to make use of confusion and distraction to get the reliable and honest information that they require. On the other hand, the trust would be lost in the relationship, making it hard to restore the relationship to its former glory.

The individual on the receiving end of both dishonesty and betrayal would always wonder about the things their partner was telling them, thinking about whether the story was true or false. As a result of this new doubt, most relationships will be brought to an end once the agent realizes their partner's dishonesty.

Types of Deception

Deception is a type of communication-based on omissions and falsehood to convince the world's subject that best fits the agent. There is a need for communication to occur. There will likewise be various kinds of deception. As per the Interpersonal Deception Theory, there are five different sorts of deception. A few of these have been revealed in other types of mind control, showing some similarities.

The five major types of deception include:

1. Lies: this occurs when the agent manufactures information or provides information that is not similar to the truth. They will give this information to the unsuspecting individual as the truth, and the individual will then see this lie to be fact indeed. However, this can be unsafe as the person being given this false information would have no idea about the falsehood. Most likely, if the subject understood that they were being given information that was not true, they would not be on talking terms with the agent, and no deception would have occurred.

2. Equivocations: this is the point at which the agent will make statements that are differing, unclear, or not direct, such that the subject becomes confused and does not understand what is going on. Also, it can help the agent to preserve their reputation, saving face if the subject returns to blame them for the falsehood.

3. Concealments: it is the most frequently used form of deception. It refers to when the agent leaves out information related to or critical to the situation on purpose or displays any such behavior that would cover up information important to the subject for that exact situation. The agent won't have lied straightforwardly to the subject. However, they will ensure that the vital information required never gets to the subject.

4. Exaggeration: occurs when the agent emphasizes too much on a fact or stretch the truth just a little to twist the story to suit them. Although the agent may not directly be lying to the subject, they will manipulate the situation such that it appears as though it is a bigger deal than it is, or they may twist the truth to make the subject do whatever they need them to do.

5. Understatements: this is the inverse of the exaggeration tool in the sense that the agent will present part of the fact as less important, telling the subject that an event is less of a deal, than it is when it really could be what decides whether the subject gets the opportunity to graduate or gets a huge promotion. As such, the agent will return to the subject, saying they had no idea how huge a deal their omission was. They get to keep their reputation, leaving the subject to look petty if they protest.

The above are only some of the forms of deception that there are. The agent of deception will use any means available to reach their final goal, the same as what happens in other types of mind control. However, these methods mentioned are not limiting, as the agent would use any means to get to their goal.

The agent of deception (who will be good at what he does) can be dangerous since the subject will not know the truth or lie.

Reasons for Deception

It has been confirmed by researchers that there are three major reasons for deceptions found in intimate relationships. These motives focused on the partner, on self-image, and focused on a relationship.

In the case of the partner-focused motives, the agent will use deception to keep their partner from harm. They could also use falsehood to save their partner's relationship with an outsider, thereby protecting the subject from worry or keeping the subject's confidence intact. This reason for the deception is often seen to be of benefit to the relationship and socially respectful.

In comparison with some of the other reasons for deception, this one is not as bad. If the agent finds out something terrible that the subject's closest friend said about them, the agent might remain quiet about it. Although this is a type of deception, it not only saves the subject's friendship but also keeps the subject from feeling terrible for themselves. This is the type of deception that is often found in most relationships and also, if found out, might not cause a lot of damage. To protect their partner, a larger percentage of couples would use this form of deception to protect their partner.

The self-focused motive for deception is not thought to be as noble as the partner-focused motive for deception, and as such, is not as acceptable as the other methods. Rather than stressing over the subject and how they are doing, the agent is going to simply consider how they are doing and about their very own self-image. Here, the agent uses deception to protect the agent from criticism, shame, or anger. Using this form of deception in a relationship is typically seen as a serious issue and offense than in partner-focused deception. This is because the agent chooses to act in a self-centered manner instead of protecting their relationship or partner.

Lastly, in the relationship-focused motive of deception, the agent uses deception to prevent any harm coming to the relationship, basically staying away from deception, relational disturbance, and quarrel. This type of deception will either help or harm the relationship, depending on the circumstances. This form of deception could be harmful because it makes things rather complex. For instance, if you do not reveal just how you feel about dinner to prevent a quarrel, this might just help the relationship. If you keep to yourself that you took part in an extra-marital relationship, the situation is only going to become more complex.

No matter the motive of deception in the relationship, deception is not advised. The agent is holding back details that may be vital to the subject; when the subject discovers it, distrust in the agent will set in, and they are left to ponder what other details the agent is keeping from them. However, the subject would not be too worried about the reason behind the deception. They will simply be vexed that they have not been told some things, causing a split in the relationship. Usually, it is best to stick with truthfulness in the relationship and not encircle yourself with individuals who don't put deception into practice in your social circle.

Detecting Deception

An individual interested in preventing deception from avoiding the mind games that come with it should learn how to detect deception when it occurs. It is not usually easy to know when deception is going on, as there are no pointers to rely on, except the agent makes a mistake and either tells an obvious lie or says something that the subject knows to be false. While it might be difficult for the agent to mislead the subject for a long time, it will usually happen regularly between individuals who know one another.

Deception can place a heavyweight on the agent's cognitive thinking because they will need to find a way to remember all their conversations with the subject on the situation. Hence, the story stays believable and dependable. Any mistake will bring the subject to the realization they are being deceived. The stress involved in keeping the story believable is much, and as such, the agent is very much likely to spill out details that will give the subject a clue that they are being deceived either through nonverbal or verbal signs.

Researchers believe that detecting deception is a process that is cognitive, fluid, and complicated and will regularly differ based on the message that is being passed across. As indicated by the Interpersonal Deception Theory, deception is an iterative and dynamic process of influence between the agent, who attempts to manipulate the information and how they need it with the goal that it varies from the truth, and the subject, who will at that point try to know if the message is true or false. The agent's activities will be concerning the actions that the subject makes after they get the information. Through this trade, the agent will uncover the nonverbal and verbal information that will signal the subject into the deceit. Eventually, the subject might have the capacity to tell that the agent has been lying to them.

Chapter 38. Techniques Used in Manipulation: Explication of Different Techniques

So far, I have briefly talked about a few manipulation techniques through personality traits and signs. However, it is important to be thorough about the techniques because there are dozens of techniques that manipulators use. Sometimes, they make up their techniques to gain control as they go through their job or relationship.

Foot in the Door Technique

The foot in the door technique is probably one of the most well-known forms of manipulation. Of course, the salespeople took the phrase a bit more literally than manipulators. While salespeople would place their foot in front of the door so the homeowner couldn't close it on them, manipulators take more of a mental and emotional stance towards this technique.

The first step manipulators use by asking for a small favor or "breaking the ice" through a small conversation. This helps the manipulators build a rapport with their target. For example, if they are trying to find a significant other, they will find a way to become compatible with their target. They will then ask the person questions about what they like and mention they enjoy the same things.

This technique is often how people get to know each other in a social setting. For example, have you ever been sitting at a club or coffee shop when someone came up to you and started small talk? They might have stated it was a busy night or a nice day. You might have agreed in some way, whether verbally or through your actions. Giving a reaction is letting the person keep their foot in the door. While you are probably just trying to be polite, they see it as a step into your life, depending on their motive.

Negative Reinforcement

Master manipulators will often use negative reinforcement to get you to stop doing something they don't like. This could be anything from going back to college or getting a job. Typically, they don't like anything that gives them a loss of control and threatens their environment.

When you start to do something they don't like, they will do something you don't like. This is the first step of negative reinforcement. They will continue to use negative reinforcement and other tactics to try to get you to stop doing what they don't like. Once they have manipulated you to stop, they will then stop.

Negative reinforcement works when the manipulator starts to do something you don't like because you won't do what they want you to do. To get the manipulator to stop doing what you don't like, you have to do what they request of you, even if you don't like it.

The main reason negative reinforcement is used is that it is more likely that you will do what they ask of you in the future without hesitation. This is especially true for manipulators who use any type of abuse to get you to stop doing something or to listen to them.

The Emotional Triangle

The emotional triangle is similar to a love triangle; however, it is used against you. The manipulator will use it to get you to do what they want. They will create a triangle with themselves, you, and a third person who is not directly involved in your relationship.

The manipulator will not hide the fact that they are interested in the third person, even if they aren't in truth. They will flirt with the person in front of you and even show affection toward the person. Sometimes they will use certain affections that you like, whether rubbing the person's back or hugging them.

While it might be obvious they like the other person. They will deny any type of affection in a confrontation. They will blame you, telling you that it is your insecurities and low self-esteem, which is making you believe this.

The emotional triangle's main goal is you become insecure about your relationship, which means you will work harder to make your significant other happy. You will do what they ask, even if you don't want to or feel uncomfortable taking on the assignment.

Establishing Similarities

The foot in the door technique can often lead manipulators into another technique where they establish similarities. For example, the manipulator might learn through observation or a friend who you like a certain coffee shop. Therefore, they will decide to run into you at the coffee shop, where they discuss how much you both enjoy the location and the coffee.

Manipulators will also mirror your actions. They will notice if you are putting your elbows on the table and do the same thing. They will notice your hand gestures and how often you smile. They will then mirror these actions as well. This is a psychological tactic that reaches into your subconscious mind. It makes you feel like you can trust the person because you feel more connected, even if you don't realize they mirror your actions and behaviors.

Fear-Relief Technique

Fear is a strong emotion and can often cause us to react in extreme ways. People are typically uncomfortable with fear, which means they will want to find a way to ease their fears. Because of this, manipulators commonly use the fear-relief technique as it allows them to gain the trust of their target by using emotion.

This technique is heavily used by manipulative people who create a fear in you to give you relief, which makes you more likely to listen to their requests time. You wait a couple of hours, and when they still don't return, you call their cell phone. They don't pick up. Another hour, you try calling them again but receive their voicemail. At this point, you start to become anxious about the situation. You have left dozens of text messages, and they don't answer their phone. You start to worry that something has happened to them. A couple of hours, they send you a text that says they are on their way home, and everything is fine.

When you confront your significant other as they walk in the door about what they were doing, they respond that you left, so they could too. They then tell you that as long as you do something like that to them, they can do it too.

Manipulators Will Put You on the Defense

Manipulators like to reach into your emotions because they are powerful. When you react with your emotions, you stop thinking, make irrational decisions, and have trouble remaining calm. This is how a manipulator wants you to react because conversations where you are calm and think rationally, are not in their favor.

Therefore, manipulators use a tactic where they will put you on the defense. This means that you will feel like you need to explain yourself. You have to defend how you feel, who you are, and what you believe. This is one of the strongest signs of manipulation, but people often don't notice it because it becomes common.

It is significant to understand that just because you find you are explaining something you believe to your significant other doesn't mean you are in a manipulative relationship. There are many times in a relationship that you might find yourself explaining why you support a cause your significant other doesn't or why you find something is fun when your partner doesn't. In a healthy relationship, you will find yourself explaining your beliefs and thoughts when your significant other wants to understand you to support you. You will also ask your loved ones to explain themselves so that you can treat them in the same way. In a manipulative relationship, your significant other will always put you on the defense, no matter what your action was. The only time you might not find yourself on the defense is if they approve of your behavior.

The Gaslighting Technique

Gaslighting is phrasing the manipulator will repeatedly use to make you believe a situation you remember is wrong. Some of the most common phrases include "You can't be serious," "I never said that," "You don't remember it correctly," "Are you crazy?" and "You imagine it." While you might feel that you are right, the manipulator will continue to stand by what they say, believe, or even give you their version of the situation. They might mix gaslighting with other tactics for you to start questioning yourself. They will continue to break you down through gaslighting or simply find a way to end the conversation.

Gaslighting is a very dangerous tactic because it is used to distort your reality. If used enough, you might start to feel that you are crazy or imagine all these situations. This will mentally and emotionally break you down even further, which will allow the manipulator to gain the upper hand as you start to distrust your thoughts, emotions, and abilities. You start to distrust your reality, making you believe that you do not see what you see, and you do not hear what you hear.

Traumatic One Trial Learning Technique

Manipulators are good at putting on an act. One technique that manipulators use to get you to listen to them better to keep you under control is traumatic one-trial learning.

When a manipulator uses this technique, they will become angry when they feel you have done something wrong. For example, if you come home later than you said you would, your significant other might yell, make you feel ashamed, or become verbally abusive. They will act in a way they know will make you fear their anger, so you are less likely to do something like that again.

Chapter 39. How To Defend Yourself From Manipulation Techniques

To avoid falling victim to manipulators, you have to build your defenses to prepare for any manipulative strategies they may try to use. The best way to build your defenses is by taking steps to improve your self-esteem and your willpower. However, as a point of caution, you should be very careful about building your defenses because you don't want to create restrictions that will keep you from living a fulfilled life.

For example, as you try to guard against manipulation, you can't act out of fear. You can't hide from the world just to avoid scenarios where someone might want to take advantage of you. Recall that the world is full of persons with dark personality traits who may harbor malicious intentions, so acting out of fear won't protect you from anyone. It will just make you more of a target. As you build your defenses, make sure that you start on the premise that you are willing to confront manipulators head-on, and you will never run away or recoil. If you act out of fear, you lose by default.

Acceptance

Acceptance is about assenting to the reality of a given situation. It's about recognizing that a certain condition or process is what it is, even if high levels of discomfort and negativity characterize it. It's about consciously submitting that something cannot be changed and that its reality is not subject to interpretation. It's about making peace with the situation that you are in. Acceptance is the opposite of denial. Denial can be a coping mechanism, one that can keep us from being overwhelmed by the reality of a given situation. However, denial does us more harm than good because unless we can accept something, we can't change it. We will be stuck looking for alternative interpretations and explanations for our prevailing circumstances.

Without acceptance, the door remains wide open for malicious people to exploit us. Take the example of a patient who is told that he/she is terminally ill. After seeking the opinions of several medical professionals and getting the same diagnosis, the patient is still left with the choice of either accepting or denying the situation. The one who accepts it will make peace and try to make the best of what little time he has. The one who stays in denial will become susceptible to tricksters who may offer "alternative cures," and he may end up losing all his savings paying such people so that in the end, he leaves his family with nothing. That is an extreme example, but it perfectly illustrates why acceptance is important in avoiding manipulation, even if the reality may seem too painful to accept.

The most crucial form of acceptance is self-acceptance. It refers to the state of being satisfied with yourself, the way you currently are. Self-acceptance is a kind of covenant that you make to validate, support, and appreciate who you are instead of constantly criticizing yourself and wishing you were someone else. Most people have trouble accepting themselves as they are. We are all in a constant strive for self-improvement. We want to be more successful, be wealthier, be more attractive, or be perceived more positively by others. Even the most accomplished among us have issues with self-acceptance.

In many ways, the desire to be a better version of yourself can be seen as a positive thing; it can help you study harder in school, work harder to earn a promotion at work or exercise more to get in shape. However, there is always room for improvement, so no matter how high you ascend, the dissatisfaction will always be there. It will make you vulnerable to manipulation by people who want to take advantage of your desires.

To defend against manipulation, you have to accept your reality, and you have to accept yourself. People tend to think that if they accept themselves, they won't try to improve—that couldn't be further from the truth. Accepting yourself means owning up to your flaws, and that gives you control over your life. With self-acceptance, attempts at self-improvement would come from within, so when you decide to change, you will.

Increase Awareness

Increasing your awareness means having a higher level of alertness when it comes to an understanding of what's going on in your environment. It means paying close attention to your surroundings and to the way people behave around you. The higher your level of awareness, the better you will be in adapting to your surroundings and understanding the motivations of the people you interact with.

When you become more aware, you will be able to catch on quickly when people try to manipulate you. Numerous of us tend to be preoccupied with our thoughts that we hardly ever notice the cues of the people we interact with. We tend to live life on autopilot, so when other people try to seize control over our lives, we only notice it when it's too late. If you increase your awareness, you will be equipped with the skills necessary to identify all the red flags, and you will be able to stop most manipulators in their tracks before they can do any real harm.

The first step towards increasing your awareness is to learn about the tendencies of manipulative people. Reading this puts you ahead of the curve; you now know enough to be able to spot people with ill motives, but you should understand that the worst kinds of manipulators are very good at concealing their motives, so you have to keep working on increasing your awareness.

To be truly aware of manipulative people, you have to approach all interactions with skepticism levels. We are not telling you to turn into a paranoid person who doesn't let anyone in; we are just saying that you should take a deeper look at each person you interact with. Try to study their body language and their words and see if they are trying to hide something.

Apart from increasing your awareness, you have to increase your self-awareness as well. Many people confuse those two things, but they entirely different concepts. Self-awareness is about understanding yourself. It's about having a clear concept of your personality. You have to examine yourself and figure out your strengths and weaknesses, values and motivations, and what kind of thoughts and emotions you are likely to have in specific situations. Self-awareness helps you understand both who you are and how other people perceive you.

Self-awareness works as a defense against manipulation because when you know who you truly are, it becomes more difficult for someone to alter your thoughts and perceptions. If you have strong and well-articulated values, it becomes harder for a manipulator to get you to abandon those values. People who like self-awareness are more likely to be gaslighted or subjected to other forms of mind control.

If you end up in a relationship with a manipulative person, self-awareness can help you keep your identity. Manipulators will try to tell you what to think and how to behave. Still, if you are self-aware, you will experience cognitive dissonance, and your brain will push back against any attempts at manipulation.

Detach with Love

Detaching with love is a defense against manipulation that is most commonly used by people who have loved ones who suffer from substance abuse problems. Even though it was conceptualized to help people deal with addicts, you can also work when dealing with manipulators.

Detaching with love is about showing love and compassion for others without taking responsibility for their actions. If the addict doesn't come home, you don't waste your time looking for them in the seedy parts of the city, you stay at home, and you do the things that benefit you and make you happy.

The point of detaching with love is to stop trying to control other people's lives, even if you are doing it for their good. The idea is that you accept that people are different from you and have their own free will.

Detaching from love can defend you from manipulation in many ways. Some manipulators want to exploit you by making you responsible for them. We have mentioned several times that some malicious people will take the submissive position in a relationship because they want your world to revolve around them. They want you to give them all your attention; that is how they control you. When you detach with love, you will learn to stop fixing everyone's problems. So, when the manipulator tries to play the victim to gain your sympathy, you will keep doing whatever is in your best interest, and you will tell him or her to take accountability for his or her actions.

Some manipulators may take up self-destructive habits because they want to dominate you by making you clean up after them. When they do this, you can detach with love by letting them follow the paths they have taken, no matter where they lead them. If they are causing you harm, you can get away from them, but leave your door open. If they find the right path in the future and regain control over their own lives, you can let them in again. You have to make it very clear that you will let them direct their own lives through your words and actions, and you won't take any responsibility for them.

Detaching with love is about accepting others for who they are and respecting them enough to let them be in charge of changing their own lives. When you feel responsible for someone, and he makes a choice that harms you both, you will frequently react with fear, anger, or anxiety. To detach with love, you have to learn to let go of those negative emotions.

Manipulators count on the fact that you will react in a predictable way to their machinations, but when you detach with love, you learn to calm yourself down and think about your role in the other person's life before you take any sort of action. This will keep you from falling into the traps that manipulators will set for you. Detaching with love builds your self-esteem because it allows you to put your own needs ahead of those trying to manipulate you.

Chapter 40. Qualities of a Manipulative Person

If you have ever heard the term "master manipulator," you might have an idea of a few manipulator personality traits. Most manipulators, especially people who are using it for their benefit, share similar characteristics. One factor to note is that there are easily noticeable traits and traits manipulators will hide well.

Manipulators Will Pressure You

A manipulator will pressure you into deciding before you are ready. They might start by doing this subtly at first and then increase their efforts. Their goal is to get you to cave as this will give them what they want.

Manipulators Are Experts at the Silent Treatment

If there is one main way to make a manipulator mad, it is not to give in. When a manipulator starts to feel threatened by your emotional and mental strength, they will resort to isolating you. For example, they might refuse to allow you to answer a question or completely ignore you.

Manipulators use this tactic to remain powerful. They want to make sure they assert their dominance.

Manipulators Will Bully You

Manipulators will do whatever they can to remain powerful, including bullying behavior. They will do whatever they can to shake your confidence as they want to make sure you don't feel emotionally and mentally stronger than them.

They will take part in this behavior anywhere; however, they often become more of a bully in public. This is because it allows them to embarrass you to the point you won't want to socialize with many people.

Manipulators Will Never Admit Their Faults

Manipulators will find someone else to blame, such as their parents, significant other, friends, and even children. They will also make up excuses when someone notices their weaknesses. For example, they might say that they didn't know certain information because someone never told them.

Manipulators Will Test Your Boundaries

No matter how strongly you discuss your boundaries with a manipulator, they will still test them. While they will act like they are sorry initially, telling you that they didn't realize this was a boundary, they don't feel this way. Testing your boundaries is a great way for a manipulator to learn what you will and will not put up with. They want to learn your breaking points to know what they can and cannot do right away. This doesn't mean that they won't cross your breaking points. They will just wait to do this until they have you within their webs.

Manipulators Don't Validate Your Feelings

Manipulators don't care about you as a person. They care about using you to get what they want. Therefore, they aren't going to spend time trying to make you feel better, ask you what is wrong, how your day went, or validate your feelings.

As humans, we need to have our emotions validated to work through them and maintain a healthy mindset. By not validating your emotions, manipulators can keep stronger control over you because you will start to lose your confidence, self-esteem, and self-image. You will become so overwhelmed with emotions; most of them negative, you will become depressed and stop caring about yourself. You might also stop talking to your friends and family. In general, you lose your interest in life.

This gives a manipulator the upper hand because you are more likely to do what they say. You will act how they want you to act. Even if you don't feel it is right, they will start to get you to believe that they are the only ones who care about you. Of course, this will further isolate you from anyone else you know and used to hang out with.

Manipulators Are Compulsive Liars

Manipulators are also known as compulsive liars. This is because they often distort facts to make them seem better than you or the best out of everyone. For a manipulator, it doesn't matter if the facts prove them wrong. They do not believe the facts.

However, their lying goes beyond facts. They will also use half-truths or withhold important information from you. This will allow them to maintain their leverage over you. For example, if you are working on a project with a manipulator, they will try to get information from their supervisor or project manager when you are not there. They will then inform you of what they were told but leave out a lot of information. They can then use this left-out information against you. They could lower your confidence in the project because you don't know everything your partner knows, or they could embarrass you in front of other people.

At this point in life, you have probably known about manipulative people. That is their mantra, many manipulative people have been practicing this art for a very long time, and as they say, practice makes perfect. Many people do not just immediately become manipulative. It can happen over time, generally, after the first time they have successfully gotten what they want, and they realize they can do it repeatedly. That is why it can be so difficult to tell when you are being manipulated because manipulators are not amateurs, so if you think you are being manipulated, remember it is not your fault. You have part of something that is much nuanced and complex, often making you feel as though you have done something wrong when that is not the case.

It would be so much easier if manipulative people signed on their backs, saying that they were indeed manipulators, but it's not that easy. They are usually very charming. One way to get you hooked is when true manipulation starts. They also adapt quickly to different situations very quickly, making it even more difficult to spot them. Unfortunately, this is all part of their game, making it even more complicated because they do change on a dime, and keeping you on your toes is what they are good at. Fortunately, they do typically stick to a certain script, if you will, that combines certain words and phrases, so that is one of the best and easiest ways to find out who in your life are the manipulators.

Traits of Manipulators

Playing the Victim

Many manipulators learn to play the victim, making it seem like they need help when they don't. They often do this by making you feel like you have caused a problem when this is not true. In reality, they are the ones that caused the issue, whatever it may be, and blame you because they do not want to take responsibility. This can be as simple as getting an apology from you or something bigger such as monetary gain. When you owed them nothing, to begin with, but they twisted it around so well, you feel as though you did do something wrong.

Hot and Cold

Manipulators can often be nice one minute and standoffish the next. This is hard to deal with because you don't know which person you will get when you see or talk to them. This is one of the easiest ways to prey on your fears and insecurities and keep you guessing. This is not a healthy friendship or relationship because the person being manipulated is constantly on their toes and worried about how they will treat them, always wondering if something they did to provoke this behavior. It might sound juvenile, but this can be very powerful in lowering someone's self-esteem, especially over a long time.

Aggressive

Many manipulators can take it passed being standoffish and can resort to being extremely aggressive or even vicious. They might not be physical, but they can wear another person down by using personal verbal attacks. All of this is done because that is how badly they want to get what they want. Often, they will not let up or stop until the other person is so worn down that they simply give in just to get the abuse to stop.

Lack of Insight

Many manipulative people lack insight when it comes to how to interact with others healthily. Instead, they truly believe that the only way to deal with situations is their way, and everyone else is wrong because their desires or needs are not being met. So, the scenarios and solutions they create will only benefit them at the expense of everyone else around them. This means that every friendship, relationship, and situation is about them, and everything else does not matter.

No Questions

Manipulative people do not question their behavior. They think they know what is right because it benefits them, which is the end of it. An average person knows how to read a situation and might understand, given certain circumstances, that their beliefs or opinion is wrong and can adjust it appropriately. A manipulative person does not do this. They just don't ask questions or wonder if the problem is them.

Lack of Boundaries

Part of being manipulative is putting their desire above everything else; part of this is not respecting other people's boundaries. They will crowd someone's spiritual, physical, emotional, and psychological space with absolutely no concern to them. This is often how they achieve their goals in the first place, by crossing these boundaries and exploiting the insecurities of others. A great way to think of this is to imagine them like a parasite, something that works in the natural world, but it is unacceptable for humans. Feeding off of someone else at their expense is weakening, demeaning, and exhausting.

Avoids Responsibility

One of the biggest traits of a manipulator is the inability to accept responsibility; everything is always someone else's fault. This does not mean that they do not know what responsibility is; on the contrary, they know what it is enough to blame someone else, just never themselves. Generally, they want you to take responsibility for their happiness, leaving you with no time or resources to get your own.

Preying on Sensibilities

Manipulators know that not everyone makes a great target, so they search out a certain type of person. They look for sensitive and conscientious people because they know this will increase their chances of trapping them into some sort of relationship. Finding the type of person who is kind, caring, feeling, and, most of all, the type of person who enjoys helping others is the perfect prey for them.

In the beginning, a manipulator will often cater to kindness and caring, usually praising the person for what a good person they are. Still, over time this will switch to praising them for what they can do for the manipulator. Again, this is not an overnight change, but one that takes time and is one reason it is so successful.

Disharmony

One common trait of a manipulator is to create disharmony amongst friend groups. They commonly talk negatively about everyone behind others' backs and enjoy stirring the pot. This keeps people uncomfortable, and they can do it in a way that makes them seem more trustworthy.

Chapter 41. Victim of Manipulation

Certain characteristics and behavioral traits make people more vulnerable to manipulation, and people with dark psychology traits know this full well. They tend to seek out victims who have those specific behavioral traits because they are essentially easy targets. Let's discuss 6 of the traits of the favorite victims of manipulators.

Emotional Insecurity and Fragility

Manipulators like to target victims who are emotionally insecure or emotionally fragile. Unfortunately, for these victims, such traits are very easy to identify even in total strangers, so it's easy for experienced manipulators to find them.

Emotionally insecure people tend to be very defensive when attacked or under pressure, making them easy to spot in social situations. Even after just a few interactions, a manipulator can gauge how insecure a person is with a certain degree of accuracy. They'll try to provoke their potential targets subtly and then wait to see how the targets react. If they are overly defensive, manipulators will take it as a sign of insecurity, and they will intensify their manipulative attacks.

Manipulators can also tell if a target is emotionally insecure if he/she redirects accusations or negative comments. They will find a way to put you on the spot, and if you try to throw it back at them or make excuses instead of confronting the situation head-on, the manipulator could conclude that you are insecure and, therefore, an easy target.

People who have social anxiety also tend to have emotional insecurity, and manipulators are aware of it. In social gatherings, they can easily spot individuals who have social anxiety, then target them for manipulation. "Pickup artists" can identify the girls who seem uneasy in social situations by the way they conduct themselves. Social anxiety is difficult to conceal, especially to manipulators who are experienced at preying on emotional vulnerability.

Emotional fragility is different from emotional insecurity. Emotionally insecure people tend to show it all the time, while emotionally fragile people appear to be normal, but they break down emotionally at the slightest provocation. Manipulators like targeting emotionally fragile people because it's very easy to elicit a reaction from them. Once a manipulator finds out that you are emotionally fragile, he will jump at the chance to manipulate you because he knows it would be fairly easy.

Emotional fragility can be temporary, so opportunistic manipulators often target people with these traits. A person may be emotionally stable most of the time. Still, he/she may experience emotional fragility when they are going through a breakup when they are grieving or dealing with an emotionally draining situation. The more sinister manipulators can earn your trust, bid their time, and wait for you to be emotionally fragile. Alternatively, they can use underhanded methods to induce emotional fragility in a person they are targeting.

Sensitive People

Highly sensitive people are those individuals who process information at a deeper level and are more aware of the subtleties in social dynamics. They have lots of positive attributes because they tend to be very considerate of others, and they watch their step to avoid causing people any harm, whether directly or indirectly. Such people tend to dislike any form of violence or cruelty, and they are easily upset by news reports about disastrous occurrences or even depictions of gory scenes in movies. Sensitive people also tend to get emotionally exhausted from taking in other people's feelings. When they walk into a room, they have the immediate ability to detect other people's moods because they are naturally skilled at identifying and interpreting other people's body language cues, facial expressions, and tonal variations.

Manipulators like to target sensitive people because they are easy to manipulate. If you are sensitive to certain things, manipulators can use them against you. They will feign certain emotions to draw sensitive people in so that they can exploit them.

Sensitive people also tend to scare easily. They have a heightened "startle reflex," which means that they are more likely to show clear signs of fear or nervousness in potentially threatening situations. For example, sensitive people are more likely to jump up when someone sneaks up on them, even before determining whether they are in any real danger. If you are a sensitive person, this trait can be very difficult to hide, and malicious individuals will be able to see it from a mile away.

Sensitive people also tend to be withdrawn. They are mostly introverts, and they like to keep to themselves because social stimulation can be emotionally draining for them. Manipulators looking to control others are more likely to target introverted people because that trait makes it easy to isolate potential victims.

Manipulators can also identify sensitive people by listening to how they talk. Sensitive people tend to be very proper; they never use vulgar language, and they tend to be very politically correct because they are trying to avoid offending anyone. They also tend to be polite, and they say please and thank you more often than others. Manipulators go after such people because they know that they are too polite to dismiss them right away; sensitive people will indulge anyone because they don't want to be rude, giving people maliciously away.

Emphatic People

Emphatic people are generally similar to highly sensitive people, except that they are more attuned to others' feelings and the world's energy around them. They tend to internalize other people's suffering to the point that it becomes their own. In fact, for some of them, it can be difficult to distinguish someone's discomfort from their own. Emphatic people make the best partners because they feel everything you feel. However, this makes them particularly easy to manipulate, which is why malicious people like to target them.

Malicious people can feign certain emotions and convey those emotions to emphatic people, who will feel them as though they were real. That opens them up for exploitation. Emphatic people are the favorite targets of psychopathic conmen because they feel so deeply for others. A conman can make up stories about financial difficulties and swindle lots of money from emphatic people.

The problem with being emphatic is that because you have such strong emotions, you easily dismiss your doubts about people because you would much rather offer help to a person who turns out to be a lair than deny help to a person who turns out to be telling the truth.

Emphatic people have a big-hearts, and they tend to be extremely generous, often to their detriment. They are highly charitable, and they feel guilty when others around them suffer, even if it's not their mistake, and they can't do anything about it. Malicious people have a very easy time taking such people on guilt trips. They are the kind of people who would willingly fork over their life savings to help their friends get out of debt, even if it means they would be ruined financially.

Malicious people like to get into relationships with emphatic people because they are easy to take advantage of. Emphatic people try to avoid getting into intimate relationships in the first place because they know that it's easy for them to get engulfed in such relationships and to lose their identities in the process. However, manipulators will doggedly pursue them because they know that they can guilt the emphatic person into doing anything they want once they get it.

Fear of Loneliness

Numerous people are afraid of being alone, but this fear is heightened in a small percentage. This kind of fear can be truly paralyzing for those who experience it, and it can open them up to exploitation by malicious people. For example, many people stay in dysfunctional relationships because they are afraid they will never find somebody else to love them if they break up with an abusive partner. Manipulators can identify this fear in a victim, and they'll often do everything they can to fuel it further to make sure that the person is crippled by it. People who are afraid of being alone can tolerate or even rationalize any kind of abuse.

The fear of being alone can be easy to spot in a potential victim. People with this kind of fear tend to exude some desperation level at the beginning of relationships, and they can sometimes come across as clingy. While ordinary people may think of being clingy as a red flag, manipulative people will see it as an opportunity to exploit somebody. If you are attached to them, they'll use manipulative techniques to make you even more dependent on them. They can withhold love and affection (e.g., by using the silent treatment) to make the victim fear that he/she is about to get dumped so that they act out of desperation and cede more control to the manipulator.

The fear of being alone is, for the most part, a social construct, and it disproportionately affects women more than men. For generations, our society has taught women that their goal in life is to get married and have children, so even the more progressive women who reject this social construct are still plagued by social pressures to adhere to those old standards. That being said, the fact is that men also tend to be afraid of being alone.

People with abandonment issues stemming from childhood tend to experience the fear of loneliness to a higher degree. There are also those people who may not necessarily fear loneliness in general, but they are afraid of being separated from the important people in their lives. For example, many people stay in abusive or dysfunctional relationships because they are afraid of being separated from their children.

Fear of Disappointing Others

We all feel a certain sense of obligation towards the people in our lives, but some are extremely afraid of disappointing others. This kind of fear is similar to the fear of embarrassment and the fear of rejection because it means that the person puts a lot of stock into how others perceive them. The fear of disappointing others can occur naturally. It can be useful in some situations; parents who are afraid of disappointing their families will work harder to provide for them. Children who are afraid of disappointing their parents will study harder at school. In this case, the fear is constructive. However, it becomes unhealthy when directed at the wrong people or when it forces you to compromise your comfort and happiness.

When manipulators find out that you fear disappointing others, they'll try to put you in a place where you sense as you owe them something. They'll do certain favors for you, and then they'll manipulate you into believing that you have a sense of obligation towards them. They will then guilt you into complying with any request whenever they want something from you.

Chapter 42. Strategies for Seduction, a Person with Manipulation

Seduction and sexual conquest are sometimes common features of dark psychology. They will show up so often that we will devote this guide to them and how they work. This is an important topic to discuss because all of us have been or know someone who has been seduced by someone else who used these dark psychological principles.

The human sex drive can be a very powerful urge, and not being able to fulfill it can sometimes lead to unhappiness, worry, and stress in a person's life. On the other side of things, some of the most famous historical figures are known for their frequent and full fulfillment of sexual urges. For example, emperors and kings have often been afforded the finest women as their reward just because of their status.

One very famous example is the powerful seducer King Henry the 8th from England. His women's appetite was so strong that he decided to create a new religion in his country to change his wife and marry any woman he chose. He also exercised utter control over all the wives he had, and many of them were beheaded when they didn't satisfy his needs or help him meet his goals any longer.

This begs the question: is all seduction a form of dark psychological seduction? Of course not! Yes, all seduction is going to involve the perusal of the other person. Those who don't have the skills of dark manipulation will clumsily do this. This is shown in some of the popular romantic comedies that come out, where the clumsy guy keeps making mistakes when they try to pursue the girl.

But a dark seducer will be someone who knows what they want and knows how to get it. They will go after the other person to fulfill their personal needs, and they often don't care how the other person feels about it. They can be charming, and they are not going to be clumsy at all, and they always know the right thing to say and do.

Why Do People Choose Dark Psychological Seduction?

One question that people will have is: why would someone want to choose this path for attraction? Isn't a better idea to go on some dates and court someone in an honest manner?

A dark seducer doesn't want to get into a relationship, at least not into the boring stuff with it. They want to just get certain things out of the area of romance. They don't care about the other person because they know they can use dark psychology techniques to find another partner if this one goes south. This allows them to approach life, and the relationship, with a non-needy and carefree mindset. If the seducer does decide to settle down with someone, they will be able to do it without feeling like they rushed or settled into the first relationship to get what they want.

So, how is a dark seducer have so much success and influence within the world of dating? They understand the dark psychology principles and have the right skills to execute these principles.

One of the key advantages that dark psychology users will have over their rivals, especially in dating, is that they understand the human mind, almost like a secret weapon. While others may feel like the human mind is impossible to understand, the dark seducer can read it like a book and get the information they want.

Someone who works on the principles behind dark psychology in the dating world may find that it will change their dating experiences compared to their past efforts. They will have a feeling of confidence and control, rather than feeling doubtful, needy, and insecure.

Sure, it may seem kind of mean. The dark seducer can jump from one partner to another, using each one in the manner that matters most to the seducer. Some people are harmed in this process, especially those looking for more of a long-term relationship or looking for more out of it.

But a dark seducer is only interested in what matters to them and nothing else. They can read the mind of their victim and be the exact person that the victim wants. However, they only do this to get their foot in the door and get what they want. As soon as the victim isn't meeting the seducer's needs, then the seducer will move on.

Where Does Dark Seduction Begin?

Now that we have an idea of dark seduction basics, it is time to move into how this seduction can work. Most dark seducers are going to have a guiding approach that is going to motivate their efforts. They will also have tactics that are going to come from their philosophy. Let's look at some of the different philosophies that a dark seducer may choose to use.

One approach is the deployment of a process that is rigid and structured. These seducers feel that they have mapped out how the sequence of attraction should be in great detail, and they may have a process that seems like it is from a flowchart. They want their seduction process to be replicable and predictable. These systems work for the dark seducer and work for others who understand these systems and learn how to implement them correctly.

These seducers are going to use a series of stages in their process. They will try to get the target to go through a range of emotions. This range is designed by the seducer to fit their own needs. They will move them through emotions such as interest, attraction, and then excitement. These seducers will see the whole process as a series of checkpoints that they need to pass through to help them reach their goals.

This method's strength is that it gives the dark seducer a feeling of certainty because they know the exact steps to take each time. They won't have any surprises that come up during the seduction, and it kind of becomes routine and habitual for the seducer. The biggest problem with this is that it doesn't consider that sometimes people will be unpredictable and won't go along with the structured emotional program that the seducer planned out.

Another option is the natural approach. This approach will involve the dark seducer cultivating a natural emotional state internal to the seducer and then expressing them freely to the one they are working to seduce. An example of this is when a person who uses this, is likely to spend some time trying to understand their own emotions and then try to perfect these. They are then going to express these to others. The philosophy behind this one is that "I can't make others feel good until I can feel good."

You can also work with hypnotic and Neuro-Linguistic Programming (NLP) seduction. NLP is a combination of neurological processes, language, and behavior. This is kind of a subset of dark seduction. Unlike the structured seduction that we talked about before or even the natural version, NLP and hypnotic seduction involve triggering specific emotional states in the victim and then linking these back to the seducer.

Let's look at an example of this. The NLP approach to seduction involves allowing people to explore their own intense positive emotions. The seducer may even try to get more of those emotions out. Then, they will work to anchor these to the seducer. That way, when the victim sees the seducer, they will naturally feel intense physical pleasure, even though they may not know why that happens.

Hypnotic seduction is another option to work with, but it can be difficult to work with regularly. This is because a few things will make someone suspicious about a seducer than the odd techniques that come with NLP. The other seduction types seem somewhat normal to the victim, but hypnotic seduction doesn't seem this way. However, some will respond to it.

Dark seduction can allow the seducer the ability to get exactly what they want out of the relationship. Those who are not looking to take advantage of others, but who are open about what they are doing and just use the techniques to give them more confidence and avoid a boring relationship can sometimes use it. However, there are plenty of dark seducers who use it as a way to use the other person, with no care about how it is going to affect the other person at all. Either way, it is still important to be on the lookout for this kind of behavior to not get into a bad relationship for you or isn't what you are looking for from the other person.

Chapter 43. Covert Emotional Manipulation: Introduction

Covert emotional manipulation is an exceptional phenomenon that can happen to anybody, even you. Behind the intensity of your mindfulness alertness is where emotional manipulation operates and restrains you emotionally, while as a victim, you know nothing about what is happening.

A skillful emotional manipulator will do to you to influence you to place into their hands all your sensitive safety and senses of self-worth. Manipulators will continually and methodically break off your self-esteem and identity until there is little left the instant you make such a severe miscalculation.

Psychopaths and manipulators manipulate much in the same way as "pick-up artists" and narcissists. As for psychopaths, they have a perception that they are in charge and look down at others as their game to suit their hunting needs. Psychopaths have no compassion, no remorse or guilt, no conscience, and no ability to love. Achieving anything they want, including money, sex, or influence and taking control and power, is a game of manipulators. Not only that, but psychopaths also destroy their victims psychologically, emotionally, physically, and spiritually in the course of their actions. They use all tactics to realize their wishes. They will get going to the next conquest after they have won the game, filled with contempt for you and getting bored.

Covert manipulators cannot have a genuine connection even though they are so smart. They have a strategy from the beginning. Apart from that, they are proficient at reading your mind. Gaining knowledge of your strengths, weaknesses, dreams, fears, and desires is so easy for them. With an armory of valuable manipulation schemes that they have chosen carefully and personalized only for you, it is not for them to hesitate to use all these against you. They yearn for control and power and will always persist to control you, even if it results in harming you.

At a point when you think your life has got the blessing of a tender bond through the magical excitement that has made a comfortable and delightful appearance, it might be that something quite sinister and different is behind it. To conceal their exact strategy and personalities is one of the skills of manipulators. The main goal of these psychopaths is to fool you into trusting that they love and ready to do anything for you so you can confide in them in the course of a frenzied process of passionate illusion. They craft this stage of deep attachment to pin you and make you susceptible to the abuse and manipulation that will ensue.

After a while, demeaning will replace loving. From then on, degrading will follow, and manipulators will confuse, exploit, and diminish your self-worth, self-esteem, and self-respect. To keep you eager to do anything to save the relationship and to let you hold yourself responsible for not cherishing a great relationship and vouching to save the affair no matter what, manipulators will make a pleasant appearance as loving individuals that hook you.

To show your devotion to the relationship, you will be eager to acknowledge sheer morsels. You won't have any thought of talking about your emotions, fears, and needs, which is not the psychopath's concern and consider unacceptable weaknesses. When things go wrong, you will shift the blame on yourself, analyzing every mood and every word, becoming quite confused about what is happening, and recalling the conversations. Your life or job will suffer and your dealings with other people and your mental and physical health.

Your manipulator will try to have you with them, waiting for the time you become a hopeless disaster. At that point, they will let you know with seething contempt and disdain how they are bored with you and don't want you anymore. They will then leave you a sensitive mess who wonders just what happened to your life, speculating your perfect affair crumbled into the gulf of hell from heaven-on-earth.

Struggling with feelings of acute emotional grief and confusion comes to all preys of this deceptive and underhanded manipulation. Many of them also experience rage, obsessive thoughts, insomnia, misplaced self-esteem, panic, anxiety, inability to trust, poor health, fear, use of drugs or alcohol, and absence of support. Sometimes, extreme and irrational behavior can happen, including withdrawal and isolation from family, friends, and society. Suicidal actions or thoughts are part of what most victims face.

The question is, do these manipulators truthfully want love in the first place? Maybe they never have any desire for love. In a situation such as this, the purpose is that of victimization. The manipulator would have had their target plans when they discovered that you are open to their advances.

On the other hand, the occasion might end up badly even if the manipulator has a real attraction for you. Because it is the incentive scheme of the brain, things and people stimulate and excite these people. In fact, for those with features of psychopathy, the system works quite well. Indeed, studies have found that far from that of an average individual, manipulators' reward system is more sensitive. Consequently, it is with the intensity that they establish a relationship.

A Deeper Look at Manipulation Tactics

Covert manipulative individuals make use of tactics to accomplish two things simultaneously:

- Conceal their intention

- Invite you to fear, doubt, and concede

Tactics that are generally the most effective in manipulating other people, especially neurotics, are a few tactics covert manipulative people use more frequently. The key to personal empowerment is to know how to deal with these manipulation methods when you recognize them.

With just about any behavior imaginable to accomplish their aims, it is amazing how capable the more skilled manipulators can be. Armed with these tactics, manipulators will thoroughly evaluate how they will manipulate their target character when the manipulators know their victim inside out and are familiar with their target's fears, sensitivities, conscientiousness level, core beliefs, and so much more. Moreover, in a covert war of dominance, manipulators will have a considerable prospect making way for them to use that person's traits, especially their most collectively attractive characteristics, against them.

It will be appropriate for us to focus our attention on the more conventional approaches they employ and give in-depth details on why the tactics are so efficient. It is not realistic to talk about different feasible behaviors covert manipulators can use to influence another person. Having a good understanding of the fundamentals of manipulation works will reinforce your insight into the various potential tactics manipulators might apply and give you superior conscious control of the nature of upsetting encounters with all manipulators.

There is a rationalization tactic, which we may call "justifying", or "excuse-making." Originated from the Freudian notion, the word rationalization indicates that, on occasion, against the fear they might have suffered by engaging in dealings that damage their principles, people defend themselves unaware. They will assuage any qualms of conscience when they find reasons that appear to make their achievement more benign, appropriate, understandable, and acceptable. However, the assumption for this situation implies that the person has a highly sensitive conscience, and this type of rationalization is a mostly unconscious process and strictly internal.

Manipulators know what they are doing when they make explanations for their actions in some situations. When this set of people is looking to validate themselves, they certainly have obvious intention in mind. They use this approach when they know that they plan to do something or have done something most people would regard as wrong. However, manipulators stay determined to do it even when they know it is wrong and how their actions negatively represent them. They have permission to do it, such as the aggressive characters' situation or the case of more self-absorbed individuals, or they may clash against the accepted rules.

Most essential to identify is that at the time, manipulators are justifying their actions; they are neither unconsciously fending off any anxiety nor defending. Instead, they are actively at war against a set of standard manipulators who know society wants them to accept. More importantly, they are also attempting to get your support. Unlike open defiance, undercover manipulators prefer this type of tactic because it not only helps to mask their manipulative goals and various revealing parts of their personality, but at the same time helps them to preserve a more positive social image by making someone else identify with the supposed rationality of their actions or have a similar perception to their own. When the person accepts their premise with this strategy, the door of wielding the mutual domination and contest of image is opening gradually.

It is not that manipulators don't understand that their actions are wrong or that most people would see them as evil; instead, they hate your negative appraisal of their personality and perhaps end any relationship with them. More importantly, they should not engage in such behavior again because covert manipulative people don't want to incorporate and allow. Even when they still apply the tactic, they oppose a standard and hold up the inculcating that standard into their social ethics. It is the visible signal that they can engage in a similar activity in any related situation.

Now, let us talk about denial, another tactic. Denial is a word that had its origin from the psychology of Freudian. Freud invented it as an unconscious and primitive resistance against intolerable emotional pain. With other tactics such as pretending that they are innocent, manipulators often will use denial. This situation is when someone you have confronted acts as if they know nothing of what you are saying or they pretend in a vain way that they did nothing of which to be guilty or ashamed. They will often use faking gullibility and denial with such apparent confidence and intensity that you start to be curious about your sanity and perception. That moment, you start out knowing that you have caught them on the action, and one way or another, using this tactic, you begin to wonder if you are making any sense at all. This tactic is quite an efficient one-two manipulation blow!

However, the main missiles in the arsenal of any manipulator are the strategy of guilt-tripping and shaming. The fact behind this analysis is that precision defines the high degree of neurotics and cannot stand thinking that their actions are shameful or wrong. As a result, making them believe that what they have done should make them feel ashamed or guilty is the perfect way to control them. Conscientious individuals sometimes attempt to shame or guilt on their prey, hoping that it will somehow induce their behavior.

Covert is when an attempt is made to communicate with the subject's unconscious mind without knowing that they will be put through hypnosis. It comprises a string of techniques such as conversational hypnosis or NLP (neuro-linguistic programming), body language, and other powerful communication and interaction strategies.

Chapter 44. Covert Manipulation in a Love Relationship

The love-bombing is hard to ignore. They will make you feel like you are the most important person in the world to them, and you will be showered with loving gestures such as poems, love letters, gifts, or just merely the fact that they always have time for you.

The first few times they overreact to something, you might be able to justify it in your mind. There is a simple stage in a relationship where a kiss and a few sappy words can fix any argument.

A narcissist cannot have a productive argument. When people in a healthy and loving relationship disagree, their goal is to learn how to communicate better and find out where the miscommunication happened this time. When it is narcissistic abuse, they want to demean and shame you.

It is one that is void of name-calling and hurling accusations at one another. An argument is also not the time to bring up past grievances. This is sometimes referred to as the "kitchen sink" method. This is a very unhealthy way of arguing, but one that is often used by narcissists. They mean to make you feel like a wrong person.

They will not hear you out if you come to them with a concern about how they treat you. They will say something like, "do you think you're perfect?" This focuses the attention away from what they have done that is hurtful to you. For example, you might tell them you don't want them to call you names. Their response is, "You're not always a ray of sunshine around me either." In this situation, they did not hear you out at all. They shut down what you were trying to say to them.

A narcissist's first impulse will always be to self-protect. They are not interested in listening to your point of view, nor do they want to reach a compromise. They want to make sure they do not have any tarnishes on their character. That is because if they are not flawless, they are worthless. That is their thought process. This is most likely because, during childhood, they were only given praise when they succeeded.

The covert narcissist will be honest with you about what their grievances are in a relationship. Instead, they will go to other people. There will often be a cheating situation that arises, but they will rally many people against their partner. They often aim to taint their mutual friends' idea of them.

Venting to a confidant such as a best friend or family member is alright and something you will need to do at times. Speaking ill of your partner is not. When you come to a confidant with a legitimate issue, you still want to preserve the relationship's integrity. This is because you are talking to someone outside of the situation and will not share what you say with other people.

While communicating with your partner is essential, you sometimes need to express that would only harm the other person. It is okay to have things to say that you don't want your partner to hear. Where it becomes morally grey is when a person consistently goes to people outside of the relationship with the intent of bashing their significant other.

There is a difference between venting and bashing. While harsh words may be said when a person is venting, they still value the other person. As humans, we will get frustrated with one another, especially if we have an intimate relationship, which will inevitably come with miscommunications and disagreements.

This is an example of venting: "It hurts my feelings when they talk on the phone at the dinner table. It makes me feel like they would rather spend their free time talking to other people besides me." On the other hand, this is bashing "They're impossible to live with. They're always on the phone, ignoring me. I always try so hard, and they never give anything in return."

In the first example, the person is expressing frustrations but not talking about the person negatively or aiming to damage their reputation. In the second example, the language is inflammatory, and it hints toward a deep resentment towards the other person.

"You always" and "you never" are terms narcissists use in arguments.

Narcissists are infamous for their jealousy. They call every interaction you have with everyone in your life, particularly towards the gender you prefer, into question. You can never reassure them enough that you are not going to leave them for someone else. Acting jealous is designed to isolate you. Everything and everyone in your life makes them feel threatened.

Jealousy is not cute. It does not mean your partner is so in love with you that it hurts them to see you talking to someone else. It might sound very romantic when they word it like that, and it might make you feel loved, but what it means is that they want ownership of you.

It is crucial to remember to keep your priorities straight when you begin college. They are trying to put pressure on you to prove to them that you are faithful to them, which will mean your attention is divided while trying to navigate through the complex environment that is college.

A jealous person will call often and want to have long conversations. You cannot do this and study at the same time. Anyone who makes you feel like you need to choose between them and pursuing your education and the things that will further your career is not suitable for your life. They might tell you that you never loved them in the first place if you choose your education, but they did not put you first if they made you feel like you need to limit yourself to keep them.

This leads to another thing a narcissist does in a relationship. They give ultimatums. They will say, "okay, fine, you either stop going to that class or we're breaking up. It's your choice!" This may sound extreme, but that is how unreasonable the demands of a narcissist will become. They will say it's your choice, but it is a threat.

Covert narcissists harbor resentments indefinitely. They might say the conflict is over, and they have moved past it, but if you do something to cause them narcissistic injury, you will hear about it again in perpetuity. This is where a double standard in the relationship begins. They can say and do extremely rude and hurtful things to you, and they will expect you to forgive them after giving you a half-hearted non-apology.

If you are in a relationship with a narcissist, you will often be compared unfavorably to other people. You will be told that you are much more difficult to get along with than these people. This is because, at their core, a narcissist has a very juvenile mentality. They want what is most beneficial to them at the moment. They also do not understand why everyone else seems to be so much easier to get along with than their partner.

They do not live with these other people who seem so shiny. They only see them when they are at their best, and when they spend time with them, it is the good times: for example, it is a neighborhood get-together, and everyone is dressed their best. Drinks are being poured, and food is on the grill. Everyone is laughing and talking, and when the party is over, everyone leaves. All the cleanup is left to the people who hosted the party. We see every side of our spouses or significant others. We only see a certain depth of our acquaintances. You will have much fewer and less intense conversations with those you don't see as often.

They look at people they only see once in a while and then compare them to the person they live with and therefore see every day in every state, even the least glamorous ones. They might be married and even have children with this person. Marriage is difficult even when the relationship is healthy, especially when children come into the equation. Now, not only are you trying to navigate through life between just the two of you, but now you are both responsible for the life, growth, and well-being of other people.

When you share responsibilities this great with someone, you are not always at your best with each other. When you have financial troubles or one of the children begins to act up, tempers will be short, and arguments will be more often. When you compare two relationships, one complex where you share marriage and children, and another relationship where you only see each other when both are well. Your partner will come out, not seeming as good as the other person. Narcissists also do not think about what habits they have that might be unappealing to their partner. They do not consider the idea that they might not be easy to live with themselves.

A narcissist does not consider these factors when they discard one romantic partner to start a relationship with another person. While they are unfaithful to their partner, they are also rude to them. This makes their partner feel completely unmotivated to try to be attractive or be intimate with them. They talk to this person like a dog and fantasize about how much better life would be cheating. They think about how much more fun they have with this person. They believe their partner is no fun, and the person they see in secret is so much more exciting than them.

Chapter 45. How the Mind Works When It Is Manipulated?

When it comes to working with dark manipulation, there will be many different methods and techniques that we can use to get what you want. Remember, we are talking about some forms of manipulation that will help us get what we want but may harm the other person in the process. This means that they may not be seen as the best options to work with, and you may feel a bit uncomfortable with them if you have not worked in dark manipulation, or even with dark persuasion, in the past.

However, working with these techniques will help you to get the results that you want. They will ensure that the other person you are using as your target will be likely to do the actions or say what you would like them to, even though it may not be in their best interests. With that said, let's take a look at some of the different dark manipulation tactics that you can use to get someone else to do what you want.

Using Isolation to Get What You Want

The first technique that can be used in mind control includes isolation. Humans are very social creatures. They like to spend some time talking with others, spending time out in public, having close friends and family, and spending time in more social situations. When we take this social aspect away from many individuals, it changes how they look at life.

Complete physical isolation can be the most powerful. This is when the subject is taken away from all contact with others, including email, social media, phone calls, and physical contact. This is something that has been seen in cults and with other groups. They will often take the person far away from others, and then the only human contact that the person can have is with the captors.

This total physical isolation can be really hard to do, and it is usually only done in really intense situations. If you are just trying to use manipulation, you usually don't want to go through and completely isolate the target. However, it is common for a manipulator to try to attempt their target mentally as much as possible.

There are many methods that the manipulator can use to get what they want with the help of manipulation. They could include some seminars that last a week and isolate them from what they usually do. They could be many criticisms of the person's family and close friends so that the target feels bad and stops seeing them. It could be jealousy that keeps the target at home and limits the influence that anyone outside the manipulator has on the person.

Once the manipulator can control the information that goes to the target, they can share information, withhold information, and do anything that they would like to continue influencing the target as much as they would like. The target will become reliant on the manipulator, and this is how the manipulator can work and get what they want from the target. There are no outside influences to tell the target that something is wrong or watch out, ensuring the target even more.

Criticism

The option to work with when it comes to manipulation is the idea of using criticism. This one is sometimes used with isolated or on its own, and it works well because it makes the target feel like they are always doing something that is wrong and that they cannot meet the high standards of the manipulator. The criticism can always show up on various topics and could include how they look, who they hang out with, their clothes, their beliefs, and anything that the manipulator thinks will work for this.

When a manipulator decides to use this tactic, they will be good at hiding it behind one of their compliments to the other person. Alternatively, they will say something nice and add this little jab at the end of it. This allows them to say all the mean things they want, and then they can say that the target misheard or misunderstood them and that they hadn't meant any harm by it. This puts the target in a bad spot because they know the manipulator is mean to them, but they are the ones who look paranoid and bad in this situation.

The criticism that the manipulator is going to use is often going to be small. They don't want to start out using really big criticisms that are obvious because the target doesn't want to be criticized. If the manipulator starts with something big, the target is going to fight back and walk away. However, when it starts small with some little comments along the way, it starts to plant a bit of self-doubt, something that the target will notice, but they often are not going to fight back against.

They will start with something that may seem like a compliment or like that will sound like they are helpful, but they are trying to be hurtful in the process in reality. They may say something like, "I didn't know that you liked the color blue. I think you should go with something else." This one will have the hidden meaning inside it that you don't look good in what you are wearing, and your clothes don't look that well.

Or maybe you bring in your favorite outfit to a meeting to make yourself feel better. You are excited and feel good about how you look and feel in the outfit, but then they are going to say something about how they liked you in some other outfit better. It isn't necessarily mean, but it is said in a manner and at a time that it ends up hurting your feelings in the process.

As time goes on, the type of criticism that is going to be used against the target is going to get worse. Moreover, the criticism will become quite a bit more obvious and add in a bit more self-doubt here. This will make it so that the target starts to rely on the manipulator a bit more. This is since the target will feel like they have so many flaws that are hard to ignore and that the only person who can like them and maybe even loves them through these flaws will be the manipulator. The fact that the manipulator is still around is a good sign that they care, which causes the target to be more willing to do what the manipulator asks.

The manipulator will find that they can use this criticism more of us against them if it works better. They could even choose to move their criticism against the outside world to claim they are superior.

When this happens, the manipulator will claim to their target that they are super lucky that the manipulator is even associating with them. The manipulator will ensure that they are important so that the target is more likely to stick around and do what they want. This alone is meant to be enough if it is done in the right manner so that the target feels lucky just because the manipulator is going to spend time with them.

Alienating the Target to Get What They Want

No one wants to be alienated. They want to feel like they are a part of the group. They want to feel accepted, as they belong, and more. This is never more apparent than when we see a newcomer. When someone is new to town, or to school, to work, or somewhere else, you will notice that they are trying to figure out how to join the group and get them to accept them. They are worried that they will be alienated, and to avoid this, they will do everything to get others to like them and go along with them, which is where the manipulator can come in and get what they want.

Newcomers who start to join a new manipulative group are usually going to receive a very warm welcome. And they will form many new friendships that seem to be much deeper and have a lot more commitment and meaning behind them compared to anything that they were able to experience in the past.

There are several reasons for this one. First, this gets the target to feel welcome and more indebted to the group and the manipulator. They are thankful that they have these deep connections, and it is usually easier to get a friend to go along with something that a stranger, so it works to the benefit of the manipulator. Add in that the target is scared to be alienated, then they are going to do what they can to keep the relationships going strong.

Simply because we do not want to be taken away from the crowd and don't want others to have anything to do with us, we will do what the manipulator wants us to. The fact that humans are very social creatures and like to be included in some kind of group all of the time, it is likely that we are going to give in to these urges to do what the manipulator wants, even if we don't feel like it is the best thing for us.

Using Social Proof as a Form of Peer Pressure

We like it when we can be a part of the group. Sometimes we center this around wanting to fit in, and we will follow the rules and do what we can to make sure that we are liked and part of the group. Even when we are more introverted and don't want to be in the group all of the time, we still want to find a group of people we can be around and fit in.

Chapter 46. Hypnosis

Hypnosis is a state of mind that individual's fall into where they are no longer in control of their actions. This is often done in therapeutic circumstances to help individuals find the peace they need within themselves to confront their deepest and darkest traumas. Hypnosis also offers a means to persuade and influence others.

Hypnosis and mind control may seem like the same thing since they involve exerting control over someone else. However, there are glaring contrasts between the two. To recognize the distinctions, you must become more acquainted with what they depend on.

Hypnosis is an artificially induced condition in which the individual reacts to inquiries or prompts from the hypnotist. The procedure can be used on an individual or a gathering of people for a specific reason. At the point when this is utilized for therapeutic purposes, the process is known as hypnotherapy. In any case, when it is being used as a type of diversion for a crowd of people, it tends to be alluded to as organized hypnosis.

Then again, personality control is the way toward utilizing a few traps in getting the ideal response you need from others. You can use the secret to get aggregate or fractional command over what is happening in someone else's psyche.

When it is utilized amid reflection, it can enable you to center around your examination subject.

You can deal with your feelings and contemplations when you participate in this sort of reflection. As a rule, incredible people who accomplished extraordinary life achievements could have excellent command over their psyches through daily reflection.

Having seen the essential meanings of hypnosis and mind control, it is obvious to pinpoint their disparities. The real contrast you'll see between these two is that hypnosis must be utilized on others. It is doubtful that there is any method by which you can hypnotize yourself. A subliminal specialist is necessary to induce hypnosis.

Then again, personality control reflection can be utilized on oneself just as on others. You can, without much of a stretch, take part in this sort of contemplation anytime. All you need is to find a tranquil spot, take a seat, and afterward think. You can influence others to concur with you on specific focuses using mind control traps.

Once more, another distinction is seen in the manner in which hypnosis is connected with mind control. In case you are having an issue of fear, smoking, or appetite, a trance specialist can enable you to opt-out if the hypnosis was done with the correct mindset at heart.

Sometimes, the hypnosis specialist may utilize a few methods in reflection to get individuals to be comfortable with capturing the reaction they need at a specific point in time. It is highly unlikely you can utilize mind control traps to spellbind somebody. It is intended for strategic purposes.

Hypnosis and mind control have clear contrasts. A few components utilized in one may likewise be used in the other, but they are not the same. Everything relies upon how you are ready to draw in the essential standards included.

Hypnosis includes two principal components: acceptance and proposals. Trancelike acceptance is the major proposal conveyed amid the hypnosis; however, it should comprise a matter of discussion.

Proposals are commonly communicated as suggestions that inspire automatic reactions from the members, who don't trust they have much control over the circumstance. A few people are likewise more susceptible than others, and specialists have discovered that they are more likely to have a decreased feeling of authority while under hypnosis.

Susceptibility to hypnosis has been characterized as the capacity to encounter proposed modifications in physiology, sensations, feelings, musings, or conduct. Neuroimaging procedures have demonstrated that these individuals show higher activity levels in the prefrontal cortex, the foremost cingulate cortex, and the mind's parietal systems amid various hypnosis periods.

These are regions of the mind associated with a scope of complex capacities, including memory and observation, feelings, and assignment learning. Be that as it may, the particular cerebrum components associated with hypnosis are as yet hazy. However, researchers are starting to sort out the neurocognitive profile of this procedure.

How would you know whether somebody has been hypnotized? Various changes indicate that the subject is in a hypnotic trance. NLP calls these profound daze markers, and they are a set of highly detailed observations one can make of the subject. Recognizing such markers requires practice and focus. Not all of these markers need to be present to establish that a subject is under hypnosis.

Hypnotic Strategies

The first step in putting someone in a hypnotic state is opening the individual's mind to suggestion. The hypnosis specialist uses a vast range of techniques and, depending on the specialist's skill and the susceptibility of the subject. The outcome may vary.

Hypnosis by relaxation is one of the most common methods of hypnosis. Have you ever heard a hypnosis specialist ask an individual to make him or herself as comfortable as possible? By doing this, the person being hypnotized falls into a relaxing state where the mind tends to shut down on immediate surroundings.

Here are some basic techniques for unwinding:

- Relax your body and mind
- Settle down
- Count in receding order in your mind

- Control what your body and mind is thinking and doing

- Feel your muscles give in to relaxation

- Tone down your voice to a whisper

The handshake strategy for hypnotism involves a hypnosis expert shaking an individual's hand. However, where you might think this is a usual way for the public to greet or welcome each other, hypnosis specialists use this for another advantage.

Instead of just shaking your hand, they will grab, twist your wrist, or pull you forward towards them, so you become unstable. When you are unstable in that split second, the perfect opportunity arises for a hypnosis specialist to control your mind.

Eye prompts can also be important in hypnosis. Talking to someone, it is only natural for one's eyes to wander to surroundings or perhaps a glimpse of something in the distance. A hypnosis specialist will take note of this and, within a short period, learn what prompts you to move your eyes left, right, up, or down. With that, they gain access to the way you think, feel, and respond to certain things surrounding you.

Another approach for the hypnosis of others includes mesmerizing proposals that aren't always obvious suggestions. This kind of suggestion is proposed by the hypnotizer and involves something they wish the subject to do. These proposals also come after the customer has already fallen into more of a stupor.

This is when they are the most open to impact. Rather than telling the hypnotized to do something, the command is masked in a mystifying suggestion. If you want someone to sit down, you don't say, "Sit down," you might say, "You should take a minute to relax in the chair over there."

One method you can do to help improve your hypnotic tactics is to record yourself doing hypnosis and listen to it. If you can fully hypnotize yourself, you can be assured you will have the skills to do this to others. Start by listening to other hypnosis recordings and determine which methods have managed to work best on you.

After this, you can write your original script. Remember, never hypnotize someone who doesn't consent to it. Hypnosis helps the other person find a state of relaxation while also helping to persuade them to do something healthy or beneficial.

Like NLP, all of these methods take practice to master. Don't be discouraged because you cannot hypnotize someone else the first time you try fully. Take note of each hypnosis session that you have, as well. What about it worked once that didn't work as well the next time?

Remember not to use information gained from another in a hypnotic state against them either. Sometimes, they might fall into such a stupor that they become in a dreamlike state. They might say something they don't fully mean, much like a person on pain medication after getting their wisdom teeth removed might.

In contrast to manipulation, these skills are intended to be used for good purposes, as well. You might find it becomes easy to hypnotize others once you have practiced, but your motivation shouldn't be primarily for your gain. There are benefits that both you and the entranced can gain from your hard-earned skill. However, you choose to use these powerful methods, along with the NLP tips, you can be helpful and empowering to both you and the person you can influence.

Understand that when you agree to hypnotize someone else, you are also given a certain responsibility. They are trusting you with a vulnerable headspace that they probably would not entrust to just anyone. Once you attempt to persuade someone, you agree to accept any negative outcomes due to your influence.

The healthy, positive influence will take time to build, and that is true even when you are using these hypnotic techniques. To have long-lasting persuasion that will benefit all parties is a great privilege, and it is up to you to find a positive way to utilize this power.

Chapter 47. Office Politics or Sociopathic Tricks? – The Workplace Manipulators

The workplace is a fertile ground for the manipulation of various types to occur. Many people will find they encounter at least several of the following types of workplace manipulators throughout their careers. It can be tough to know how to draw the line between normal workplace politics, gossip and banter, and actual manipulation. Classifying some of the main types of manipulators within the world of work can help potential targets stay away from the wrong type of colleague before finding their world turned upside down and their professional life damaged beyond repair.

The Blackmailer

The Blackmailer is a type of workplace manipulator that can have a serious impact not only on their victims' careers but also on their mental wellbeing and overall sanity. The basic method of the blackmailer is to appear friendly and highly trustworthy at first. This is usually achieved by finding a newcomer to the workplace or someone who does not fit in with others particularly well.

Once an appropriate target has been identified, the blackmailer will invest a serious amount of time and effort to win over their target and deceptively earn their trust. This is often done by taking a new member of staff under their wing and offering to mentor them and make their new life at the company as easy as possible.

The blackmailer will often form friendships with their intended target that occurs outside of work and inside work. This is essential for the blackmailer's manipulation to be effective. It must involve the target seeing the blackmailer more as a trusted friend than simply as a colleague.

Over time, the blackmailer will begin to elicit sensitive information from their target subtly. This could involve controversial opinions about the other people that the two work with or even sensitive details of the victim's personal life, such as their sexual orientation or political views. The blackmailer will keep going until they feel they have accumulated sufficient information to use against their victim.

Once the blackmailer has some powerful information to hold against their target, such as a covert phone recording of them saying something disparaging, or a photograph of the target behaving controversially in some way, the blackmailer will begin to hold it against them. They may make threats such as planning to reveal sensitive information to others within the workplace or even the target's loved ones and family.

The blackmailer will often demand increasing money or favors from the victim to keep their secrets safe. The victim lives in a continuous state of fear as they do not know when and if they will have their secrets revealed. This has a destructive effect on the victim's mental health and can lead to breakdowns and major anxiety levels.

The False Ally

The false ally is a type of workplace manipulator who is skilled at hiding their true intentions. They will seem to be a keen ally of their target. They are likely to suggest that they go to big places in the workplace and support each other's climb up the career ladder.

The false ally will often begin by making an over the top show of helping out their intended target. This is designed to ensure that the target sees them as trustworthy figures and feels a debt of gratitude towards the false ally. Once the false ally feels they have earned the trust and respect of their target, they will begin to exert subtle levels of control over them.

Some typical plays in the playbook of the false ally include coercing a victim into acting in the ally's self-interest and not of the victim. This will usually take place under the guise of doing 'what's best for both of us' when it will be anything but. This type of manipulation is especially effective if the victim is naive and idealistic. The false ally can tap into the victim's desires and ambitions to gain their compliance in carrying out the false ally's bidding.

The endgame of the false ally is typically to see their career advance while their targets either stalls or are damaged irreparably. This often takes the form of the false ally gaining some form of recognition, like a promotion, at the target's expense, but due to the efforts and choices the target has been coerced into. Often, the victim has no knowledge that they have been played like a puppet until it is too late, and the false ally has already benefited.

The Abuser of Power

It is a well-known fact that power has the potential to corrupt human beings. The office is one of the most common arenas for such behavior to occur. The abuse of power can take many different forms, but they all involve someone unfairly wielding a position of hierarchical authority over another person.

Some common examples of power abuses include those in supervisory or management positions asking for inappropriate or over the top levels of support and compliance from those they have power over. This can take less serious forms, such as getting workers to put in hours that they are not paid for, or take more serious forms such as pressuring female employees into sexual liaisons to promise promotions and job security.

It is important to distinguish between someone who legitimately exerts power and someone who abuses it. To cross the line into the realms of covert emotional manipulation, it must fulfill the following criteria for the wielding of power to cross the line. Firstly, the manipulator must have authority over their targets, such as their manager or some other formal authority position. Secondly, the manipulator must use their power in a way that is intended to control their victim through the manipulation of their emotions. Abusers of power can draw on their victims' feelings of job insecurity or doubt about their future.

Abusers of power are particularly dangerous types of manipulators as they have very little chance of being caught. This is owed to the point that it can be difficult for someone to blame their boss or superior for their actions. Unless clear evidence exists, which is very rare to happen, it is likely to come down to the victim's word in contradiction of the manipulator's word. Sadly, this is rarely sufficient evidence for a company to take any action against the person who has abused the power they hold.

The Sexual Predator

Sexual predators can take the form of almost any other type of workplace manipulator and exist on their own. Simply put, a sexual predator seeks to act in an inappropriate sexual way towards someone they work with. This can range in severity.

At one end of the scale, workplace sexual predators may simply make another member of staff feel uncomfortable. This can be through looks, gestures, or inappropriate physical contact. Despite this being the mildest type of sexually predatory behavior that can occur, it is still unbelievably serious and should be avoided at all costs.

Sadly, many workplace sexual predators take things a lot further than merely making a victim feel uncomfortable. Many sexual predators will coerce their victims into carrying out a sexual nature that they feel pressured or forced into doing. To ensure that their victim stays quiet about what has occurred, the predator will often gather some kind of compromising evidence, such as photographs. The predator threatens to expose the victim's colleagues and family if they cause any predator problems.

Although many workplaces have policies intended to protect against any type of inappropriate sexual behavior in the workplace, they are rarely enough to stop the worst predators from going about their manipulation. This is owed to the fact that skilled predators of this nature can ensure they do not leave any evidence whatsoever. They are also likely to choose victims who have low self-esteem or have some other reason that makes them unlikely to tell others what has taken place.

The Bully

Bullies may seem to be a fairly trivial workplace manipulator, but this is far from the case. Bullying can severely impact someone's happiness and well-being. Is often hard to detect, and even harder to stop. This is owed to the detail that a skilled manipulator engaged in the practice of bullying is likely to mask their actions as friendship or advice underneath the friendly veneer. However, something far more dangerous and sinister is occurring. Bullying can range in severity. On one end of the scale, a bully may seem to be making jokes that just happen to involve the victim. However, this is not what is happening. What seems like a joke is often an attempt to gradually erode the victim's confidence and leave them vulnerable and doubtful. Cognitive dissonance is created in the victim's mind as, on the one hand, they are aware that the comments or actions of the bully are hurting them, but on the other, they do not want to appear overly sensitive or thin-skinned. This often results in the victim begrudgingly accepting the bullying taking place, even if it is hurting them in the long path. For bullying to work, the manipulator chooses their target carefully. They are likely to select someone who lacks self-confidence and is not particularly popular within the workplace. This is owed to the point that the victim will put up with the bullying, as it is often the only form of attention they have received in the workplace up until that point. Bullying can have severe consequences in the long run. It can chip away at the victim's confidence and happiness and, perversely, create a sense of dependency on the manipulator and the attention they provide. The effects can be with a victim for the rest of their life. They may have severe difficulty trusting another again and forming any type of healthy relationship in the future. This is because they will have fallen into the pattern of seeking approval and validation via negative attention.

Chapter 48. Human Behavior and Manipulation

Once you have gotten a decent read on a person, the step to mastering your environment and analyzing your potential in each situation is learning how to manipulate another person's feelings and reactions through subtler cues, both verbal and non-verbal. This will create an environment where your suggestions can thrive.

Don't beat yourself up for thinking outside the box when it comes to analyzing and influencing people. While some people might call it manipulation, you can simply tell them that you are extremely persuasive. What's more, there is nothing to say that the person you are influencing wasn't waiting for an excuse to move forward in the direction you suggested anyway. It is your creativity in constructing a good plan or formula that turns resistance into compliance.

Besides emotion, successful manipulation is all about the imbalance of power. There may be times when getting what you want from another person means using the home-court advantage, which means keeping the person in an environment where you have primary control. This includes your home, car, office, or even your side of town. This makes it harder for your target to do things such as dodge a conversation or even decide that they think they might hurt your feelings.

While it may seem surprising, letting people dominate the conversation is a good thing when you want to have the upper hand with them. You can establish their underlying weaknesses and strengths by listening to their stories and throwing in limited questions from time to time, which will also ingratiate you to them further. It makes you look as though you are supremely interested in what they have to say. However, you don't want the conversation to be one-sided, which means you want to tell them enough about your situation to make them feel comfortable, while at the same time hiding any information that weakens your point of view or that can be contorted to mean something else. Don't be afraid to lie to protect any weaknesses in your argument.

If someone is pushing you for more than they need, you can use a humble tone and explain that there are things about your no one would understand or that you aren't interesting enough to warrant talking about. This will make them curious, and it will also make them a little nurturing, which is where you can snag them. This is known as flipping the script, and it can be a very effective technique when used selectively.

Suppose you have to speak about facts and statistics. Ramble about as many as you can to be a bit overwhelming. At this time, you need to show interest in their part but establish that if you are to go along with whatever they are suggesting, you will have your own rules. Depending on the state you are currently in, this may be enough for them to "decide" to complete the task in question or give in to your suggestion because it is easier than going along with your stipulations.

Another way to manipulate a person is to change the modulation of your voice. If you are trying to intimidate a person, you will want to be loud. If you are seeking sympathy, lose the loud tone for a depressed, defeated tone instead. Most people are inclined to help a person who is feeling down. Now that you have their sympathy, ask for something. Suggest what you want in a way that seems impossible to achieve. Wait for their response, which should be some variation of, "I want to help you." Some people will want to offer up advice as a way to soothe you. To avoid losing control of the situation, you will need to consider their advice and find that their logic is faulty to ensure things remain under your control.

Manipulation Tools for Specific Situations

A key to pulling off any form of manipulation is to see what drives the person you are dealing with. For example, is it a religion? If so, you would need to focus on their devotion and find a creative way to get your point across using their religion. It is a good way to reinforce their opinion of themselves, most likely that they are godly and intelligent. As long as you focus on their utopian visions and aspirations, you will find this technique to be very effective.

Another tool that is useful from time to time is sarcasm. It allows you to express your discontent with someone while maintaining a doorway out as if you were just joking. However, be cautious, as sarcasm can be insulting and hurtful if misused. After you have been given a chance to vent, turn it around to the sarcastic "what if." This allows the person to hear your opinion, and it comes across like you are just defeated. Now they can save you. When they offer their help, humbly tell them it is not their responsibility, but that you need their support. It is helpful to add, "What would I do without you?"

You must keep in mind that you are being manipulated every day. The news, media, and those in power all deploy tactics to keep your attention or threaten your security for non-compliance. You are bombarded with images and stories that tug at your heart, anger your soul, and move you either into action or into seclusion. Just seeing how easily you can have the same effect on a person will allow you to recognize when it is being done to you. Awareness is life-changing. At this moment, you realize you have tried conventional methods of persuasion, being genuine and truly caring. Formerly, you got nothing in return, but you will from now on.

Be Creative

You will need to focus on your creativity for these manipulative tactics. Your goal is to transform someone's reality and alter their beliefs. Every situation is different, which means you will need to be creative and think on your feet. You must observe the cues a person is giving you. You must observe their reactions to you and others, as these can be very telling. Sometimes, just watching your target interact with others can give you more insight into how to manipulate them.

For example, if you see how a coworker reacted to a customer, you can use that to make them feel justified by adding your opinion to explain how they reacted. They will repeat the excuse you provided them. This can be used against them. If you are trying to get them to do something for you, just point out how they overreacted to that customer, which should shame them into following your suggestion. They should act in the way you suggest to minimize their past actions.

Sometimes all you have to do is create an image. Think of a spin on something that would suggest the person you are dealing with is a victim. Encourage them to see how others have been unappreciative and lazy compared to them. Suggest a course of action and reap the benefits.

If you are dying to know what someone feels about a situation, for example, in politics or religion, make up a story that you read on the internet that is sure to rile them up. Sit back, watch their reaction, and start agreeing with them. Be sure to add your perspective to draw them out of the shocking story into your plan. You might just be harvesting information to keep a profile on someone who is a threat to your vision of success. Building your profile, you will be able to understand their weakness in most situations.

Take Your Time

You can be sure to pay special attention to their strengths and find ways to undermine them. Don't proceed it so far as to where others observing can figure out what your intentions are, and instead always take the high road in public so that at the end of the day, most people will only ever see the public face you decide to show them.

Keep in mind that everyone just wants to be happy, which means they seek to understand and support people around them. They think it is rare for someone to take an interest in them without wanting something in return. This is where patience becomes your ally. You cannot act like someone has to be available at a moment's notice. Anyone can figure out that you have selfish motives if you display this impatient tendency. It might be killing you to lie in wait for the perfect opportunity, but it would kill you more to be seen as a fake. So, wait. Even encourage them to ask others about the situation. Once you have proven that you are only worried about them or want to see them succeed, then you can wiggle into their mind with subtle manipulation.

While playing on the heartstrings of another, you weaken their response. You cannot simply ignore that they might say no to your request or idea. You have to come across as genuine in trying to help or care about them. Find a way to make their "no" seem unreasonable without saying it directly. You will have to point out that if someone else acted as they did, they would see it as being stubborn or pig-headed with their closed mind. Let them know that the brain has a chemical response to doing something new and brave. Tell them that the brain lights up like a Christmas tree when changes are occurring.

The bottom line is that there is potential for manipulation. It is a creative process. It takes a little planning and observing, but if mastered, it can change your life. You will feel powerful every day. You will start to see every rejection as a canvas. It is your starting point. A word for word or gesture-by-gesture guarantee that you are in control.

Self-preservation is an important aspect of manipulation. You do not want to be perceived as a manipulator. You want to be known as the neutral person who sees all sides but uses logic to decide why your decision is more valid. Maintain a solid reputation for being thoughtful, and people will seek your opinion often. This is an advantage from the start. In a new group of people, you can find a way to agree with everyone and make a statement that you were always taught to show respect and think of all sides before making a decision.

Chapter 49. Psychological Manipulation

Covert psychological manipulation is essential to the art of dark psychology. Many of the methods utilized with dark psychology will utilize this type of emotional manipulation, whether in part or entirely. As you learn a bit more about the world of dark psychology and its various symptoms, you will soon begin to see the signs of CPM. This is why it is so crucial to comprehend what CPM is precisely so that you can watch out for it in your daily life.

Covert psychological manipulation, or CPM, will attempt by a single person to attempt and influence the feelings and ideas of the other person in a manner that is considered deceptive and undiscovered by the one who is being manipulated. Being able to break down each of the words in CPM is very important to help you understand this subject's structures. Covert refers to the way that a manipulator can conceal their intentions. They wish to have the ability to hide the true nature of all their actions. Remember that not all types of influence and psychological manipulation will be classified as hidden. The victims of the concealed type, though, will usually not realize they are being controlled and will not have the ability to comprehend the way the manipulation is performed. Sometimes, they are not even able to look and determine the motivation of their manipulator.

This is why CPM is such a stealth bomber in the world of dark psychology. Its point is to prevent detection and defense up until it is far too late for the victim. The psychological side of the manipulator is going to be the specific focus of that manipulator. Other kinds of manipulation might include things like the other person's self-discipline, beliefs, and habits. Numerous manipulators will concentrate on this area of impact as they know that the other person's feelings are essential to the other elements of their character. Being able to manipulate the feelings of the other individual is essential. If a person has emotional control over the other individual, they will have complete control over them. The last piece of CPM is manipulation. It is typically thought that manipulation and impact are the same things. This is not true, though. Manipulation refers to the surprise and underhand process of influence outside the awareness of the one who is being controlled.

The objective behind this compared to someone who has the intent to influence can be a huge difference. They will enter into this with an influencer with the idea of "I wish to assist you in deciding that benefits you." With the manipulator, they have the thoughts of "I want to control you to supply advantage to myself secretly." As you can see, both of these are quite a bit different, so comprehending the objective behind any offered behavior is going to be a big part of choosing whether the scenario is hidden psychological manipulation or not.

Manipulative Circumstances

There are four primary situations in which CPM can take place. These consist of the household, romantic, individual, and professional parts of your life. Among the most typical kinds of CPM is romantic, and it can sometimes be the deadliest. There are some less obvious kinds of CPM that you can discover anywhere, and because they are less typical, they can often be the most unsafe. A good example of CPM is a managing romantic partner. If a woman remains in a relationship and her partner is trying to control her, she will be revolted by what is going on as soon as she figures it out. She might wish to discover a way to leave the circumstance. Thus, many times the controlling partner is going to exercise their impact as covertly as possible. They don't desire their partner to understand they are being managed, or the victim leaves, and there is nobody delegated control. If the manipulator achieves success, their spouse or sweetheart will continue to be a psychological manipulation victim. They might have difficulty recognizing that it is going on. This permits the manipulator to keep the control that they want with no danger of being found and losing the other person for good.

This can likewise occur with a buddy who would use CPM to get the outcomes they want when they have a relationship with another individual. In this group, one of the common types of manipulators will be covertly induced feelings of obligation, compassion, and guilt in a pal. The friend is being controlled in this way without understanding that they are being influenced. They may understand that they are acting differently to that buddy; however, they won't have the ability to explain why and how. You will discover that the expert part of your life can be another place for hidden emotional manipulators. Many people have worked for an employer or another person who had authority, who seems to set off some unidentified sensations of duty, worry, and regret in them.

Individuals who are manipulated in this manner might never identify why these feelings exist or where they come from, and in the world of CPM, the family can be the most troublesome. A proficient manipulator can discover a victim, even within their household, and the amount of influence they exercise can be dangerous. This is because the manipulator and the victim will have a very deep connection together. After all, they are related. When blood relations are included, the amount of influence and control can increase a fair bit. These family circumstances are so matched to utilizing CPM because most people currently feel a social responsibility to help their own family. They are willing to go a little more to guarantee the requirements of their family are addressed. Because of this predisposition, covert psychological manipulative practices will give you a malleable victim.

The (Bad) Love Giver

This consists of the severe, unforeseen, and robust expression of positive feelings towards a victim. It may, in the beginning, seem counterintuitive. Why do they behave so intensively positive at first if that individual is attempting to damage them? Since it matches its functions—that's why! This produces a deep sense of self-confidence, affection, and appreciation from a specific victim to their manipulator, and this is the principle behind love providing. Based on the manipulator's analysis, the degree to which enjoy providing is utilized, and the people on whom it is pre-owned forms the basis. A lonely, helpless victim who seeks help and consolation is most likely to be more love-bombed by the manipulator because the manipulator will know the victim will be more responsive to it. The more the victim is grounded, the less effort the manipulator will have to put into positivity. The meaning of the love giving technique offers two essential lessons on Emotional Manipulation. Firstly, the covert nature of Emotional Manipulation is well shown. Envision is trying to comprehend that love giving is an unfortunate thing. "Well, this guy was very sweet to me, and he made me feel very good." The red flags or warning signs of abuse are unlikely to be raised by such a declaration. This is a textbook example of how something can be provided as something favorable but has a negative result. The second general lesson pertinent to Emotional Manipulation that can be learned from love offering is how emotional manipulation is formed to suit every unique circumstance. Experienced manipulators have discreetly tested and learned from lots of encounters in their history. In any given scenario, you understand the strength and timing of each Emotional Manipulation strategy.

What is Empathy

Empathy is the capability to put yourself in another person's shoes and consider their emotions and sensations. An empath is an individual who can interact with others on several levels to experience their emotional wellness with precision. How empaths have this capacity has yet to be comprehended to many individuals, but numerous believe it is innate and transmitted through our DNA. As for how it runs, everything in deep space resonates with electrical energy; empaths are believed to can perceiving the shifts in the electrical energy around them. Empaths are usually considered compassionate, loving, sensitive to other individuals' feelings, and sympathetic. Would you be astonished to learn there's a dark side to being an empath? The essence of compassion itself makes sure that lots of are helped and supported by an empath. It likewise means empaths can see the world a lot more than we do, and as such, issues can happen in various areas of their lives. The dark side of empaths is that their sensations can't be managed. You might believe they are well versed in emotions, but the truth is they are in a constant fight to keep them under control. Sometimes, it can bring them down to depression since they so strongly feel others' feelings, specifically others' grief. They discover it difficult to separate their feelings and others and find other empaths to reveal their sensations. Empaths can accommodate a large amount of information from their sensitivity to electrical energy when managing negative energy resulting in fatigue. This can puzzle and exhaust them badly while attempting to understand everything. They are particularly prone to negative energy, as it greatly upsets them. They will easily end up being tired when all they can feel is negative energy. They are used by the less scrupulous amongst us because empaths are compassionate individuals who always believe in people's good nature. Empaths are generous and kind; they will attract only those who take and never return.

An empath can quickly fall under deep anxiety when they discover they have been conned. Because empathy tends to give to others instead of getting, it is most likely that they overlook their wellness, including their bodies and minds. This is the dark side all frequently since it's all too easy to forget how to appreciate them because of the pressure of what they feel. They keep back a little piece of their heart just if they're wounded in the future.

They can't permit themselves to fall deeply in love because they are terrified of all that love. After all, it could be a lot for them to manage.

Empaths are selfless people who are day-to-day bombarded with sensory info, so they typically feel like they carry a heavy load.

Chapter 50. Turning the Tables

Whether you're the victim or the one who is doing the manipulating, there's one thing that's for certain. Manipulation is abusive, and no one, especially not the victim, deserves to be subjected to that kind of treatment. Since most manipulators are unlikely to see the error of their ways or want to become a better person, it is up to the victim to do what they can to keep themselves as safe as possible. Cutting all ties with the manipulator will not always be immediate or easy; some relationships take time before you can sever the bonds and walk away for good. In the meantime, what do you need to do to protect yourself from being taken advantage of in that way? Perhaps turn the tables and deflect the manipulator's techniques can onto them.

Manipulation is an emotional and mental game of cat and mouse, but just because you may be the mouse in the scenario, it doesn't mean you're completely at their mercy. The savvy mouse with a few useful strategies up their sleeve can flip things around and take the power dynamic away from the manipulator. Just when the manipulator thinks they have you within their grasp, turn the tables on them and let them know you're not going to tolerate whatever it is they're trying to do to you. It's time to gain payback on the manipulator and let them know you're not as easily fooled as they might think.

Shut down the manipulator's attempts by standing up for your fundamental rights. Among the fundamental human rights that we are all entitled to include the right to be respected, the right to say no without having to feel guilty about it, the right to express your opinions and your feelings, and the right to protect yourself when you feel you might be threatened emotionally, physically or mentally among other things. These basic rights are what you need to remember when fighting back against manipulation because we so often tend to forget when we let others pressure us and play on our emotions to get their way. We forget that we have a right to protect our hearts, minds, and bodies from the people who would trample all over us if given a chance. Make these rights part of the boundaries that you set in your dealings with others, and strengthen your defenses against the manipulator using the following techniques:

Say No, Thank You - Do not feel guilty if you have to say no to the manipulator. They're trying to take advantage of you, and you are well within your rights to say no to them. They do not have any rights to pressure you into deciding or taking action with something you're not comfortable with, and when you firmly say no, remember that you don't owe them an explanation. You can make your own decisions, your own choices, and if you choose to say no, go right ahead. Some manipulators will still attempt to push the boundaries and try to persist despite you telling them no, and you're going to have to be firm and stand your ground. Make it politely but firmly clear that you're not going to change your mind, and you would appreciate it if they could respect your decision. Say no, thank you, and end the conversation there and then.

Saying No to Buy Time - If you have ever been pressured into deciding on the spot without having enough time to think things over, you'll be familiar with that uncomfortable, dissatisfied sensation that often follows when you're not quite sure what you agreed to or whether you've made the right choice. This is the manipulator's favorite tactic to force you into complying with their schedule, and they'll hold you to your agreement. Try to back out of it, and they'll immediately lash out at you, painting you as the "bad guy" because you're backing out on your word. The most effective tactic to stem off this unwanted pressure is to say no to buy yourself some time repeatedly. Tell them firmly that you need time to think things over, and you don't appreciate being put on the spot like that. If they try to make you feel guilty by pretending to be upset or angered at your resistance, let them know you're sorry they feel that way, but you are still sticking to your answer, and you need time to think things over. When they try to bully or intimidate you, once again firmly but politely tell them that you don't appreciate being intimidated into making a decision. They need to respect your need to take some time. At the first sign that you might be onto what they're trying to do, the manipulator would usually retreat.

Avoid Them - The most straightforward way to stop manipulators is to avoid them in the first place. Of course, this is often easier said than done since sometimes these manipulators exist within your own immediate family. Since they're family, it can be hard to sever all ties with them completely, so the best thing you can do is avoid them. Do everything that you can to stay away from them where possible. During those few moments where they're unavoidable, such as family gatherings, for example, minimize your contact with them by surrounding yourself and keeping busy with the other non-toxic family members. They might not be entirely avoidable (unless you were to leave the company for a better job), so the best thing you can do is once again minimize the contact you have with them. Communicate through emails to avoid interacting with them directly, and when you do need to, try to get another colleague to come along with you as a witness of sorts. This leaves the manipulator with little chance of twisting their story or denying what they said.

Fire Back at Them with Questions - If there is one thing that manipulators avoid, it is having others discover what they're really up to. The minute you start firing back at them with probing questions each time they try to force you into meeting an unreasonable demand, flip it around back on them and probe them with questions they'll be reluctant to answer. Since their requests or statements will be unreasonable most of the time, it is an opportunity for you to let them know that you're fully aware of what they're trying to do. Put them on the spot by asking questions that include whether they believe this request is fair or reasonable and how this arrangement will benefit the two of you mutually. These questions will make them uncomfortable, and they won't answer them without revealing themselves. When they're dismissive of your questions, be firmer and keep pressing the issue, making it clear you expect them to answer. An effective way to get them to back off and stop putting so much pressure on you.

There's so much to remember and be mindful of in your dealings with the manipulator. However, there is one reminder that you shouldn't forget, and that is never to blame yourself or feel guilty that you were a victim. Making you feel that way is exactly what they want, but don't let them get inside your head. They're deceptive and conniving, willing to do many things that most people would not, and anyone could have easily become a victim just as much as you were. Just because they picked on you, it doesn't mean that there is anything wrong with you. We all have our strengths and weaknesses; it's part of the dynamic that makes us human. Blaming yourself is playing right into their hands, and if you are beating yourself up over it, don't do it.

Effectively Dealing with the Silent Treatment

Here's something you need to know about manipulators who use the silent treatment. They're emotionally stunted people who resort to this childish approach over choosing to have a mature conversation to resolve any kind of problem. They may look like adults, but their behavior reflects a childish, underlying personality beneath it. They're so used to getting what they want that they kick up a fuss when things don't go their way. Pretty much like what a child would do. Besides ignoring them and refusing to play their game (meaning groveling and begging for their forgiveness the way that they are hoping you would), here's what you can do to stomp on the manipulator's attempts at trying to abuse you with the silent treatment emotionally:

Point Out Their Behavior - They're not going to be used to people calling them out on their bad behavior, since most of the time, the general reaction that tends to follow the silent treatment is the victim continuously trying to reach out to them, asking them what's wrong and what they can do to make things better. Manipulators want to feel in control, and very rarely are they going to encounter someone who pushes back by saying, "I know what you're trying to do, and it's not going to work with me." Whenever they revert to the silent treatment to get you to submit, do the exact opposite. Let them know that you're not going to tolerate being emotionally abused with the silent treatment this way, and when they're ready to have a proper conversation about it, they can come and talk to you. If they choose to keep sulking and ignoring you, let them be, it is not your responsibility to try and fix a situation caused by their bad behavior. Eventually, which is often when they need you, they'll come around, and that's when you move onto the point below.

Discuss Their Behavior - Once they're done throwing their little temper tantrum and start behaving like an adult again, have a discussion with them about what happened. They'll do everything that they can to avoid the subject, but be persistent and let them know that you're not going just to sweep this under the rug. Talk to them about how abusive you through their behavior was (this will put them on the alert, worried about being discovered again), and how you see this affecting your relationship with them. They will try to turn things around and make it out to be your fault that they behaved this way because you were the one who angered them or upset them in the first place. When they do, shut them down and say while you do feel sorry that they felt that way, it was still no way to treat you when they could have chosen other ways of dealing with the issue. Make it clear that regardless of how they felt, silent treatment abuse was never the right approach to take. The manipulator will wake up when they realize that their maneuvers do not as easily fool you as they initially believed.

Don't Resort to Tit for Tat - Dealing with manipulators can be unbelievably frustrating. On several occasions, you may be tempted to give them a taste of their own medicine, use the same approach they are taking with you, and treat them the same way.

Chapter 51. Stages of a Relationship with a Covert Narcissist

A relationship with a narcissist doesn't have the natural flow and is characterized by stages absent in healthy relationships. The natural balance of giving and take is disrupted. Relationships with such individuals start with infatuation and idealization, only to end devaluation, rejection, and complete discard of narcissist's partner. In psychological and therapeutic practice, there are three main stages of a relationship with a narcissist: the idealization phase, devaluation, and discarding.

Idealization

During the idealization stage, the narcissist earns their target's trust by showing them affection, appreciation, praise, and adoration. They lift the other person, cheer for them, offer unlimited support, a shoulder to cry on, act as a friend in need, and a perfect lover who just knows how to make things right. This is called love bombing, and during this phase, narcissists aim to recreate the ideal relationship and earn the trust and loyalty of their targets.

Covert narcissists have a fluid identity that allows them to transform like a chameleon and adapt to any person they are to gain their respect and trust. They are perceptive, analytical and will investigate the target carefully to create the perfect scenario that gives them the green light to the phase of a relationship we will soon talk in the text. It is in a narcissist's interest to be liked, and so they create the persona that is likable as the only thing they care for is admiration. This first stage is about their target's identity to get the admiration they believe they deserve. The behavior almost resembles a teenager who desperately wants to fit in with a group of popular people, just to be popular and liked themselves. Emotional detachment and infertility allow them to reflect on the person they are with, quickly attaching their needs and wants to the other person—they are giving because they know it will be appreciated and make them likable. Needing acceptance and admiration from you, a narcissist will do anything to get it and go about it so smoothly that you will hardly notice they are mirroring who you are. In other words, they will do it covertly.

The love bombing is based on acts and words of adoration that are excessive and "too good to be true." The survivors of narcissistic abuse often say that the relationship with covert was like heaven in the beginning. "It was perfect." "It felt like a fairy tale." "Our relationship was ideal." "I thought I finally found someone who gets me." "They made me feel special." "They seemed like the person I have been waiting for all my life." "I thought I have finally found my soulmate." "We were the best couple." "We had so much in common." "Back then, I felt so lucky I found them." They identify how to target your weaknesses and use them to manipulate you, at this stage by earning your trust by building you up in those areas you feel insecure about. When love bombing, they will realize you and the relationship, make you feel very special and worthy of love, only to make you feel opposite at the two stages of the relationship.

It is very common for survivors of narcissistic abuse to say that they were very impressed by their covert having the same interests, lifestyle, and hobbies. A narcissist does detailed research on their targets and will spend time learning about and absorbing their interests, tastes, likes, and dislikes. While there is a natural incarnation, people have to be open to learning about interest people they like to have. In the light of a narcissistic personality disorder, this is not a result of curiosity, but a lack of identity and the desire to be so desperately liked and worshiped. Many love bomb others by taking care of their needs, giving them gifts, compliments, praise, taking them places, or being overly helpful even when there is no real help needed. This behavior has a certain level of pushiness, but because it seems genuine, the person who is being love-bombed perceives the narcissist as the nice person who just wants to love and care for them. Many of their former partners say they felt unexplainably uncomfortable for receiving so much attention and needing to return the affection or favors but couldn't recognize it as a red flag back then.

Ultimately, in the love-bombing stage of a relationship, the narcissist treats the other person as they were the same. Although it is never a conscious process in their mind, the people they are targeting are seen as an extension of themselves. In the beginning, this person is the extension of their praise-needy, self-important, "ideal" side of the personality, a boost to their ego that shows how valuable they are. The other person is a "replica" of himself or herself. They are a replica of that person, their interests, thoughts, and feelings. This process is called mirroring or projecting the aspects of self to the other person. However, it is a two-way street. At this first stage, a narcissist's target will feel very special, beautiful, respected for their talents, important or praiseworthy—which is exactly what narcissists think about themselves.

Everything they do, they need to be returned and in double or triple doses. If they do a lot of helpful things for you in the beginning stages of a relationship, rest assured they will require you to do little or big favors for them and make you feel guilty when you are not able to put a pause on your life and deliver what they need when they need it. The idealization phase is a base a narcissist builds to create a safe zone where they can be admired while gradually revealing their true selves as the relationship progresses. The paradox of this disorder is that the narcissist knows that connecting with other people is open, empathetic, and interested in the other person. Therefore, they use it to create an environment where they can be who they are—the empathetic, closed-off person who doesn't care about the other. The final goal is to make the target comfortable enough to refocus the relationship towards themselves gradually.

This stage, just like the other two, is as present in work and family environment as much as it in love relationships and friendships. For instance, covert narcissists are often praised and respected members of society, many of which are very involved with charity work or are in important positions. They care about their status and what others think of them, so naturally; many will opt for careers that allow them to be in the spotlight in one way or another. Covert colleagues and bosses will be the first ones to hop in to help you with tasks, help you get things done, and even take on your part of the job on themselves. This, however, lasts only during the first stage, when you get to know them. They appear agreeable, kind, generous, charismatic and everyone seems to love them. Remember, no matter what place they take in your life, there are always three stages of a relationship with the present. Don't be surprised that once the appreciation bombing phase is over, you get criticized, unappreciated for things you were once praised for, or if they take the credit for your ideas or give it to someone else. They want your full trust and give you praise and help whenever you need and don't need it, only to twist the reality and diminish your ambition, work drive, and health.

Devaluation

At this stage, little things they adored about you suddenly become flaws and something you are ashamed of. Once the relationship is established, and the covert has created a haven by gaining your loyalty and trust, they gradually start expressing their dissatisfaction with the relationship and you. Because they have first carefully analyzed your weaknesses and built you up, they will start using your fears and insecurities against you. Although never or rarely openly, they slowly diminish their target's self-confidence by planting the seeds of self-doubt, fear, and even self-hate in them. This happens periodically. It is hard to pinpoint and even harder to understand because it is done subtly and entwined with sporadic acts of love and kindness, especially at the beginning of this stage.

The trouble here is that a covert narcissist devalues their partners subtly and appears completely innocent in the process. Most often than not, this devaluation manifests in little things they don't do for you rather the things they say directly and openly, especially at the beginning of this stage. Because it is a covert narcissist we are talking about, this phase can revolve simply around them not acknowledging your needs, wants, and desires, showing less and less interest in your life and you as a person. They will not shout, be cruel in obvious ways, yell or say mean things. Instead, they will damage your self-esteem in little, subtle ways, turning to more serious manipulation techniques. Devaluation can go from little things like not replying to text messages, not calling when agreed upon, or prioritizing other people or things to give silent treatments, criticizing, nitpicking, or blaming others.

The reason for devolution is to make them feel better about themselves because that is the level of emotional maturity the narcissist operates on.

This can manifest as falling from the number one worker to the average one, comparing or praising other employees who put in even less effort than you do. At the beginning of his career at the company, Richard was his boss's favorite employee, always prized for his ambition, problem-solving skills, and efficiency. It was his dream job, so he tried his best to put all his enthusiasm into it. However, as time went on, he could hear his boss complaining about the little mistakes he made in the prospects, the tidiness of his office, or his time-management. These were nothing new, but unlike before, where such tiny mistakes weren't recognized as major, which they are not, were now seen as Richard's lack of professionalism and capability to meet required criteria. He did extra hours and took on more responsibilities than he should prove his dedication, only for his boss to blame it on him for not finishing even more.

Chapter 52. Covert Emotional Manipulation Methods

In a manipulation method that is entirely based upon triggering emotions, it should come as no surprise that at the end of the day, there are nearly endless ways that you can go about manipulating the emotions of others. We will take a look at five different methods that can be used to toy with other people's emotions, allowing you to understand that you will need to use them in any way that may work best for you. We will be going over the use of fear, obligation, and guilt to keep people under your thumb with emotional blackmail. We will look at how you can play the victim, invalidate your target, gaslight, and use a love bombing method and devaluing. These will create emotions within the other person you can use to get exactly what you want or need to see.

Emotional Blackmail

Emotional blackmail is a common way that people can be controlled. When you do this, you are using the threat of either fear, obligation, or guilt to try to get everyone around you in line. Essentially, you will be relying on the fact that fear, obligation, and guilt are all incredible motivators. They can be used to trigger that motivation to make the negative emotions end through, making it a point to trigger them by failing to do what you wanted in the first place. Each of these works in their ways, but at the end of the day, they require you to have some sort of leverage over the other person that can directly be used to control them. That leverage will be what you use to trigger one of these responses.

Fear

When you are using fear, you need to have a credible way to make the other person feel afraid. You may use the fear of losing you. For example, you can threaten to break up with someone. You may use the fear of some sort of punishment or abuse. You may use the fear of just about anything to get someone moving and in line.

Obligation

This is most commonly used in relationships or amongst families. When you attempt to use an obligation to try to get someone working toward what you want them to do, you somehow make what you want them to do an obligation or responsibility of theirs, so they feel like they have no choice but to do so. Frequently, you see this in relationships in ways such as saying, "But you owe me after everything that I did for you!" This is meant to make the other person feel like they do have no choice in the matter—if they do not live up to your expectations, they are left feeling guilty and, therefore, responsible for what has happened or are left feeling like it is otherwise all their fault. Still, either way, it is a struggle for them.

Guilt

Finally, when you use guilt as a weapon, you are frequently telling the other person that it is their fault that things did not work out. You may say that you are now in a very tight or bad spot because of their inaction in doing something, or you may try to make it the other person's fault when something goes wrong. For example, if you need money for something, you could guilt the other person into paying for it by letting them know how badly you need it, but you cannot afford it. You may have been able to afford it just fine—but you will never let the other person know that. You may also try to put down the guilt in other contexts as well—perhaps you remind the other person that they are responsible for their children's safety, so they owe it to their children to buy the most expensive car they are approved for, even if it is going to be pushing their budget a bit more than they are comfortable doing. The guilt they would feel at not buying that car with more safety features is enough to push them toward making it a point to buy the other car instead, despite not wanting to initially.

Playing the Victim

Another common way to emotionally manipulate other people is to play the victim role. When you switch yourself into the victim role, you are essentially making it a point to make the other person feel guilty for whatever they have done. For example, you may be in a situation in which you have messed up somehow. Maybe you forgot to pay a bill, and your partner is now angry about the addition of a fee that would otherwise not have to be paid due to the bill being late at this point. You know that you are at fault, but do you want to take the fall and the blame? Most people would prefer to avoid that blame altogether, so what you have to do is figure out how to redirect somehow. You need to be no longer seen as the perpetrator or the one at fault, but rather to be seen as the victim of some sort of unfortunate circumstance.

When you can shift the attention in that way, you can then take back control. You can no longer be the one at fault, but rather the one who was victimized instead. Perhaps you do this by pointing out how you had tried to pay the bill and that you thought the bill was paid, so it must be a banking error. Maybe you bring up how, on the day that it was due to be paid, something extreme happened that prevented you from paying for said bill. Maybe you even try to reverse the situation to make your partner the one at fault instead.

When you reverse the situation, your partner is the one at fault. This is known as DARVO—Deny, attack, and reverse victim and offender. When you follow these steps, you can make sure that you remain the one that is pitied or seen as the victim in the situation, which then allows you to defend yourself.

Deny: you start by denying the claim somehow. You say that you did not forget what had happened, or you say that you did not avoid paying the bill for some reason. You are going to refute whatever claim has been thrown at you. You could very easily substitute not paying a bill for claims of abuse, for example, or any other fault, whether you have done it or not. Denying it is the first step in the process.

Attack: now, you need to shift the burden onto the other person. You may say that your partner was the one that was responsible for those bills, or you claim that your partner was the one that was abusive or toxic toward you instead. The task here is to put your partner or whoever you are talking to on the defensive—you want them to suddenly feel like they have to refute your claim instead of asserting their own, which allows you to remain shielded.

Reverse victim and offender: finally, in this last stage, you are sort of rewriting the narrative—you are making it clear that you did not cause the problem, but rather, you are the one that is now having to pay more in fees due to the other person's incompetency or whatever else you are blaming. At this point, you want to assert that the other person is the offender and that you are the victim in this particular situation. If you played your cards right, the other person would be so busy trying to prove that they are not, in fact, the ones at fault that they will not realize what you have done.

Invalidation

Another common method to mess with the emotions of someone else is to use invalidation. When you are doing this, you make the other person feel like they are at fault for some reason. You are making them feel like they cannot trust themselves, and then you are preying on that doubt. One such form of this will be gaslighting, which we will be looking at shortly.

When you are using invalidation, you are essentially always saying things to use plausible deniability when they do try to blame you or call you out for the way you are treating them or acting. For example, imagine that you hear someone trying to manipulate say that they have just done something good eventually. Perhaps they are happy about the job that they just got hired for. If you want to make them feel invalidated, you would then shrug it off and mention how you did something better. If they try to tell you that you are hurtful, you can deny this and say that you were just sharing your successes.

You can also invalidate people by constantly pointing out why they are wrong, how they are wrong, and why they should change up what they say or why they are saying it. You can also make snide jokes and sarcastic comments. When they say something about what you have said hurting their feelings, you can then deny it all together—you simply tell them that they are too sensitive and not to be so willing to be hurt over something that was not meant to be taken that way in the first place. When you do this, reminding the other person that you did not do anything that was intended to be hurtful, you make them feel wrong and invalidated. They are stuck, feeling like they cannot defend themselves without looking petty or too sensitive.

Gaslighting

Gaslighting is a very specific form of invalidation. When you are using gaslighting, you are intentionally trying to make the other person doubt their perceptions around them. They may tell you that you did something, and you deny it, saying they are wrong. They may eventually believe the narrative that you are trying to push, and they made a mistake somewhere along the line, and that they are entirely wrong.

Usually, you start small—you correct them about where things came from or where you found something. This does not have to be significant—it just has to plant the seed that they are mistaken regularly. Slowly, you will up the stakes—you will start to remind them that they were wrong about when they did something or if something happened in the first place. Over time, you will eventually plant the idea that they cannot get what is going on around them right. They will stop questioning you when you suggest something and instead look at how they are always wrong. They will not trust themselves, which means that you would be able to lie to their faces about something that just happened practically, and they would take your narrative over their own.

Chapter 53. Knowing Yourself

The key to being able to avoid manipulation is to know yourself. You will not be able to know yourself unless you experience failure in the world. Most people experience enough failure when they become adults to know how they deal with it and learn how to keep going. If you don't know yourself, you will repeatedly use people who don't care a lick about you. They are just more focused on their own goals. When you know yourself, you can know other people better. You will be able to tap into that voice that tells you this is not worth it, that you are being manipulated. If you know yourself, you are less vulnerable to deceit and lies.

This is because people are very self-repressed, and they don't learn about themselves. By not learning about yourself, you are opening yourself up to the worst of interactions and relationships. Relationships are shallower when you are like this. They lack depth and concentration. When you know yourself, you can analyze what is happening to you and other people. When you know yourself, you can protect yourself.

Analyzing people involves keeping knowledge of how we see the world and how we move to observe others. This is why knowing yourself is so important. It takes a lot of effort to understand how other people see you globally, cueing you into their behavior. One way to start this is to look at the Enneagram of personality and see what line up mostly with you. This can tell you about the drives you have in your personality that you might not even realize. When you are trying to find out what type of personality you are, you are engaging in a self-reflexive behavior that will have you become a better person. It will help you to know yourself, and your intuition will be increased as a part of this.

Another way to know oneself is to participate in the art of watching or listening to art. A movie can tell us the story of a world. It is a way by which we understand the world. Every time you speak, you tell a story, either in words or as you say them. This can help you realize your strengths and weaknesses.

When you are reading a great novel, you become immersed in that book, and you get to share a little bit of the writers' world in your imagination. The writer and reader create a continuum, wherein the writer's consciousness is being followed directly by another person. They say that literature is the art that most people can escape their world and get into another person's consciousness. You start to learn the characters, and you start to predict what they are in to do. Characters in the story can be compared to people you know in real life, and the book can give your ideas of how to behave and change the world through your actions. As you get into the story, you are experiencing a ride that is the most positive way of expressing ourselves. This is art. Art is a mysterious way that we participate in the world. Art has the power to incite wars and peace. It is a way to disturb people deeply, and you can keep them happy and calm. Art (we are talking here about the art with a big A, as to mean every category of art, from dance to film to sculpture) is a way that we are in the world that lets us start a feedback loop with the world, and it becomes a source of communication with the world and with others. This is a way that we can find solace and express ourselves to the world.

Art is also a way that we immortalize ourselves. Each human is subject to the lifespan that they are given on this planet, and when you realize when your life is going to end eventually, you start to realize that the world will move on without you. This means that you might be forgotten, at least according to our primal fear. So, we try to do things to counteract this. The most primal and animal way is to have children because then you'll live on in the world through the people who you have created to carry out their own goals and happiness in the world.

Having children is a simple way that people leave a legacy, and it is the ultimate creative act in the world. All other forms of art are underneath this one. That is because art comes from consciousness. That is why humans are not art. We are conscious, we have the power of gods, and when we create another person, we use our power as gods. We are also using the power of gods when we create art, but it is slightly lesser.

Art is a way that you can analyze yourself to deeper levels. Remember the Rorschach test, a way of analyzing people where we look at blobs of ink of paper and say whatever comes to mind first? Well, all art is sort of like that, as a creator and as a viewer. As a creator, when you are creating art, you are creating the ink blob. Sometimes it is very clear what the artist is talking about. When you look at a Norman Rockwell painting, you understand the scene that he has created because he is putting you right there in a scenario that you can recognize and understand. The artist often puts you in a place where you can't understand because you aren't meant to. This kind of art can help us explore what it feels like for other people to experience tarts o fat world's tarts. Abstract art is not about telling you things but rather gets you to think. Many people say that literature is how you can most experience another persons' consciousness, out of all of the art forms. Think about the best book you ever read. You were so into it that you couldn't put it down, and when you read it, you were nowhere else except in the world created by the writer. You were a citizen in his world, and there was nothing to do except to be there in the story and experience whatever was going on.

When you do this, you are experiencing a human mode called flow. Flow is when you are just in the moment, when you are only experiencing something that you are doing, like meditating, playing the piano, running, driving, or something else. It is a state of focus and a state of creativity.

To know yourself, you have to be able to experience the extremes of life. You must have been able to understand the anger and express it. You must know when you feel angry and understand what that feels like to you. You must be able to experience joy at the highest level, for this is an extreme human feat. You must be able to take deep pain and failure and also accept the beauty in life. You must immerse yourself in the book and then pay some bills that you have lying around, which is just menial work that you have to do. You have to deal with all sorts of things that are big and small, and none is less important. It might seem that the small stuff is less important, and in many ways, it is, but the details are something that you can be vigilant with, and they are ways for you to let yourself experience each part of life.

The number-one way to do this concretely every day and learn about you is journaling. You can journal every day but never write the same thing twice. Journaling doesn't have to be your homework. It can be fun, it can be creative, and it can be a way to release yourself from the shackles of what binds you.

When you write about yourself, you are looking at yourself through the lens of another person, or at least not through your own. By writing about yourself, you are also able to tell your story. Let's talk about both of these aspects of writing.

When you write about yourself, you get to look at yourself through your own eyes, but more objectively. Or at least, that's the hope. When you open up the journal and start writing about yourself, and it is all negative stuff, you should tell yourself that you have a problem there. When you are writing about yourself, try to be as subjective as possible. When you find that you cannot do this, it might mean that you are too much up in your head.

You see, we start to develop ideas and concepts about ourselves that may or may not be true. Even if they are true, they might not be so good to dwell on. Many people have problems with intrusive thoughts or automatic negative thoughts. If you are one of these people, just take your writing and see if you notice these thoughts in writing, and see if you can stop yourself and try to write out thoughts that are kinder and more accurate. By talking about ourselves more objectively, we can get more in touch with ourselves regarding our real desires, goals, and ways of living. When we are in our heads, we don't get a really good idea of our perceptions vs the world's perceptions around us. When we are all up in our heads about how we are, the world seems like a movie that we are starring in. When we write about our lives, you are writing a movie. An objective perspective will let you talk about yourself as a friend rather than yourself. You can start to think of this guy or girl as a person who is closer to the world than to your own experience, and when you do that, you reduce the number of feelings and thoughts that might get mixed up with the perspective.

When you take out the emotions and thoughts and just go with the facts, you'll find that you can be fairer and more realistic about yourself.

Some people will find that they have self-esteem issues that they need to deal with. Others will be more on the side of narcissism, and they will need to learn about how to reduce their selfishness and start to think more about others. Telling a story is another big part of writing that is so beneficial to us. Writing a story can give you some narrative that will let you be expressive and real about your life. Telling the story tells you how you feel about yourself. You can see yourself as a character in a play or movie. What is the character like? Is he or she an antagonist or protagonist? What are the character's values, their role in life, and their role in the story?

Chapter 54. Psychological Tricks to Examine Human Beings

You must have heard it a lot of times already that communication is the key to everything—be it your relationships or your business deals. Everything is carefully balanced on how you choose to communicate with people, but it's easier said than done. It can be really hard to handle people the right way, but certain psychological tricks can come in handy. They help you examine the people around you to understand their motives, and they will also make your overall life much easier.

By now, you must have already understood that humans are not at all easy to understand, and they are quite complex. However, there are certain patterns in behavior that can be studied to make conclusions. If you think that examining someone can only be done through psychoanalysis and not otherwise, you are wrong because it can also be done through other tricks, which are relatively easier. Even if a person raises an eyebrow or stands in a particular manner, there is meaning to it, and this meaning, when deciphered, will help you understand that person.

I know what you must be wondering. It is just like any other skill you learn. Understanding and examining a human being is not any different. With time, as you keep practicing, you will notice that you have developed an inner intuition that will always guide you in the right direction. Whether you want to understand how you should approach your boss or in what way you should speak to please your client, all of those tactics can be mastered through some simple psychological tricks. Do you know who the top performers in a company are? They are not the ones who are the smartest in the room. They are the ones with the best people skills and know-how to communicate.

You simply need to practice every day to tune in and understand what every person is thinking or how they are as a person. If you want your relationship-building skills to improve, there are different ways to make educated guesses about people from now on.

Let us look at some of these tips and tricks, and I hope you can apply them to the person you meet.

Look Into Their Eyes

I have to say that looking into someone's eyes is the first and foremost trick that everyone should learn. Eyes are the doorway to the mind, and they convey much more than we can imagine. You will often come in situations where you do not particularly prefer the answer you got, and when that happens, you do not understand why things happened the way they did. You might have expected a different answer, and now that the opposite happened, you can't seem to figure out why. Sounds familiar? Well, then you are in luck here because looking into that person's eyes can get you the answer you are looking for. The first reaction that most people have in such a situation is that they ask the question again, but that is most likely to get you the same answer once again. You should look deep into that person's eyes and try to understand what you see. When you do that, the person is automatically going to feel as if they are cornered. In short, they will feel a bit of stress, and this stress itself will bring you a lot of answers. Most of the time, in such situations, the person tries to elaborate on why they said what they said.

Apart from the situation, I just explained, looking into someone's eyes will help you take a peek into their mind. If someone is trying to dismiss what you are saying or is not liking the conversation, you can make it out if you truly look into their eyes.

Now, let us go into some of the details. One of the first things you should keep in mind is to watch for any changes in the pupil's size. I am going to give you an example from a study that was published in the year 1965. It was conducted to show the difference in the pupil's size in response to the people (Eckhart H. Hess, 1965). The psychologists had produced semi-nude pictures belonging to both sexes to female and male participants. There was an increase in the size of the female participants' size when they saw men's pictures. Similarly, there was an increase in the size of the male participants' size when they saw women's pictures.

Subsequent studies were done by the same psychologists to find more information. Homosexual participants were included, and the same result was obtained. Their pupils increased in size when they saw pictures of men in semi-nude condition. Simultaneously, when pictures where mothers were coddling babies, were shown to women, their pupils dilated. So, do you see where this experiment is heading? It is not the only arousal depicted by pupils' dilation, but it also shows whether the information shown is interesting and relatable.

Now, let us move on to something much more complex—when you become an expert at reading the eyes, you can also determine whether a person is telling the truth or lying by simply looking at their eyes. In the year 2009, another study was conducted in which one group of participants did not steal, and the other had stolen $20 (Andrea K. Webb, 2009). Whether the participant had stolen the money or not, every one of them was asked to say the same thing that they had not stolen anything. The detection of a thief was possible when pupil dilation was examined for denying the theft. When the pupil dilation of both groups was compared, it was noticed that the ones who were lying witnessed an increase in pupil size, which was 1 mm more than those who did not commit the theft.

Another thing about the eyes that you should keep in mind is that when people close their eyes in the middle of a conversation, it is usually because there is some feeling that they are trying hard to bury inside themselves. It can also be that they are trying to hide from the chaos of the outside world. However, what you should remember is that closing the eyes does not necessarily mean that the person is afraid of you. It is quite the opposite. They might be finding you annoying, or something about the conversation is irritating them, which is why they want to shut you out. It makes them feel that even when you are in front of them, closing their eyes means that they can shut you out momentarily and not have to see you.

Find the Hot Buttons

If you want to understand someone and their motives, you have to find out more about their hot buttons. It starts with recognizing the hot buttons first. Hot buttons are people's pain points, and they help you understand what they are thinking. The best way to recognize these points is to ask the right questions, and for that, the first step is to build a rapport and a good bond with the person. In short, you have to be a good listener first and a small mouth.

Whenever you want to know more about a person, the trick is to ask questions that give the person room to answer away. These are called open-ended questions. Asking questions whose obvious answers are yes or no is not going to help you here. Questions that require the person to speak about them, their challenges, and their strengths are what you need. Another way to approach this situation is to talk to the person and share stories from your own life where you have done something helpful for other people. Most of the time, you will find people telling you that they have been facing something similar in their life, and this conversation will help you a lot. For starters, it will help you to understand what this person truly needs.

One of the first mistakes that people make is that they think not everyone has triggered, but you are wrong here—everyone has them. The only difference is that some people are good at hiding their triggers. If it is of any help, I am going to give you examples of some of the most common hot buttons that people have:

Fear

I am mentioning fear at the beginning of this list because it is the most powerful hot button. Two of the most common situations, when fear shows itself as a hot button in a person, are avoiding pain or trying to seek pleasure. However, you also have to keep in mind that fear does not act in the same way for everyone. What you fear in life might not be the same for someone else and vice-versa. Fear depends on the experiences that people have in their lives. If you notice this hot button in the person, you have to use it to your benefit. Give them a solution that removes their fear, and this option should eliminate all doubts.

Anger

Anger is something we all experience in our daily lives, and to be honest, quite frequently. However, what is important here is that you have to notice how someone is reacting to this emotion and how it affects their ability to form decisions. If there are any choices that you are looking to change, then you have to keep an eye on how anger is influencing those choices in the person. But if you want to use this hot button for your benefits, the first thing that you should do is try and understand it.

Greed

We make the mistake of thinking that only some people are capable of greed. But no, greed is present in some form in all of us. The degree of greed in a person varies, and yet, it is still there. Greed is mostly about a fear that you won't get anything out of a situation and that you will be left lonely. This gives rise to the thought that no one can take things from you when you have everything. This makes people go to great lengths just because they are looking for approval and acceptance.

Chapter 55. Basic Body Language Signals

Now that you are aware of the "what" and the "why" of body language, let's get into the "how." How can we start to pick up on people's body language? What different secrets are waiting to be discovered within the way that somebody holds their body? It's not easy to know exactly what somebody is trying to tell us, but the more we focus and study these aspects, the easier it will be to get what people are trying to say.

Closed-Off Body Language

Everybody has their reason for wanting to get to know what different body language signals mean. Suppose you are an individual who plans to have closer relationships with people and more successful business interactions. In that case, we must understand what closed-off body language looks like.

Often, when we might be interacting with somebody, the other person could feel a little anxious or reserved because they don't want to share certain parts of their life. While they might continue to talk to you, you could start to pick up how they might be closed off from you so that you can better understand whether or not they want to be in this active conversation or if they're trying to be a little bit more avoidant.

With the use of an arm cross, you can also notice that they might be crossing their legs in the same instance. Because we are primates and animals in general, we focus on self-preservation. This means that we will often protect ourselves and our bodies no matter what we might be feeling at any certain moment.

What you also have to understand is that there are certain times when we might simply be cold. It's not in a metaphorical sense. We can merely experience times where the temperature is low, and we want to warm ourselves up.

There is another important area we can look at when deciding whether somebody is being closed off or if they are just the type of person who is a little bit more reserved. You can take notice of the tension in their mouths.

Those who are closed off and who do not want to be open with you will have stiff shoulders and flexed muscles. If somebody is cold, they might have little self-soothing habits they're doing, such as touching their arms a little bit or even rubbing their hands together.

When somebody is a little bit more open, then they'll keep their arms to the side and their chest exposed to you. This is because they are not afraid of what you might do to them. When somebody feels comfortable and confident within a situation, they won't exhibit the easily identifiable closed-off body language signals.

Remember, the reason that someone might close themselves off is not necessarily because they are afraid of the other person. Still, rather they could do this is because sometimes they just want to hide or have some other generalized anxiety within that moment and simply do not wish to allow the other person to see what we are doing.

If you want to make somebody with closed-off body language a little more open, you can begin to mirror their behavior. This means that you can mimic how they're closed off and holding their bodies in one instance, and then as they become more comfortable with, you switch into a little bit more of an open body language.

Preening and Repeating

One thing that many humans and other animals frequently do is they will go through an act of preening. Preening is when we are subconsciously cleaning and preparing ourselves for other people. Acts of preening include fixing up somebody's hair. Maybe they are playing with their hair by pulling stray hairs out or smoothing it down as they sit there and talk to you. They might run their fingers through their hair, move it to the side, throw it up in a ponytail, or do anything else that will indicate that they are fixing their hair from a state of what it was to state where it's a little bit cleaner and more presentable. This could also be seen through how we might pick ourselves while we are talking to other people. Some people pick at mini scabs on their faces. They might also be picking at their chapped lips or fidgeting with their hands and picking at the cuticles around their fingernails.

Perhaps they are going through short periods of scratching as well. Scratching isn't always a preening way and can sometimes display that the person is itchy or nervous. Sometimes we scratch ourselves when we're nervous because it feels as though we might be doing some active preening on a smaller scale.

Scratching yourself is a way to heal, but it's something that feels good and alleviates some of the pain or tension we might be feeling from different discomforts in our body.

Think of how dogs need to wear cones after surgery or go through another experience where they might have a wound or sore. Though it might not itch all the time, they might still try to scratch it as often as possible. The dog doesn't realize that this can make things worse; they do it because it's a natural feeling we have inside ourselves to alleviate some of the wound's discomfort.

This feeling gets twisted around in our brains, and we'll do the same kind of action when we're feeling nervous or anxious. It's a form of preening in some instances, but it could also simply indicate that the person is feeling uncomfortable or uneasy. Preening is also seen in how we might pamper ourselves or prep our looks using different products or makeup. Many individuals often associate trimming with women trying to be a little more romantic or flirtatious. The thing that we have to remember about preening is that it doesn't mean that another woman is attracted to you and trying to get your attention. She could only be feeling insecure and want to make herself feel better.

Preening in front of other people can also indicate that there is some form of competition. For example, suppose a woman chose to go into the women's restroom where it's a little bit busier and freshen up her makeup in front of other people. In that case, some might take this as a subconscious signal that she's letting others know that she is the top competition. She's fixing herself up and making sure that those around her know just how beautiful or powerful she might be. Preening is also seen in how we can sometimes clean up the area around us or rub imaginary lint off our bodies when talking to other people.

We go through some acts of preening because we want to feel more confident with our appearance, or we might be showing our worth through our attraction from other people.

If somebody is presenting in front of you, then it could be a sign of insecurity. It could also be a sign that they are making themselves more desirable for you.

Understanding the context of the situation will help you determine the intention of their preening. We also have to consider the repetition movements that somebody is using in their body language. Specific individuals might do the same kind of move over and over again. That could be somebody trying to persuade you, and they want to reiterate a point so that you are more likely to be convinced by the things they're sharing.

This can also be seen in how people are preening if somebody is constantly trimming while in front of you, it could be a sign that they are simply anxious. For example, you might have a friend who's always picking and touching her hair. Maybe she is a little bit more insecure. She might put a high weight on her hair because she identifies herself with these looks.

It's vital to notice repetition in how people use their body language to understand their intention better.

Mirroring Body and Speech

Mirroring body language is something that we have already touched on; however, let's take a more in-depth look into why we reflect and how we can use it to help other people connect with us further. Mirroring is the act of mimicking somebody else's body language. It's as if you are a mirror, and you pick up how they're moving and doing that yourself.

Mirroring happens from the moment we're born. We start to mimic the emotions and facial expressions of the people who raise us because we learn how to feel. For example, if you walked up to any baby between six months and 12 months old and started smiling at them, there's an excellent chance they're going to smile back. They have no idea why they're smiling, but they're going to do it because somebody else is showing them this act.

Mirroring is very normal. If you notice somebody mirroring you, that's not necessarily a sign that they're trying to control you. However, mirroring can be used as a tactic to get closer to somebody. Mirroring can be a way to connect with somebody and let them know that they are in a safe and comfortable space

Mirroring frequently happens subconsciously as a way to connect with other people. It helps remind us that we are not alone and that we are similar to others. In a world where we can sometimes feel like an outcast, we must focus on looking for ways to connect with others. Mirroring can also be very influential. If you are in a situation where you want to help somebody get into a different state, you can start by mirroring them.

For example, let's say that you're talking to a friend and they are having an awful day. They're feeling down about themselves; nothing seems to be going right; they're upset, and they're on the verge of tears. As a good friend, you want to help cheer them up; you want to better mood. So, you would start by mirroring the position that they're in at that moment. They might be hunched over with their arms around their legs, looking down and feeling sad. You don't want to do the same position because that's too obvious; however, you can hunch over as well. Let your arms hang or rest on the top of your knees and maybe tilt your head to the side as you talk to them.

You're letting them know that their feelings are valid and that they aren't alone. You're there to support them, and you're going to help work through these emotions with them. After you mirror their body language and pick up on this, you can change their body language after a few moments and sit like this and let them spill their feelings; maybe you sit up straight.

Chapter 56. Strengthen or Change the Views of Others

If you say anything that is consonant with my views, I, of course, agree with you. The fact is that it is easier to argue an already established opinion than to acquire a new one. Besides, every time you formulate a belief to yourself, it is a little more firmly fixed in your brain. If you tell others about it, it becomes almost impossible for the brain to restructure.

Therefore, wanting to influence a person, try to find out exactly his convictions. If your neighbor thinks that you bake the most delicious cakes in the city and you would like to support this opinion in every way, try to make her conviction even stronger: ask her to tell others about your cakes, preferably to the widest possible range of people. Moreover, even better if she puts out a photo of pastries with praise on Instagram for all her friends. Publishing our views is the most powerful way to convince ourselves that we think so. It does not matter that the judgment was initially not very well thought out —if we wrote it down and shared it with others, it would take a lot of effort to take our words back. Therefore, the keyboard or pen and the public who can read are your best helpers when you need to strengthen someone's rather weak beliefs: for example, that you are the best or that communism is great. (Believe it or not, but this was used by Chinese military leaders during the Korean War, forcing American prisoners of war to write and then read aloud that they renounced capitalism and became true radical socialists. It led to a change of political views: many soldiers returned to the US as Communists. However, the Chinese army overlooked the fact that similar beliefs were used in the United States, so soon, the former prisoners had turned back to capitalism.)

If in this way, you manage to strengthen the person in his views, he will defend them. Even if they try to convince him otherwise, he will persist—just to not look like an idiot, spreading unsubstantiated opinions.

And what if you need not back up the conviction but form it? If the neighbor does not like your cakes, it is necessary to prepare the ground for her to change her mind. Then make sure she doesn't do any of the above. Let him keep his opinion with him and not tell anyone about him. Do not ask what she thinks of her cakes—because then she will be even more convinced that she is right. The less chance she has of expressing her views, the more chances you have to change them. Act as Chinese commanders (although this appeal does not apply to other situations): bring to her the opinion you need—and in full compliance with covert reception, show that there are quite a few people who think the same way.

The neighbor will then be easier to abandon their former weakly expressed opinions and join the "wise" majority's point of view.

Influencing Opinion, Distracting Attention

I suspect that everyone who has an adoring sports partner in life often uses this feature for their good. They know that when a match is broadcast over the radio, the partner loses the ability to hear something else. This phenomenon has deeper roots than adherence to the colors of the local football club. Here we discuss the redistribution of brain resources, which cannot support several active states' functions.

For example, suppose you want to convince your partner that it is very different from his opinion. In that case, it is very useful to distract him from other impressions while you present him with your argument.

It is much easier to incline to your opinion a person who is watching TV while you are talking to him—even if the sound is muted. After all, the interlocutor's brain must process information coming from you and visual information (a football match). So, he can no longer allocate sufficient resources for the search for weighty counter-arguments. Similarly, it is much easier to convince you to buy many things on Amazon.com if you, while wandering around the site, simultaneously talk on the phone.

This conclusion is confirmed time after time. A diffuse consciousness (that is, a brain that performs several operations at once) is easier to manipulate and subject it to changes than when it is focused on one thing.

Dispelling the attention is not difficult. If you make a presentation in your company, you put a model next to you; you will notice that you can get any nonsense out of your audience. You can do the same as in the example with the TV—wait until the one you want to convince of your rightness is distracted by something, and at that moment strike.

However, such distracting techniques are not always convenient to apply in practice. If a distracting object is too noticeable, for example, if only models are wearing swimming trunks from a swimsuit, you risk that the rest will not be up to you. As a result, you will not receive any objections or approval. Meanwhile, there are subtler ways to dispel attention than just turning on the TV or simultaneously talking on the phone. Strictly speaking, it is enough to use random words. When we hear something different than we expected to hear, the brain seems to be dramatically slowing down at full speed and thinks "Stop, what else is that?"

Consider an example. If we discuss the price with you, then there are certain rules by which this discussion is based. Among other things, it usually sounds like the word "crowns." If you suddenly declare that the thing you want to sell is nine thousand cents (instead of ninety dollars, as I expected to hear), my thought will turn off for a moment from the well-groomed road. At this second, you will have the opportunity to turn my desire to buy something in the right direction—for example, saying: "It's fabulously cheap!" Confirmed by experiment: several researchers, selling Christmas cards, almost doubled sales when they started calling prices cents instead of dollars.

Pay attention: it is not enough just to knock the client's thoughts off the beaten path; thus, you only create a "window" in which you can influence the brain. For the reception to work, you must embed your message into the interlocutor's mind about how good or cheap a certain product is or how this person needs it. Researchers went up sales only when they began to pronounce the phrase "This is very cheap!" indicating their postcards' price in the cent. (When they called the price in dollars, nothing happened, no matter how much they claimed that the postcards were cheap.) The man who sold mini-muffins managed to increase sales, distracting customers with the unusual word "half-muffins," followed by the phrase that formed the conviction "They are amazingly delicious!"

Regardless of whether you use a sophisticated version, uttering unusual words, or are discussing plans for a vacation with might and main, with a person immersed in Dark Souls 2, dispersing attention, in any case, is a great way to make others more pliable.

It remains only to tell them what opinion they should hold.

Form "Others" About Them

You may not believe me, but your idea of yourself is largely based on what others say about you. The most famous experiment on this topic was conducted in one of the schools, where pupils of one class were told that their intelligence level was higher than of other children. Delighted with this news, the children immediately began to show much better results in the controls.

For example, this means that you can change your cousin's identity by treating her as if she has already become what you want her to be. With this technique's help, you can influence those around you, so that they correspond to your ideas and act as you need. Perhaps you want to convince someone to vote for your party. Join your church community. Get undressed already on the first date. Or just support your proposal at a workshop on Monday. Think about what type of personality is required to perform such an action. Then, make it clear to the one you have chosen to target that he is the carrier of precisely such value orientations.

It may seem difficult at first glance, and people will resist—they probably have some idea of what they are. However, nothing is easier. For example, a colleague suggests taking a test on personality traits, and then, showing him mysterious figures that are difficult to interpret, explain that he is conservative and prefers well-tested solutions (and therefore should be captivated by your offer). Or—that he is a man of an adventurous warehouse and has nothing against a certain amount of risk (if you need such a turn). Just forget to speak convincingly, leaving no reason to doubt your words.

However, in reality, there is no need to go so far and carry out pseudo-diagnostics. It is enough to talk about what your partner is doing in everyday life and describe his actions, taking into account the value orientations currently beneficial. "Oh, you chose a new sort of ice cream? So it seems to you to always try new things." "You can make an adventure out of everything." "It is very typical for you always to take risks." If a colleague hears several times that his actions indicate a propensity to take risks, he will begin to perceive himself as an adventurous person. He will then easily decide to press the big red button when you ask him about it (or what other actions you have to incline him).

If you need to encourage belonging to a different type of personality, emphasize its inherent qualities. Do you want a colleague to feel like a person with developed empathy? In this case, you ask "You took me coffee too? You, like anybody, always think of others." Alternatively, do you need strategic thinking? Then you will say, "An excellent thought is to drink something cold when it is so hot outside. It is noticeable that you are used to planning everything." When a colleague does something that does not fit the type of personality that you want to encourage, you will, of course, just keep silent.

You do not need much effort to make the desired changes. Secret advice for dating in a bar: First, make a woman interested in you feel like an adventurer—ask her to tell you about the various difficult situations she has been in, and then ask her to show you how much she likes to take risks. Between us, it is much faster and cheaper than to treat her to drinks at the bar.

Chapter 57. The Art of Persuasion

Persuasion, as an art, should be subtle and unnoticed. Less forceful than manipulation, more palatable than coercion, persuasion carries the assumption that those persuaded act out of their own 'fully informed' will and usually in a way that works towards the embitterment of all involved. This is not necessarily the case. However, framing an idea in an altruistic way of thinking is a good place to start. The following methods of persuasion are focused on being passive in our persuasion. We wait for the right time, consider their feelings, values, and standpoints. These tactics complement and support each other to create a practically impossible strategy to see through. So, they cannot be directly argued against or attacked with violating socially agreed-upon rules of conduct.

Using an honorable cause is a great way to get someone's attention. Still, an honorable cause alone is rarely enough to convert others to your way of thinking. To truly convert them, we must shift their focus away from the cause to their self-interest. Linking a great cause to the self-interest of listeners is an overwhelmingly powerful motivator. Once the listener begins to think about what they may get out of modifying their opinions or reassessing their loyalties, the cage door is closed.

As a rule, anyone can be persuaded of anything providing the timing, approach, and context are correct, but there are limitations such as time constraints. Before any attempt at persuasion, analyze the context of the situation as a whole and devise an acceptable approach based around the current underlying mood or general atmosphere, otherwise known as the emotional 'flow' of the situation. Do not go against the flow of the situation. Instead, use the emotional flow to your advantage. Frame your ideas as exciting when people are optimistic and as safe and pre-emptive in times of reflection. Going with the flow in this way allows you to siphon the already existing emotions in the room directly into your initiative. This method is ultimately more effective than simply trying to change the conversation topic to serve your purpose.

Timing is another pivotal factor when persuading others. The time of day greatly affects the expected desires of any particular person. For example, if we try to corner someone at work at 4 pm on a Friday, all they can think about is likely leaving work for the weekend, and so a large part of their brain will have already left the building. This could work to our advantage or against it depending on the goal. The timing of an approach extends beyond hours and days to weeks, months, and years. The longer we can plan, the greater our overall chances of success.

Identify those who are 'on the fence' or easy to influence and concentrate your efforts on these individuals in the same way politicians focus on 'swing' voters.

Most people are their own worst enemy, give them enough rope, and they will only be too happy to tie the noose. Ask questions that get people talking, and they will quickly voice opinions and values that can then be mirrored back at them in the present or used at a date to obtain their consent. Being cordial will cause people to open up to you. They will provide the information needed to devise an approach that speaks directly to their personally held beliefs and values. At that point, they will be powerless to refuse you or refute your way of thinking.

Do's and Don'ts of Arguments

We should be able to avoid most conflicts through clever maneuvering and planning. Still, there will be times when unpredictable people and events catch us off guard and are forced to either publicly or privately defend our position. By not instigating such situations, we automatically begin in a position of power from which we can choose exactly how to respond and set the tone for the rest of the interaction. If someone is attempting to start an argument or become abusive, it is likely caused by uncontrolled emotions, which implies that they have not planned. There are many ways to use this to your convenience, from passively listening (to obtain ammo) to deliberate provocation (to cause someone to lose their temper). From simple distraction to appealing to values, all have their benefits. However, some methods, such as baiting someone into a temper tantrum, will not win over your opponent and should only be used when attempting to influence the audience and as a last resort. The tips include actions and behaviors that should be avoided due to blatant nature and their futility, and the detrimental effect on influence and persuasion.

Do's

Keep Cool

It's easy to become caught up in a passionate moment or feel frustrated when faced with an argumentative and unreasonable individual. However, even a momentary lapse in composure can set us back massively, and it also gives those with an eye an opening to exploit. We do not need to restrain ourselves to the point that we are far removed; a little emotion helps keep the thought process flowing. It is a matter of balance; we must place ourselves somewhere between stoicism and enthusiasm without emotionally engaging any other individual or their point of opinion. Do not resist others' arguments, seek to augment them to your purpose by playing the long game, always be aware of the end goal, and remember that losing your temper is a sign of powerlessness.

Use Slick One-Liners Whenever Possible

Cleverly placed, hard-hitting one-liners can completely throw a person's chain of thought. A smart cliché or witty observation can completely demotivate an opponent for a few seconds, enough time for you to take control of the interaction. These seemingly spontaneous and intelligent interjections need not always make clear sense but sound reasonably sincere. You do not want to be seen as a heckler needlessly interrupting the flow of an otherwise relevant conversation. Here are a few of my favorite examples:

- Don't you think this will come back to bite us?

- Right or wrong, it's still beside the point.

- But what does that mean in the real world?

- What exactly are the parameters?

- You seem defensive.

- You're comparing oranges and apples.

- What research did you do?

- Use tactical contradiction.

When discussing matters in front of an audience, it is possible to convert those who are still undecided by dissecting and contradicting your opponent's proposal's specific points. By contradicting them, we have an opportunity to discredit their entire initiative. Even the 'airtight' points can be undermined through the association with premises that can be proved faulty or, even better, foolish. Don't be afraid of a little humor bordering on the theatrical. The audience will enjoy it; however, take care not to get carried away and become disruptive to proceedings.

Make an Appeal

From time to time, you will find yourself in a situation where you have exhausted your logic, expertise, and powers of persuasion. When this happens, it is no doubt since we missed a step along the way, leaving the listener/audience room for critical thinking. It is almost impossible to reverse engineer the interaction and start over immediately and mush in the same way that it is easier to win a new chess game than to recover one after a few poorly considered moves. In these cases, we can appeal to higher values, which will buy us valuable thinking time and also strengthen our position, so that we can then reapproach the issues from a slightly different angle by following up with some questions like:

- "Don't you think that this would make things safer for everyone involved?"

- "Shouldn't we be working together on this?"

- "Yes, but what kind of world do we want to leave for our children?"

- Practice pinpoint listening skills

People get emotional when they speak, and because of this, they make slip-ups, huge ones. Many people are terrified of speaking in front of others, and those who are not afraid of public oration are often overly confident in either themselves or their message. By intently listening to someone, we will at once be aware of their emotions. We can choose to 'pump' these emotions with questions directed to either excite or annoy. At this point, by pretending that you will concede a good point if only they see your point of view, they are likely to openly agree with you. The instant they do, undermine or contradict their point or objective. This simple 'bait and switch' technique will leave the opposition annoyed and confused, allowing you to take control and move on to other issues in the assumption that you have won this time. The people present will assume the same, and when the opposition sense this, they will internally admit defeat rather than go against the group consensus.

Play Devils' Advocate

By playing the part of the Devil's advocate, we can infuriate our opponent, prodding them until they lose their composure and the debate. Playing Devil's advocate consists of gently arguing against and questioning an idea relentlessly, even if we secretly agree with the point being made. It is a tactic that can also be used on your ideas. Question yourself in the way that you believe an incessantly annoying skeptic would and bolster the foundation of your position, and find better ways to protect and strengthen it. Doing so builds resistance to the negative comments, needless questioning, and others' behavior, which so often drains many of us of our creative juices and sometimes even confidence. When playing Devil's advocate to annoy an opponent, do so with a hint of ridicule and ask questions that severely stretch the premise of your opponent's position until the distortion causes it to appear absurd.

Don'ts

Indulge Distractions

Skeptics, disbelievers, and dissenters will often try to distract you with phoney and half-hearted arguments, and the truly argumentative may even attempt to push extreme examples of your ideas to distort them so that they seem ridicules or even reckless in the hopes of either redirecting your argument or causing you to lose your composure. Avoiding such distractions is not always easy, especially those that carry an emotional edge, but by being firm and focused, you can avoid deviations like digressions and subject changes. Resist the urge to dismiss or stifle others. Allowing others to opine is essential in so many ways. Thank them for their valued input, and Segway through some connection or other back to your original point, ideally using the interjection to strengthen your own ideas.

Make Personal Attacks

Lowering yourself and making personal attacks won't win advocates or arguments. You won't convert a person you've just offended, and anyone else present, will automatically assume that your ideas, as well as your integrity, lack substance.

Chapter 58. Influence Without Manipulation

Of course, not all social influence has to be manipulative either. There are several different ways that you can engage in influencing other people without ever having to step into the realm of manipulation if you would prefer to avoid it. These methods are largely more ethical and are meant to be beneficial to the other person, so you are not only taking advantage of another person for your benefit.

Influence can be particularly useful in situations that are not suitable for manipulation or when manipulation would likely violate any contracts or job descriptions you have now. Overall, you can think of many of the persuasive methods that will be here as the ethical, work-appropriate techniques that can be used without losing a license to practice medicine, sell a product, or practice law.

Principles of Persuasion

The principles of persuasion refer to a set of six different techniques that people find inherently persuasive. Using these persuasion principles, you can convince people to do things legitimately and honestly simply by appealing to one of six different principles. Of course, using any of these is not a guarantee for success, but rather it ups your chances of naturally convincing the other person to do whatever it is you are requesting of them. The six principles of persuasion are reciprocity, likability, authority, social proof, scarcity, consistency, and commitment.

Reciprocity

Reciprocity refers to the idea that people naturally want to return favors after they have had one done for them. Think of the feeling of obligation you may get when someone gives you a birthday present—you feel the need to return the favor when the other person's birthday rolls around. This is for a specific reason: you are convinced through reciprocity. This sort of nature's failsafe to the selfless behavior that humans have developed throughout evolution. With reciprocity, humans feel the need to return the favor whenever anyone helps them in any way.

Good, strong leaders recognize reciprocity as an inherent way the human mind works, and they will frequently bank on it—this is why you will see people ask, "What can I do for you?" when you come in somewhere. They are making it clear that they are interested in helping you, and hopefully, in return, you will help them as well. Good, emotionally intelligent leaders will almost always ask what they can do to help someone else before they ever ask the favor they had in mind. You can do this as well—offer to do something for someone. They will think that you are doing so out of the goodness of your heart. You may be, at least in part, but you will still have an ulterior motive. You can then ask the other person for a favor when you need it. For example, if you need to have your shift changed for a concert you want to attend in two months, you may volunteer the following time one of your coworker's mentions needing time off and needing a shift covered to get it approved. Your coworker then will probably offer to do something if he can repay you, at which point you can mention that you need your shift covered for the concert you want to go to, and your coworker agrees to do so. Now, you are left satisfied because your shift is covered, and you were not required to use manipulation to make it happen.

Likability

Likability refers to the fact that people naturally are more inclined to be persuaded when they like the person doing the persuading. After all, would you rather do a favor for your spouse, who you presumably love, or that coworker that you cannot stand? The answer is almost definitely that you would rather do something for your spouse, and the biggest reason for that is because you like your spouse.

Studies have shown that people are more likely to reach agreements in negotiations when all members take a moment to introduce themselves with some small tidbit of information about themselves that makes them more relatable. The biggest reason for this is because they become relatable, and when you relate to someone, you are more likely to want to come up with a compromise with them because you are more likely to feel empathetic toward them.

Luckily, there are three surefire ways to establish yourself as likable, even if your interaction with someone is relatively short. You will only need to take a few moments to do three simple things. You must first make yourself relatable, such as offering a small detail about yourself into the conversation naturally. Following, you should offer some sort of honest compliment to the other person. Lastly, you need to establish yourself as willing to cooperate to reach the same goal, effectively creating a team mentality. These three things can be the difference between landing that sale at work or failing to close.

Authority

People most often are willing to respect authority. They are usually willing to listen to someone who has established himself as an authority. For that reason, those viewed as authority figures are typically seen as more persuasive than those who are not. After all, you are more likely to listen to your dentist about how to save that tooth than the random cashier at the grocery store. This is due to your inherent bias that the dentist is more knowledgeable about dentistry than the cashier, and you are likely right. However, it is possible (and highly unlikely) that your cashier did go to school for dentistry.

When you want to make yourself an authority, you want to clarify that you know what you are talking about. You can do so by displaying your diplomas and other licenses you may have acquired during your career in your office. You can display awards that show just how good at your job you are. You could try including your credentials on your name placard on your desk or nametag. You could even have a secretary whose job is to sing your praises when answering the phone or greeting prospective clients. Suppose all of that is impractical with your job. In that case, there are other methods you can utilize as well—you can drop hints toward your experience in whatever topic you are discussing in a way that is natural with the client, such as mentioning that when you studied business back in graduate school, you learned certain concepts relevant to the conversation you are having. Simply dropping your experience in conversation makes it clearer that you do have some sort of experience, and therefore, your judgment should be trusted.

Social Proof

Social proof refers to the fact that people are largely more influenced by their peers than simply being told what to do for no real reason. This is essentially utilizing peer pressure to control someone else or recognizing that peer pressure principles are relevant to social interactions. For example, people are more likely to go along with their peers' behaviors than when they feel out of their element.

This can be used in manipulation and persuasion—you can hint that other people in a similar position made a choice similar to whatever you want the other person to do. For example, suppose you want to sell a mother of three children a car. In that case, you may point out that many of the parents that you sell to in the same boat as the mother repeatedly buy a minivan or SUV for the extra space for supplies for sports and extracurricular activities or even just to make up for the fact that children grow and may even outgrow a smaller car, feeling completely cramped if they do not have a third row to spread back toward. The mother may feel pressured as you mention this and be a bit more inclined to defer to what other people are doing simply because she was unsure anyway, and if other people are doing it, it likely works well.

Scarcity

The principle of scarcity is little more than supply and demand—people think that scarce things are more valuable simply because they are not as easily attained. With that in mind, you can make something seem more desirable or valuable simply by creating an artificial scarcity of the item. Companies do this frequently—you will see companies with business models that surround selling seasonal or limited time only items, and they draw out massive amounts of attention simply because everyone wants to get their hands on that new limited edition item, or they have been dying for that seasonal drink for months now. They are thrilled that it is finally available again.

When you want to use scarcity to control someone else, you can do so simply by making yourself scarce. Particularly in relationships, you see this utilized in one partner threatening to break up with the other, making it clear that their presence and commitment to the relationship is not guaranteed. If the other person cannot figure out what they are doing, then the person creating the request is willing to walk away altogether.

Consistency and Commitment

The last of the principles of persuasion is consistency and commitment. This refers to the fact that humans naturally value consistency. The easiest way to get that consistency is through commitments meant to motivate the individual to go through with what was committed to becoming consistent simply. For example, someone who has committed to doing something for you will likely follow through because with commitment comes obligation, and failing at obligations begets guilt, which most people want to avoid. If you want someone to do something, you must first start with a small commitment. It does not have to be particularly significant—even asking to borrow a pen would start this process. When that first commitment has been made, the individual is already in the mindset to continue saying yes, enabling you to continue asking for whatever you need. You can then attempt to get the other person to do something else, and you are somewhat more likely to get them to agree if you have already asked them to do something that they agreed to do.

Ethos, Pathos, Logos

Alongside the principles of persuasion, there is also the theory of ethos, pathos, and logos— three Greek words refer to appeals to different aspects of life to convince other people.

When using these, you are essentially creating arguments in which you convince or compel someone to agree to do something because your argument is simply too compelling to deny.

Ethos

Ethos means ethics—it refers to appeals to ethical or moral duties. When you make an argument rooted in ethos, you are arguing for ethics. You are making it a point to spell out exactly why it is important to do things a certain way to avoid violating any inherent values of right vs wrong.

Chapter 59. Escape or Die

Y ou may not die in the sense that your life will end, although that is a very real possibility. However, your freedom is sure to die. Your happiness will die. Your sanity will die. You will suffer a fate that is worse than death. If you were dead, you would be at peace. You would not have to suffer the endless misery that comes with being stuck in a manipulative situation. Instead, your body lives, but your spirit does not. You are trapped in an invisible prison, forced to suffer each day without the promise of ever getting free.

Of course, literal death is a tragic but very real possibility as well. At least three women each day are killed in the USA due to being in an abusive relationship. Countless more choose to end their own lives as it is the only escape from their torment that their broken mind allows them to see.

It doesn't have to come to this. There are several ways that you can retake your freedom and live the life of happiness that you deserve. Is escaping easy? No. Is it worth it? Absolutely. Your choice is none other than that of freedom or a slow, miserable, spiritual, and emotional death.

A strong word of caution must be emphasized before we begin to share how to escape a manipulative situation. Manipulative people are dangerous and devious. They will often stop at nothing to regain control of a situation. For such people, their victim escaping their clutches represents the ultimate loss of control. Many manipulators will stop at absolutely nothing to restore things to the way they want. If they find out that this is not possible, they may resort to acts of violence, stalking, and other forms of extremely dangerous criminal behavior.

That is not to say that these people cannot be escaped from—quite the opposite. Thousands of people each year find the courage and strength to take their life back. By following the advice of this, you will be able to experience the joy of your escape without running the risks that come with escaping in the wrong way.

Before the Escape

The exact nature of your escape from a manipulative person, and situation, depends heavily upon the type of manipulator you find yourself with and the details of the situation. However, every escape has in common is the need to plan very carefully before carrying it out. A well-planned escape makes all the difference between success and failure. Also, more importantly, planning makes the difference between danger and safety. So let's discover how to plan properly.

The first thing to realize when planning an escape is that very few people must know about it beforehand. People have a way of being unable to keep secrets or giving away the wrong information to the wrong person. Even if you tell people and they have your best intentions in mind, they may accidentally let the wrong thing slip at the wrong time.

There is also another key reason for telling as few people as possible about what you have planned. Many manipulators do not respect personal boundaries in any way whatsoever. They may go through your phone, your email, and your social media regularly without you having any idea. If they discover what you are planning, then you are placing yourself in a position of immense physical danger.

Even if you think that your manipulator is not going through your phone or your social media and that you have covered your tracks by deleting messages, there is no way that you can be sure. Did you know that software exists, which can be discretely installed on a PC or phone and allows someone to spy on you in real-time? As you are typing, each button you press could be being transmitted directly to your manipulator. There is no way you would know this is happening, and therefore there is no clear way to protect against it.

That is not to say that you should not tell anyone what you are planning. Rather, it is important to tell one trusted person only. This could be a best friend or a member of your family. You must trust this person with your life, as this is effectively what is at stake. You need to know this person will not let anything slip, even accidentally. The reason for telling them is that they can first support you through the process in any way you need, and secondly so that if anything goes wrong, they can inform the police what has happened and who is responsible.

Choosing the right person to let know what you are up to is only the first stage of the planning process. It is also absolutely vital to choose a physical place you can escape to and spend some time in the aftermath of your escape. This, ideally, will be somewhere out of town, preferably as far away as possible. This is because the manipulator is likely to look everywhere they can think of in the aftermath of you escaping the situation. The place you choose should be far away geographically and somewhere that the manipulator will not be able to figure out easily.

Preparing financially for life without a manipulator is another key aspect of planning. This can be very difficult as some types of manipulators are incredibly controlling when it comes to finances. Ideally, you will have one to two months' expenses saved up and be able to access them in a way that will not arouse suspicion. If this is not possible, your one trusted friend or family member should

be asked to help you out. You will be able to repay them after you have got clear of the situation. This is just a temporary measure. If you are in a situation where you live with your manipulator and want to move out, planning to take the things you need with you is important, but difficult. Anything that is replaceable should be left behind. Only essential things like valuable jewelry, identity documents, and other similar things should be taken. Ideally, you should only take as many things as you can fit into one bag. This makes the practical side of the escape much easier.

In the period leading up to your escape, you should put together a duffel bag or similar sized bag of new purchases from outside of the home. For example, you should pack some underwear, clothes, toiletries, and other similar items. They should not be taken from the home as their absence would likely arouse suspicion. Instead, they should all be new purchases. When you have carefully put together your bag, it is vital to find a safe place to store it. Some good ideas for such places include with your one trusted person or at some kind of rental locker space, such as a gym locker.

The above steps are the essentials you need to consider when planning your escape from a manipulative situation. There may be other steps you need to consider in light of your particular scenario, or some of the above ideas may not apply if you are sure to follow the advice, though. You are putting yourself in a position of preparedness and safety ahead of your escape.

Now that you have made practical preparations for your escape, it's time to plan the escape itself.

The preceding of this gave you all of the information you need to make some preparations ahead of your escape. While essential, it is not enough. Equally, if not more important, is to plan the actual escape. This includes the escape's nature, the escape's timing, and what you will do if something goes wrong. Having a clear plan in mind for the period after the escape is also essential. After the escape, this is often the most difficult time as the manipulator will know what has happened and look for revenge.

The first key step in this process is understanding exactly what an escape means to you. Every situation is different, and not all of them require a dramatic escape, which involves hiding out in some remote location. We will now look at some of the more appropriate escape methods depending on the type of manipulative situation you are trying to get away from. Suppose you are with one of the more serious types of relationship manipulators.

Suppose you are with one of the more serious types of relationship manipulators, such as someone who is violent, or gaslighting, or denying reality. In that case, it is vital to put physical distance between yourself and your manipulator. This is because these types of manipulators are the ones who will cross the line into violence and even murder if they are provoked. This is the most serious type of manipulative situation you can find yourself in, so make sure to leave nothing to chance when attempting to escape it. Some types of relationship manipulators are less dangerous, but you still should err on the side of caution. For example, suppose the person you are with manipulates you through lying and minimizing. In that case, you may not need to plan such a dramatic and comprehensive escape from this type of scenario. It may be enough to break up with such a person from a distance and make sure they know you will go to the police if they attempt to remain in contact with you.

Other types of situations require a different approach. If you are stuck in a manipulative workplace situation, you may find that changing jobs is the only way you can get out. It may be tempting to quit in the heat of the moment, but this is the wrong way to go about it. It is vital to have another job, known as a parachute job, lined up before you quit. Otherwise, you will face serious financial trouble after quitting the manipulative situation. Schedule interviews for days off from the office and consider using vacation time for all your new job interviews into two weeks. This can allow the job search process to be less stressful for you.

Conclusion

A healthy life with a narcissist is impossible. They do not know how to communicate with others in a way that is not manipulative. This is likely because as a child, they could not get their needs met by asking for them and had to go about it in an underhanded way, and as an adult, they continue this behavior. They will likely use these stories of childhood tragedies as a way of playing on your sympathy and getting you not to leave them. You can feel compassion for what they endured as a child, but you owe it to yourself not to tolerate abuse from who they have become as an adult.

It cannot be stressed enough how important it is that a survivor does not contact the narcissist. This means they cannot share phone calls, messages, or visit this person. It will only be detrimental to their mental health and put them right back into the position they worked so hard to get out of. They need to keep themselves out of the risk of breaking no contact.

This means their time needs to be filled with something else, so they won't have time to think about and contact the person they are trying to distance themselves from. This is the time to make new friends and reconnect with old ones. Taking up a new hobby or a class will take up your time and introduce you to new people.

Everyone who dealt with a covert narcissist knows the pain, toxicity, and hardships such an individual brings. As a result of being exposed to narcissistic abuse for a prolonged period, victims, future survivors face many challenges. They are faced with a great task: to leave it all behind and heal from what has transpired due to that relationship. Healing from abuse is never easy as it leaves deep marks on one's personality and diminishes their wellbeing. Covert narcissism is a set of destructive behavioral patterns that harm everyone involved with a person who harbors these behaviors. Unfortunately, because it is a personality disorder that is very much conceived, there are no proven ways to foresee you are dealing with one unless you've experienced being abused by a narcissist in your past.

Hard to diagnose, covert narcissists, because they are so well-liked and accepted in society represent a real threat to everyone they are involved with, as their destructive patterns, manipulation techniques, and controlling behavior can be extremely damaging to one's mental, physical, and emotional body. Being part of the Cluster B spectrum, covert narcissism represents a real danger to one's sense of self, self-worth, and mental health in general. It is threatening, disturbing, which is why a healing process for those who suffered from narcissistic abuse is a lengthy process that is never light and easy.

One of the most important things to do to heal from narcissistic abuse is to create and strengthen interpersonal relationships with others. You need to be focused on something outside of the relationship between you and a toxic person. If a bond does not replace the bond you break with them with someone else, it will be effortless to break no contact.

Realizing what led you to the place you are now is the first step to getting to a different one. Many times those who get into prolonged relationships with a narcissist, were raised by one. In reality, they were most likely raised by two. One parent was the overt narcissist who victimized the child with their rage, while the other parent allowed their child to be mistreated.

You have every right to be angry with a parent who mistreated you. However, you also need to permit yourself to be angry with the parent who kept that parent in the house and refused to leave them. This is a natural feeling, and you cannot feel guilty about it. Even if there were extenuating circumstances, the parent who allowed you to be exposed to narcissistic abuse throughout your upbringing did not do right by you. You probably also had to be a therapist for them. They needed to vent to you so that they could go on another day.

They will talk of the burden they bore for you, but there was also a burden you bore. Often, the child carries the heaviest weight throughout the entire family in a dysfunctional situation. There were probably times this parent turned the narcissistic parent's anger away from you and onto them, but there were also most likely times when they couldn't handle it anymore, and so it was "your turn" to deal with it. That act was abuse from them. A family is not supposed to be a dynamic to where there is a parent who flies into rages, and the child has to take the brunt of it on days when the other parent has had all they can stand.

A child who grew up with a parent who was prone to angry outbursts might internalize that behavior. Not realizing their parent's behavior came from within, they will think they were responsible for it. This theory will be confirmed by the fact that sometimes making themselves as small as possible, groveling, and going along with whatever the parent wanted would give them a reprieve. When this child grows into an adult, they will think they are responsible for other people's anger. They will feel a sense of guilt when another person gets angry and insults them. They will think, had they not done something wrong. They wouldn't be getting treated like this.

When a person has had long-term dealings with a narcissist, they come out of it with wounds that will take time and work to heal. There is an argument that a form of PTSD forms after suffering this type of abuse. Anxiety management is something you will need to learn while recovering from narcissistic abuse. Studies have shown that people are breaking away from a relationship with a narcissist exhibit symptom reminiscent of post-traumatic stress disorder.

They are hyper-vigilant because they never knew what would set off the narcissistic rage. People who are recovering from narcissistic abuse invariably have high levels of anxiety. They are traumatized by the way they have been treated. This is why it is essential to seek ongoing treatment for a little while after breaking free from psychological abuse.

While there is anxiety, there is also a feeling of numbness. This is another aspect of trauma. You cannot handle the sheer amount of stress you are under from the house's amount of tension. To feel all of it would be overwhelming to feel, so you choose not to feel it and then go into survival mode. Your mind is on getting through the situations that are thrown at you throughout the day.

There is a sad reality that people who were raised by a narcissist has to face. They have to watch out for narcissistic tics, also called fleas. These terms are used to refer to the tendencies they learned from their narcissistic caregiver. It is a way they further damage the children under their care. It is not enough to put them through the wringer that is narcissistic abuse. They also, whether it is conscious or not, try to teach their children narcissism. It can become a legacy if the child does not monitor their behavior as an adult. Humans respond to their environment and learn from the examples set for them by their caregivers.

Before you start to panic, be reassured, a tic does not mean you have become a narcissist. It means you have learned certain behaviors from those who raised you, as we all do. You are not a bad person because you were told lies as a child.

Think about it this way. A person raised by people who held prejudices against a specific religious or ethnic group would have been taught incorrect lessons about an entire population of people.

Their family went through a lot of trouble to program this person into thinking similarly to them. When you are a small child, you think your own family is a representation of all families. However, when you get out into the world, you will start to notice there are beliefs your family held that are not shared by other people. In the case of a person raised by a prejudiced family, they would have to learn some harsh truths about how they were raised.

They would discover that the belief they had always been taught to have was frowned upon by society and morally incorrect. It would be a complicated process for them to shed this thought process and take on a healthier one because our minds do not have switches that can be turned back and forth at our convenience. The person would go through a most likely lifelong journey of monitoring their biases and recognize when the old thought patterns were trying to creep their way back in.

Now let's apply this lesson to a person who had picked up a narcissistic tic from a parent. Melissa's mother was a covert narcissist. She had a very manipulative way of navigating through her relationships with others and yet would portray herself as a victim. As covert narcissists tend to do, she would seek out the company of overt narcissists. She would choose the same type of man to start a relationship with over and over again and be just as devastated every time these men let her down in the same ways as the ones did.

It is difficult to make connections in a situation when you are going through it personally. Melissa did not realize the similarities between her behaviors and that of her mother. When she thought about her, she felt a deep-seated resentment because she gave her a difficult childhood. When she started cognitive behavioral therapy, she began to realize her relationship patterns went the same way as her mother did—abrupt and ending chaotically. Her therapist reminds her that a child sees what is presented to them as normal.

They think the example their parents set for them is representative of how it is supposed to be and what everyone else does. She comes to realize she doesn't know what a healthy relationship looks like. She decides to take a break from dating until she learns how to choose better partners, be a better partner herself, and navigate through relationships in a more productive way. She realized she had developed thought patterns that were wrong due to her raising and is now working towards transforming these beliefs into healthier ones. That is the goal of cognitive-behavioral therapy.

www.ingramcontent.com/pod-product-compliance
Lightning Source LLC
Chambersburg PA
CBHW081345080526
44588CB00016B/2380